ADVANCED TEXTS IN]

General Editors

Manuel Arellano Guido Imbens Grayham E. Mizon
Adrian Pagan Mark Watson

Advisory Editors
C. W. J. Granger

Panel Data Econometrics

MANUEL ARELLANO

OXFORD
UNIVERSITY PRESS

OXFORD

Great Clarendon Street, Oxford OX2 6DP
United Kingdom

Oxford University Press is a department of the University of Oxford.
It furthers the University's objective of excellence in research, scholarship,
and education by publishing worldwide. Oxford is a registered trade mark of
Oxford University Press in the UK and in certain other countries

© Manuel Arellano 2003

The moral rights of the author have been asserted

Reprinted 2013

All rights reserved. No part of this publication may be reproduced, stored in
a retrieval system, or transmitted, in any form or by any means, without the
prior permission in writing of Oxford University Press, or as expressly permitted
by law, by licence or under terms agreed with the appropriate reprographics
rights organization. Enquiries concerning reproduction outside the scope of the
above should be sent to the Rights Department, Oxford University Press, at the
address above

You must not circulate this work in any other form
and you must impose this same condition on any acquirer

British Library Cataloguing in Publication Data
Data available

Library of Congress Cataloging in Publication Data
Data available

ISBN 978-0-19-924529-1

To Olympia, Manuel, and Jaime

Contents

Preface

The objective of this book is to review some of the main topics in panel data econometrics. It deals with linear static and dynamic models, and it is aimed at a readership of graduate students and applied researchers. Parts of the book can be used in a graduate course on panel data econometrics, and as a reference source for practitioners.

I have tried to survey as many modelling ideas as possible, rather than trying to present them with the greatest generality. Modelling ideas are often the key input in applied econometrics, and although the book is concerned with econometric methodology, an effort has been made to motivate techniques in the context of applications.

Familiarity with linear regression analysis and basic concepts in probability theory is required. For the most part I adopt a generalized method of moments (GMM) approach, and I make frequent use of instrumental variable arguments. When available, I also present likelihood approaches drawing links to their regression or GMM counterparts. Since the degree of exposure of economists to GMM varies with cohort and style of undergraduate training, I have included two appendices, one on GMM and another on optimal instruments, in order to make the book reasonably self-contained. These two appendices are a revised version of the notes I have used over the years in teaching graduate students at CEMFI.

Acknowledgements I started writing this book in the Winter of 2000 during a stay at the Faculty of Economics and Politics, University of Cambridge, whose hospitality I am pleased to acknowledge. It was finished at CEMFI two years later, and I gratefully thank my colleagues for their forbearance. Its existence owes much to Andrew Schuller's belief that I was capable of writing at book length on panel data; my warmest thanks to him for his encouragement and patience. Over the years I have been fortunate to be close to teachers, colleagues, and students that provided decisive stimulus to my work. My teachers and mentors, Steve Nickell and David Hendry, and especially my Ph.D. adviser, Denis Sargan, greatly influenced my understanding of econometrics. I have enormously benefited from close interaction with Richard

Blundell, Steve Bond, Olympia Bover, Costas Meghir, and Enrique Sentana. Martin Browning, Gary Chamberlain, and Whitney Newey had particularly large intellectual impacts in my views on the subject of this book. My former research students Lola Collado, César Alonso-Borrego, Victor Aguirregabiria, Raquel Carrasco, and Javier Alvarez have also been a constant source of fruitful interaction. I am also pleased to acknowledge my co-authors, notably Bo Honoré, as I have drawn heavily on our joint work. I am most grateful to Javier Alvarez, Jesús Carro, Tony Lancaster, Francisco Peñaranda, and Frank Windmeijer, who read parts of the manuscript and made valuable comments, and to James Davidson for his advice on the technical composition of the manuscript. Special thanks are due to Pedro Albarrán, Olympia Bover, and Enrique Sentana for their comments, help, and willingness to discuss every aspect of the preparation of the book throughout. I am, of course, solely responsible for the failings that remain. Finally, my deepest gratitude to Olympia, Manuel, and Jaime for their staunch support.

M.A.
Madrid, July 2002

1

Introduction

At one time exotic, the use of economic data with both time series and cross-sectional variation has now become common place in modern econometric practice. The term *panel data* is used for a wide variety of situations in econometrics. It refers to any data set with repeated observations over time for the same individuals. "Individuals" can be workers, households, firms, industries, regions, or countries, to name a few.

If we pool together the national accounts of several countries we obtain a country panel. Data of this kind have been prominent, for example, in recent research on models of growth and convergence. Moreover, much interest has been directed to cross-country or cross-state panels because these data can sometimes provide exogenous variation in institutions or policies that facilitate the identification of parameters of economic interest.

Not surprisingly, some of the econometric issues arising in this context are closely related to time series econometrics. In aggregate panels, the cross-sectional and time series dimensions are often of a similar magnitude. A central modelling issue is how best to accommodate heterogeneity across units. A central statistical issue is the impact of cross-sectional variation for the choice and sampling properties of estimators.

Another class of data sets are household or firm level panels, which are based on surveys, census, administrative records, or company balance accounts. These are usually referred to as "micropanels". Typically, these panels consist of large cross-sections of individuals observed for short time periods. Examples are the Michigan, Essex, and European Community household income panels,[1] or the rotating panels on household expenditures conducted in the US and some European countries.

---

[1] The Panel Study of Income Dynamics of the University of Michigan (PSID), the British Household Panel Survey of the University of Essex (BHPS), and the European Community Household Panel Survey (ECHS).

Interest in the latter, originally evolved from cross-sectional econometrics in such areas as labour economics, demand analysis, and the analysis of cost and production functions. In this context a number of specific techniques for "large N and small T" panels have been developed (although there are also panels where neither N is very large nor T is very small). It is important, nevertheless, to bear in mind that from a substantive point of view it is not T itself that matters but the nature of the variation over the period, or the relevance of the frequency of the observations for the analysis (quarterly, annual, etc.).

Household or firm level data sets may overcome aggregation problems in identifying individual agents' rules of behaviour. Moreover, panel data may provide the exogenous variation that is required for the identification of structural parameters through comparisons across periods covering policy changes. These remarks would be also true of data consisting of time series of independent cross-sections. What is specific about panel data is the possibility of following the same individuals over time, which facilitates the analysis of dynamic responses and the control of unobserved heterogeneity.

In the econometrics of panel data there tends to be an emphasis in the modelling and implications of heterogeneity, which is not surprising given that we are dealing with different units. Aside from that, the field has expanded to cover almost any aspect of econometrics. Structural equations, dynamics, time series models, discrete choice, selectivity, unit roots: all the standard econometric tools have been reassessed for use with panel data. Thus, it is increasingly more difficult to regard panel data analysis as a special topic within econometrics having a unified theme. Rather, most econometric developments are potentially relevant for panel data. Furthermore, given the variety of existing panel data sets and the diversity of objectives economists may have in using them, there is no such thing as *the* methodology for analysing panel data, but a collection of disparate techniques that have accumulated from a series of heterogeneous motivations in theoretical and applied econometrics.

This book has two main concerns. One is the analysis of econometric models with non-exogenous explanatory variables. This includes strictly exogenous variables that are correlated with unobserved permanent effects, variables subject to measurement error, and variables that are predetermined or endogenous relative to time-varying errors.

The other main concern is dynamic modelling and, more specifically, the problem of distinguishing empirically between dynamic responses and unobserved heterogeneity in panel data models.

Static and dynamic linear models are covered. With the exception of error-in-variable problems, most results can be made extensive to nonlinear models with additive errors, and I make this extension explicit at times. However, nonlinear models with non-additive errors are outside the scope of this book. Some of these models, like discrete choice and sample selection models, are important tools in empirical work. Unfortunately, very little is known about nonlinear panel data models with explanatory variables that are predetermined, endogenous, or measured with error. A review of recent work on nonlinear panel data models can be found in Arellano and Honoré (2001).

The main text is divided into three parts. Part I deals with static models and Parts II and III with dynamic models. Part II discusses pure time series models, whereas dynamic conditional models are considered in Part III. In the econometrics of panel data two different types of motivations have converged. One is the desire to control for unobserved heterogeneity; the other is the possibility of modelling dynamic responses and error components. The three parts of the book are organized around these two themes and their interrelations.

Finally, Part IV contains two appendices that review the main results in the theory of generalized method of moments estimation, and optimal instrumental variables.

The introductory material in each of the chapters will be useful to anyone interested in panel data analysis. Many topics are discussed from both small and long T perspectives, and I present empirical illustrations for both micro and macro panels. There is, however, an emphasis in the econometrics of micro panels. This emphasis is reflected in both the organization of the material and the choice of topics.

Part I

Static Models

2

Unobserved Heterogeneity

The econometric interest on panel data, specially in microeconometric applications, has been the result of at least two different types of motivation.

- First, the desire of exploiting panel data for controlling unobserved time-invariant heterogeneity in cross-sectional models.

- Second, the use of panel data as a way of disentangling components of variance and estimating transition probabilities among states, and more generally to study the dynamics of cross-sectional populations.

These motivations can be loosely associated with two strands of the panel data literature labelled *fixed effects* and *random effects* models. We next take these two motivations and model types in turn. First in the context of static models in Part I, and then in the context of dynamic models in Parts II and III.

2.1 Overview

A sizeable part of econometric activity deals with empirical description and forecasting, but another part aims at quantifying structural or causal relationships. Structural relations are needed for policy evaluation and often for testing theories.

The regression model is an essential statistical tool for both descriptive and structural econometrics. However, regression lines from economic data often cannot be given a causal interpretation. The reason being that in the relation of interest between observables and unobservables we might expect explanatory variables to be correlated with unobservables, whereas in a regression model regressors and unobservables are uncorrelated by construction.

There are several instances in which we would expect correlation between observables and unobservables. One is the classical supply-and-demand simultaneity problem due to time aggregation and market equilibrium. That is, a regression of quantity on price could not be interpreted as a demand equation because we would expect an unobservable exogenous shift in demand to affect not only purchases but also prices through the supply side effect of quantities on prices.

Another is measurement error: if the explanatory variable we observe is not the variable to whom agents respond but an error ridden measure of it, the unobservable term in the equation of interest will contain the measurement error which will be correlated with the regressor.

Finally, there may be correlation due to unobserved heterogeneity. This has been a pervasive problem in cross-sectional regression analysis. If characteristics that have a direct effect on both left- and right-hand side variables are omitted, explanatory variables will be correlated with errors and regression coefficients will be biased measures of the structural effects. Thus researchers have often been confronted with massive cross-sectional data sets from which precise correlations can be determined but that, nevertheless, had no information about parameters of policy interest.

The traditional response of econometrics to these problems has been multiple regression and instrumental variable models. Regrettably, although the statistical theory of the problem is well understood, we often lack data on the conditioning variables or the instruments to achieve identification of structural parameters in that way.

A major motivation for using panel data has been the ability to control for possibly correlated, time-invariant heterogeneity without observing it.

Suppose a cross-sectional regression of the form

$$y_{i1} = \beta x_{i1} + \eta_i + v_{i1} \tag{2.1}$$

such that $E(v_{i1} \mid x_{i1}, \eta_i) = 0$. If η_i is observed β can be identified from a multiple regression of y on x and η. If η_i is not observed identification of β requires either lack of correlation between x_{i1} and η_i, in which case

$$Cov(x_{i1}, \eta_i) = 0 \Rightarrow \beta = \frac{Cov(x_{i1}, y_{i1})}{Var(x_{i1})},$$

or the availability of an external instrument z_i that is uncorrelated with both v_{i1} and η_i but correlated with x_{i1}, in which case

$$Cov(z_i, \eta_i) = 0 \Rightarrow \beta = \frac{Cov(z_i, y_{i1})}{Cov(z_i, x_{i1})}.$$

Suppose that neither of these two options is available, but we observe y_{i2} and x_{i2} for the same individuals in a second period (so that $T = 2$) such that

$$y_{i2} = \beta x_{i2} + \eta_i + v_{i2} \tag{2.2}$$

and both v_{i1} and v_{i2} satisfy $E(v_{it} \mid x_{i1}, x_{i2}, \eta_i) = 0$. Then β is identified in the regression in first-differences even if η_i is not observed. We have:

$$y_{i2} - y_{i1} = \beta(x_{i2} - x_{i1}) + (v_{i2} - v_{i1}) \tag{2.3}$$

and

$$\beta = \frac{Cov(\Delta x_{i2}, \Delta y_{i2})}{Var(\Delta x_{i2})}. \tag{2.4}$$

A Classical Example: Agricultural Cobb–Douglas Production Function (Mundlak, 1961; Hoch, 1962; Chamberlain, 1984) Suppose equation (2.1) represents a production function for an agricultural product. The index i denotes farms and t time periods (seasons or years). Also:

y_{it} = Log output.

x_{it} = Log of a variable input (labour).

η_i = An input that remains constant over time (soil quality).

v_{it} = A stochastic input which is outside the farmer's control (rainfall).

Suppose η_i is known by the farmer but not by the econometrician. If farmers maximize expected profits there will be a cross-sectional correlation between labour and soil quality. Therefore, the population coefficient in a simple regression of y_{i1} on x_{i1} will differ from β. If η were observed by the econometrician, the coefficient on x in a multiple cross-sectional regression of y_{i1} on x_{i1} and η_i will coincide with β. Now suppose that data on y_{i2} and x_{i2} for a second period become available. Moreover, suppose that rainfall in the second period is unpredictable from rainfall in the first period (permanent differences in rainfall can be made part of η_i), so that rainfall is independent of a farm's labour demand in the two periods. Thus, even in the absence of data on η_i the availability of panel data affords the identification of the technological parameter β.

A Firm Money Demand Example (Mulligan, 1997; Bover and Watson, 2000) Suppose firms minimize cost for a given output s_{it} subject to a production function $s_{it} = F(x_{it})$ and to some transaction services $s_{it} = \left(a_i m_{it}^{(1-b)} \ell_{it}^b\right)^{1/c}$, where x denotes a composite input, m is demand for cash, ℓ is labour employed in transactions, and a represents the firm's financial sophistication. There will be economies of scale in the demand for money by firms if $c \neq 1$. The resulting money demand equation is

$$\log m_{it} = k + c \log s_{it} - b \log(R_{it}/w_{it}) - \log a_i + v_{it}. \tag{2.5}$$

Here k is a constant, R is the opportunity cost of holding money, w is the wage of workers involved in transaction services, and v is a measurement error in the demand for cash.[1] In general a will be correlated with output through the cash-in-advance constraint. Thus, the coefficient of output (or sales) in a regression of $\log m$ on $\log s$ and $\log(R/w)$ will not coincide with the scale parameter of interest. However, if firm panel data is available and a varies across firms but not over time in the period of analysis, economies of scale can be identified from the regression in changes.

An Example in which Panel Data Does Not Work: Returns to Education   "Structural" returns to education are important in the assessment of educational policies. It has been widely believed in the literature that cross-sectional regression estimates of the returns could not be trusted because of omitted "ability" that if correlated with education attainment would bias returns (cf. Griliches, 1977). In the earlier notation:

y_{it} = Log wage (or earnings).

x_{it} = Years of full-time education.

η_i = Unobserved ability.

β = Returns to education.

The problem in this example is that x_{it} typically lacks time series variation. So a regression in first-differences will not be able to identify β in this case. In this context data on siblings and cross-sectional instrumental variables have proved more useful for identifying returns to schooling free of ability bias than panel data.

This example illustrates a more general problem. Information about β in the regression in first-differences will depend on the ratio of the variances of Δv and Δx. In the earnings–education equation, we are in the extreme situation where $Var(\Delta x) = 0$, but if $Var(\Delta x)$ is small regressions in changes may contain very little information about parameters of interest even if the cross-sectional sample size is very large.

Econometric Measurement *versus* Forecasting Problems   The previous examples suggest that the ability to control for unobserved heterogeneity is mainly an advantage in the context of problems of econometric measurement as opposed to problems of forecasting. This is an important distinction. Including individual effects we manage to identify certain coefficients at the expense of leaving part of the regression unmodelled (the one that only has cross-sectional variation).

Note that the part of the variance of y accounted by $x\beta$ could be very small relative to η and v (5, 80, and 15 per cent would not be an unrealistic situation

---

[1]Writing the firm's cost as $\mathcal{C}_{it} = p_t x_{it} + R_{it} m_{it} + w_{it} \left(s_{it}^{c/b} a_i^{-1/b} m_{it}^{-(1-b)/b} \right)$, equation (2.5) results from the first-order condition $\partial \mathcal{C}_{it}/\partial m_{it} = 0$ or

$$R_{it}/w_{it} = s_{it}^{c/b} a_i^{-1/b} m_{it}^{-1/b} (1-b)/b.$$

in, for example, intertemporal labour supply models of the type considered by Heckman and MaCurdy (1980)).[2] In a case like this it is easy to obtain higher R^2 by including lagged dependent variables or proxies for the fixed effects. Regressions of this type would be useful in cross-sectional forecasting exercises for the population from which the data come (like in credit scoring or in the estimation of probabilities of tax fraud), but they may be of no use if the objective is to measure the effect of x on y holding constant all time-invariant heterogeneity.

An equation with individual specific intercepts may still be useful when the interest is in forecasts for the same individuals in different time periods, but not when we are interested in forecasts for individuals other than those included in the sample.

Non-Exogeneity and Random Coefficients   The identification of causal effects through regression coefficients in differences or deviations depends on the lack of correlation between x and v at all lags and leads (strict exogeneity). If x is measured with error (Chapter 4) or is correlated with lagged errors (Chapter 8), regressions in deviations may actually make things worse.[3]

Another difficulty arises when the effect of x on y is itself heterogeneous. In such case regression coefficients in differences cannot in general be interpreted as average causal effects. Specifically, suppose that β is allowed to vary cross-sectionally in (2.1) and (2.2) so that

$$y_{it} = \beta_i x_{it} + \eta_i + v_{it} \ (t = 1, 2) \ \ E\left(v_{it} \mid x_{i1}, x_{i2}, \eta_i, \beta_i\right) = 0. \qquad (2.6)$$

In these circumstances, the regression coefficient (2.4) differs from $E\left(\beta_i\right)$ unless β_i is mean independent of Δx_{i2}. The availability of panel data still affords identification of average causal effects in random coefficients models as long as x is strictly exogenous. However, if x is not exogenous and β_i is heterogeneous we run into serious identification problems in short panels.[4]

2.2   Fixed Effects Models

2.2.1   Assumptions

Our basic assumptions for what we call the "static fixed effects model" are as follows. We assume that $\{(y_{i1}, ..., y_{iT}, x_{i1}, ..., x_{iT}, \eta_i), i = 1, ..., N\}$ is a random

---

[2]Since $x\beta$ and η are potentially correlated, the variance of y need not coincide with the sum of the variances of $x\beta$, η and v.

[3]See Griliches and Mairesse (1998) for a cautionary tale on fixed effects solutions, and an assessment of empirical production functions based on firm panel data.

[4]Chamberlain (1992a) considers the estimation of random coefficients models with strictly exogenous variables. The problem of identification from short panels with non-exogenous x is discussed in Chamberlain (1993), and Arellano and Honoré (2001). Estimation from long heterogeneous panels is considered in Pesaran and Smith (1995).

sample and that

$$y_{it} = x'_{it}\beta + \eta_i + v_{it} \tag{2.7}$$

together with

Assumption A1:

$$E(v_i \mid x_i, \eta_i) = 0 \ (t = 1, ..., T),$$

where $v_i = (v_{i1}, ..., v_{iT})'$ and $x_i = (x'_{i1}, ..., x'_{iT})'$. We observe y_{it} and the $k \times 1$ vector of explanatory variables x_{it} but not η_i, which is therefore an unobservable time-invariant regressor.

Similarly, we shall refer to "classical" errors when the additional auxiliary assumption holds:

Assumption A2:

$$Var(v_i \mid x_i, \eta_i) = \sigma^2 I_T.$$

Under Assumption *A2* the errors are conditionally homoskedastic and not serially correlated.

Under Assumption *A1* we have

$$E(y_i \mid x_i, \eta_i) = X_i\beta + \eta_i \iota \tag{2.8}$$

where $y_i = (y_{i1}, ..., y_{iT})'$, ι is a $T \times 1$ vector of ones, and $X_i = (x_{i1}, ..., x_{iT})'$ is a $T \times k$ matrix. The implication of (2.8) for the expected value of y_i given x_i is

$$E(y_i \mid x_i) = X_i\beta + E(\eta_i \mid x_i)\iota. \tag{2.9}$$

Moreover, under Assumption *A2*

$$Var(y_i \mid x_i, \eta_i) = \sigma^2 I_T \tag{2.10}$$

which implies

$$Var(y_i \mid x_i) = \sigma^2 I_T + Var(\eta_i \mid x_i)\iota\iota'. \tag{2.11}$$

A weaker set of assumptions is

Assumption A1':

$$E(v_i \mid x_i) = 0 \ (t = 1, ..., T).$$

Assumption A2':

$$Var(v_i \mid x_i) = \sigma^2 I_T.$$

Although we shall often rely on the weaker assumption $E(v_{it} \mid x_i) = 0$ for convenience—since many results of interest can be obtained with it—in many applied instances it will be difficult to imagine how $E(v_{it} \mid x_i) = 0$ would hold without $E(v_{it} \mid x_i, \eta_i) = 0$ also holding.[5]

Another possibility is to replace mean independence assumptions by lack of correlation assumptions, but similar remarks apply: in practice it may be difficult to imagine the linear projection conditions $E^*(v_{it} \mid x_i) = 0$ or $E^*(v_{it} \mid x_i, \eta_i) = 0$ holding without the stronger mean independence conditions also holding. Nevertheless, lack of correlation may still be a convenient way of providing a focus for the presentation of essential identification results.

Notice that under Assumptions *A1'* and *A2'* we have the same expression for $E(y_i \mid x_i)$ as in (2.9) but a different one for $Var(y_i \mid x_i)$ since η_i and v_i may be conditionally correlated given x_i:

$$Var(y_i \mid x_i) = \sigma^2 I_T + Var(\eta_i \mid x_i)\iota\iota' + Cov(\eta_i, v_i \mid x_i)\iota' + \iota Cov(\eta_i, v_i' \mid x_i). \tag{2.12}$$

A1 (or *A1'*) is the fundamental assumption in this context. It implies that the error v at any period is uncorrelated with past, present, and future values of x (or, conversely, that x at any period is uncorrelated with past, present, and future values of v). *A1* is, therefore, an assumption of *strict exogeneity* that rules out, for example, the possibility that current values of x are influenced by past errors. In the agricultural production function example, x (labour) will be uncorrelated with v (rainfall) at all lags and leads provided the latter is unpredictable from past rainfall (given permanent differences in rainfall that would be subsumed in the farm effects, and possibly seasonal or other deterministic components). If rainfall in period t is predictable from rainfall in period $t-1$ —which is known to the farmer in t—labour demand in period t will in general depend on $v_{i(t-1)}$ (Chamberlain, 1984, 1258–1259). Conditional models without strictly exogenous explanatory variables will be considered in Part III.

Assumption *A2* is, on the other hand, an auxiliary assumption under which classical least-squares results are optimal. However, lack of compliance with *A2* is often to be expected in applications. Here, we first present results under *A2,* and subsequently discuss estimation and inference with heteroskedastic and serially correlated errors.

As for the nature of the effects, strictly speaking, the term *fixed effects* would refer to a sampling process in which the same units are (possibly) repeatedly sampled for a given period holding constant the effects. In such context one often has in mind a distribution of individual effects chosen by the researcher.

---

[5]Note that a formally even weaker assumption would be

$$E(v_{it} - v_{i(t-1)} \mid x_i) = 0,$$

since this would be equivalent to saying that $E(v_{it} \mid x_i)$ could be an arbitrary function of x_i which does not vary with t. However, if $E(v_{it} \mid x_i) = \varphi(x_i)$ for any t, we could always redefine η_i and v_{it} as $\eta_i^\dagger = \eta_i + \varphi(x_i)$ and $v_{it}^\dagger = v_{it} - \varphi(x_i)$, respectively, so that $\eta_i^\dagger$ would still be fixed over time and $E(v_{it}^\dagger \mid x_i) = 0$.

Here we imagine a sample randomly drawn from a multivariate population of observable data and unobservable effects. This notion may or may not correspond to the physical nature of data collection. It would be so, for example, in the case of some household surveys, but not with data on all quoted firms or OECD countries. In those cases, the multivariate population from which the data are supposed to come is a hypothetical one. Moreover, we are interested in models which only specify features of the conditional distribution $f(y_i \mid x_i, \eta_i)$. Therefore, we are not concerned with whether the distribution that generates the data on x_i and η_i, $f(x_i, \eta_i)$ say, is representative of some cross-sectional population or of the researcher's wishes. We just regard (y_i, x_i, η_i) as a random sample from the (perhaps artificial) multivariate population with joint distribution $f(y_i, x_i, \eta_i) = f(y_i \mid x_i, \eta_i) f(x_i, \eta_i)$ and focus on the conditional distribution of y_i. So in common with much of the econometric literature, we use the term fixed effects to refer to a situation in which $f(\eta_i \mid x_i)$ is left unrestricted.

2.2.2   Within-Group Estimation

With $T = 2$ there is just one equation after differencing. Under Assumptions *A1* and *A2*, the equation in first-differences is a classical regression model and hence ordinary least-squares (OLS) in first-differences is the optimal estimator of β in the standard least-squares sense. To see the irrelevance of the equations in levels in this model, note that a non-singular transformation of the original two-equation system is

$$E(y_{i1} \mid x_i) = x_{i1}'\beta + E(\eta_i \mid x_i)$$

$$E(\Delta y_{i2} \mid x_i) = \Delta x_{i2}'\beta.$$

Since $E(\eta_i \mid x_i)$ is an unknown unrestricted function of x_i, knowledge of the function $E(y_{i1} \mid x_i)$ is uninformative about β in the first equation. Thus no information about β is lost by only considering the equation in first-differences.

If $T \geq 3$ we have a system of $T - 1$ equations in first-differences:

$$\Delta y_{i2} = \Delta x_{i2}'\beta + \Delta v_{i2}$$
$$\vdots$$
$$\Delta y_{iT} = \Delta x_{iT}'\beta + \Delta v_{iT},$$

which in compact form can be written as

$$Dy_i = DX_i\beta + Dv_i, \tag{2.13}$$

where D is the $(T-1) \times T$ matrix first-difference operator

$$D = \begin{pmatrix} -1 & 1 & 0 & \cdots & 0 & 0 \\ 0 & -1 & 1 & & 0 & 0 \\ \vdots & & & \ddots & & \vdots \\ 0 & 0 & 0 & \cdots & -1 & 1 \end{pmatrix} \qquad (2.14)$$

Provided each of the errors in first-differences are mean independent of the xs for all periods (under Assumption $A1$ or $A1'$) $E(Dv_i \mid x_i) = 0$, OLS estimates of β in this system given by

$$\widehat{\beta}_{OLS} = \left(\sum_{i=1}^{N} (DX_i)' DX_i \right)^{-1} \sum_{i=1}^{N} (DX_i)' Dy_i \qquad (2.15)$$

will be unbiased and consistent for large N. However, if the vs are homoskedastic and non-autocorrelated classical errors (under Assumption $A2$ or $A2'$), the errors in first-differences will be correlated for adjacent periods with

$$Var(Dv_i \mid x_i) = \sigma^2 DD'. \qquad (2.16)$$

Following standard regression theory, the optimal estimator in this case is given by generalized least-squares (GLS), which takes the form

$$\widehat{\beta}_{WG} = \left(\sum_{i=1}^{N} X_i' D' (DD')^{-1} DX_i \right)^{-1} \sum_{i=1}^{N} X_i' D' (DD')^{-1} Dy_i. \qquad (2.17)$$

Moreover, note that in this case GLS itself is a feasible estimator since DD' does not depend on unknown coefficients.

The idempotent matrix $D' (DD')^{-1} D$ also takes the form[6]

$$D' (DD')^{-1} D = I_T - \iota\iota'/T \equiv Q, \text{ say.} \qquad (2.18)$$

The matrix Q is known as the *deviations-from-time-means* or *within-group* operator because it transforms the original time series into deviations from time means: $\widetilde{y}_i = Qy_i$, whose elements are given by

$$\widetilde{y}_{it} = y_{it} - \overline{y}_i$$

[6]To verify this, note that the $T \times T$ matrix

$$\mathcal{H} = \begin{pmatrix} T^{-1/2}\iota' \\ (DD')^{-1/2} D \end{pmatrix}$$

is such that $\mathcal{H}\mathcal{H}' = I_T$, so that also $\mathcal{H}'\mathcal{H} = I_T$ or

$$\iota\iota'/T + D' (DD')^{-1} D = I_T.$$

with $\bar{y}_i = T^{-1} \sum_{s=1}^{T} y_{is}$. Therefore, $\widehat{\beta}_{WG}$ can also be expressed as OLS in deviations from time means

$$\widehat{\beta}_{WG} = \left[\sum_{i=1}^{N} \sum_{t=1}^{T} (x_{it} - \bar{x}_i)(x_{it} - \bar{x}_i)' \right]^{-1} \sum_{i=1}^{N} \sum_{t=1}^{T} (x_{it} - \bar{x}_i)(y_{it} - \bar{y}_i). \quad (2.19)$$

This is probably the most popular estimator in panel data analysis, and it is known under a variety of names including within-group and covariance estimator.[7]

It is also known as the *dummy-variable least-squares* or "fixed effects" estimator. This name reflects the fact that since $\widehat{\beta}_{WG}$ is a least-squares estimator after subtracting individual means to the observations, it is numerically the same as the estimator of β that would be obtained in a OLS regression of y on x and a set of N dummy variables, one for each individual in the sample. Thus $\widehat{\beta}_{WG}$ can also be regarded as the result of estimating jointly by OLS β and the realizations of the individual effects that appear in the sample.

To see this, consider the system of T equations in levels

$$y_i = X_i\beta + \iota\eta_i + v_i$$

and write it in stacked form as

$$y = X\beta + C\eta + v, \quad (2.20)$$

where $y = (y_1', ..., y_N')'$ and $v = (v_1', ..., v_N')'$ are $NT \times 1$ vectors, $X = (X_1', ..., X_N')'$ is an $NT \times k$ matrix, C is an $NT \times N$ matrix of individual dummies given by $C = I_N \otimes \iota$, and $\eta = (\eta_1, ..., \eta_N)'$ is the $N \times 1$ vector of individual specific effects or intercepts. Using the result from partitioned regression, the OLS regression of y on X and C gives the following expression for estimated β

$$\left[X'\left(I_{NT} - C(C'C)^{-1}C'\right)X \right]^{-1} X'\left(I_{NT} - C(C'C)^{-1}C'\right)y \quad (2.21)$$

which clearly coincides with $\widehat{\beta}_{WG}$ since $I_{NT} - C(C'C)^{-1}C' = I_N \otimes Q$.

The expressions for the estimated effects are

$$\widehat{\eta}_i = \frac{1}{T} \sum_{t=1}^{T} \left(y_{it} - x_{it}'\widehat{\beta}_{WG} \right) \equiv \bar{y}_i - \bar{x}_i'\widehat{\beta}_{WG} \ (i = 1, ..., N). \quad (2.22)$$

We do not need to go beyond standard regression theory to obtain the sampling properties of these estimators. The fact that $\widehat{\beta}_{WG}$ is the GLS for the system of $T - 1$ equations in first-differences tells us that it will be unbiased

---

[7]The name "within-group" originated in the context of data with a group structure (like data on families and family members). Panel data can be regarded as a special case of this type of data in which the "group" is formed by the time series observations from a given individual.

and optimal in finite samples. It will also be consistent as N tends to infinity for fixed T and asymptotically normal under usual regularity conditions. The $\widehat{\eta}_i$ will also be unbiased estimates of the η_i for samples of any size, but being time series averages, their variance can only tend to zero as T tends to infinity. Therefore, they cannot be consistent estimates for fixed T and large N. Clearly, the within-group estimates $\widehat{\beta}_{WG}$ will also be consistent as T tends to infinity regardless of whether N is fixed or not.

Fixed effects or analysis-of-covariance models have a long tradition in econometrics. Their use was first suggested in two Cowles Commission papers by Hildreth (1949, 1950), and early applications were conducted by Mundlak (1961) and Hoch (1962). The motivation in these two studies was to rely on fixed effects in order to control for simultaneity bias in the estimation of agricultural production functions.

Orthogonal Deviations   Finally, it is worth finding out the form of the transformation to the original data that results from doing first-differences and further applying a GLS transformation to the differenced data to remove the moving-average serial correlation induced by differencing (Arellano and Bover, 1995). The required transformation is given by the $(T-1) \times T$ matrix

$$A = (DD')^{-1/2} D.$$

If we choose $(DD')^{-1/2}$ to be the upper triangular Cholesky factorization, the operator A can be shown to take the form $A = diag[(T-1)/T, ..., 1/2]^{1/2} A^+$ where

$$A^+ = \begin{pmatrix} 1 & (1-T)^{-1} & (1-T)^{-1} & \cdots & (1-T)^{-1} & (1-T)^{-1} & (1-T)^{-1} \\ 0 & 1 & (2-T)^{-1} & \cdots & (2-T)^{-1} & (2-T)^{-1} & (2-T)^{-1} \\ \vdots & \vdots & \vdots & & \vdots & \vdots & \vdots \\ 0 & 0 & 0 & \cdots & 1 & -1/2 & -1/2 \\ 0 & 0 & 0 & \cdots & 0 & 1 & -1 \end{pmatrix}.$$

Therefore, a $T \times 1$ time series error transformed by A, $v_i^* = Av_i$ will consist of $T-1$ elements of the form

$$v_{it}^* = c_t[v_{it} - \frac{1}{(T-t)}(v_{i(t+1)} + ... + v_{iT})] \tag{2.23}$$

where $c_t^2 = (T-t)/(T-t+1)$. Clearly, $A'A = Q$ and $AA' = I_{T-1}$. We then refer to this transformation as *forward orthogonal deviations*. Thus, if $Var(v_i) = \sigma^2 I_T$ we also have $Var(v_i^*) = \sigma^2 I_{T-1}$. So orthogonal deviations can be regarded as an alternative transformation, which in common with first-differencing eliminates individual effects but in contrast it does not introduce serial correlation in the transformed errors. Moreover, the within-group estimator can also be regarded as OLS in orthogonal deviations. In terms of the within-group algebra it makes no difference whether forward or backward orthogonal deviations are used. However, forward orthogonal deviations will turn out to be specially useful in the discussion of dynamic models.

2.3   Heteroskedasticity and Serial Correlation

2.3.1   Robust Standard Errors for Within-Group Estimators

If Assumption *A1* holds but *A2* does not (that is, using orthogonal deviations, if $E(v_i^* \mid x_i) = 0$ but $Var(v_i^* \mid x_i) \neq \sigma^2 I_{T-1}$), the ordinary regression formulae for estimating the within-group variance will lead to inconsistent standard errors. Such formula is given by

$$\widehat{Var}(\widehat{\beta}_{WG}) = \widehat{\sigma}^2 (X^{*\prime} X^*)^{-1} \tag{2.24}$$

where $X^* = (I_N \otimes A)X$, $y^* = (I_N \otimes A)y$, and $\widehat{\sigma}^2$ is the unbiased residual variance

$$\widehat{\sigma}^2 = \frac{1}{N(T-1)-k}(y^* - X^*\widehat{\beta}_{WG})'(y^* - X^*\widehat{\beta}_{WG}). \tag{2.25}$$

However, since

$$\left(\frac{1}{N}X^{*\prime}X^*\right)\sqrt{N}(\widehat{\beta}_{WG} - \beta) = \frac{1}{\sqrt{N}}\sum_{i=1}^{N} X_i^{*\prime} v_i^*$$

and $E(X_i^{*\prime} v_i^*) = 0$, the right-hand side of the previous expression is a scaled sample average of zero-mean random variables to which a standard central limit theorem for multivariate *iid* observations can be applied for fixed T as N tends to infinity:

$$\frac{1}{\sqrt{N}}\sum_{i=1}^{N} X_i^{*\prime} v_i^* \xrightarrow{d} \mathcal{N}\left[0, E(X_i^{*\prime} v_i^* v_i^{*\prime} X_i^*)\right].$$

Therefore, an estimate of the asymptotic variance of the within-group estimator that is robust to heteroskedasticity and serial correlation of arbitrary forms for fixed T and large N can be obtained as

$$\widetilde{Var}(\widehat{\beta}_{WG}) = (X^{*\prime}X^*)^{-1}\left(\sum_{i=1}^{N} X_i^{*\prime}\widehat{v}_i^* \widehat{v}_i^{*\prime} X_i^*\right)(X^{*\prime}X^*)^{-1} \tag{2.26}$$

with $\widehat{v}_i^* = y_i^* - X_i^*\widehat{\beta}_{WG}$ (Arellano, 1987). For large T and fixed N, however, such an estimate of the variance would not be consistent and an alternative estimate will be required. We next discuss this case.

Robust Standard Errors for Large T and Fixed N The previous distribution theory for small T and large N allowed for arbitrary time series dependence but relied on cross-sectional independence. With large T and fixed N we can allow for arbitrary cross-sectional dependence by relying on sufficiently weak time series dependence.

Let $\widehat{\delta}_{WG} = \left(\widehat{\beta}'_{WG}, \widehat{\eta}' \right)'$ denote the within-group estimator of β and η, and let $w_{it} = (x'_{it}, d'_i)'$ where d_i is a $N \times 1$ vector with one in the i-th position and zero elsewhere. Moreover, let

$$V = \plim_{T \to \infty} \frac{1}{T} \sum_{t=1}^{T} \sum_{s=1}^{T} \sum_{i=1}^{N} \sum_{j=1}^{N} v_{it} v_{js} w_{it} w'_{js} \tag{2.27}$$

or equivalently

$$V = \plim_{T \to \infty} \frac{1}{T} \sum_{t=1}^{T} \sum_{s=1}^{T} W'_t v_t v'_s W_s \tag{2.28}$$

where

$$W'_t v_t = \sum_{i=1}^{N} w_{it} v_{it}.$$

A positive semi-definite estimator of V of the type suggested by Newey and West (1987) takes the form

$$\widehat{V} = \widehat{\Omega}_0 + \sum_{\ell=1}^{m} \omega(\ell, m) \left(\widehat{\Omega}_\ell + \widehat{\Omega}'_\ell \right) \tag{2.29}$$

where $\omega(\ell, m) = 1 - [\ell / (m + 1)]$,

$$\widehat{\Omega}_\ell = \frac{1}{T} \sum_{t=\ell+1}^{T} \sum_{i=1}^{N} \sum_{j=1}^{N} \widehat{v}_{it} \widehat{v}_{j(t-\ell)} w_{it} w'_{j(t-\ell)} = \frac{1}{T} \sum_{t=\ell+1}^{T} W'_t \widehat{v}_t \widehat{v}'_{t-\ell} W_{t-\ell} \tag{2.30}$$

and $\widehat{v}_{it} = y_{it} - x'_{it} \widehat{\beta}_{WG} - \widehat{\eta}_i$. The effect of the weight function $\omega(\ell, m)$ is to smooth the sample autocovariance function by assigning declining weights to sample autocovariances as ℓ increases.

Provided the data are a mixing sequence, and the bound m on the number of autocovariances used to form $\widehat{V}$ is chosen as a suitable function of T, $\widehat{V}$ can be shown to be a consistent estimator of V as $T \to \infty$ for fixed N using Newey and West's Theorem 2.

Therefore, an estimate of the asymptotic variance of the within-group estimator of β and η that is robust to cross-sectional dependence, heteroskedasticity, and serial correlation of arbitrary forms, for mixing data with large T and fixed N can be obtained as

$$\widetilde{Var}(\widehat{\delta}_{WG}) = T \left(\sum_{t=1}^{T} \sum_{i=1}^{N} w_{it} w'_{it} \right)^{-1} \widehat{V} \left(\sum_{t=1}^{T} \sum_{i=1}^{N} w_{it} w'_{it} \right)^{-1} \tag{2.31}$$

2.3.2   Optimal GLS with Heteroskedasticity and Autocorrelation of Unknown Form

Returning to a large N and fixed T environment, if $Var(v_i^* \mid x_i) = \Omega(x_i)$ where $\Omega(x_i)$ is a symmetric matrix of order $T-1$ containing unknown functions of x_i, the optimal estimator of β will be of the form

$$\widehat{\beta}_{UGLS} = \left(\sum_{i=1}^{N} X_i^{*\prime} \Omega^{-1}(x_i) X_i^* \right)^{-1} \sum_{i=1}^{N} X_i^{*\prime} \Omega^{-1}(x_i) y_i^*. \qquad (2.32)$$

This estimator is unfeasible because $\Omega(x_i)$ is unknown. A feasible semi parametric GLS estimator would use instead a nonparametric estimator of $E(v_i^* v_i^{*\prime} \mid x_i)$ based on within-group residuals. Under appropriate regularity conditions and a suitable choice of nonparametric estimator, feasible GLS can be shown to attain for large N the same efficiency as $\widehat{\beta}_{UGLS}$ using the results in Robinson (1987).

A special case which gives rise to a straightforward feasible GLS (for small T and large N), first discussed by Kiefer (1980), is one in which the conditional variance of v_i^* is a constant but non-scalar matrix: $Var(v_i^* \mid x_i) = \Omega$. This assumption rules out conditional heteroskedasticity, but allows for autocorrelation and unconditional time series heteroskedasticity in the original equation errors v_{it}. In this case, a feasible GLS estimator takes the form

$$\widehat{\beta}_{FGLS} = \left(\sum_{i=1}^{N} X_i^{*\prime} \widehat{\Omega}^{-1} X_i^* \right)^{-1} \sum_{i=1}^{N} X_i^{*\prime} \widehat{\Omega}^{-1} y_i^* \qquad (2.33)$$

where $\widehat{\Omega}$ is given by the orthogonal-deviation WG residual intertemporal covariance matrix

$$\widehat{\Omega} = \frac{1}{N} \sum_{i=1}^{N} \widehat{v}_i^* \widehat{v}_i^{*\prime}. \qquad (2.34)$$

2.3.3   Improved GMM and Minimum Distance Estimation under Heteroskedasticity and Autocorrelation of Unknown Form

The basic condition $E(v_i^* \mid x_i) = 0$ implies that any function of x_i is uncorrelated to v_i^* and therefore a potential instrumental variable. Thus, any list of moment conditions of the form

$$E\left[h_t(x_i) v_{it}^* \right] = 0 \ (t = 1, ..., T - 1) \qquad (2.35)$$

for given functions $h_t(x_i)$ such that β is identified from (2.35), could be used to obtain a consistent GMM estimator of β.

Under $\Omega(x_i) = \sigma^2 I_{T-1}$ the optimal moment conditions are given by

$$E\left(X_i^{*\prime} v_i^*\right) = 0 \qquad (2.36)$$

in the sense that the variance of the corresponding optimal method-of-moments estimator (which in this case is OLS in orthogonal deviations, or the WG estimator) cannot be reduced by using other functions of x_i as instruments in addition to (2.36).[8]

For arbitrary $\Omega(x_i)$ the optimal moment conditions are

$$E\left[X_i^{*\prime} \Omega^{-1}(x_i) v_i^*\right] = 0 \qquad (2.37)$$

which gives rise to the optimal GLS estimator $\widehat{\beta}_{UGLS}$ given in (2.32).

The k moment conditions (2.37), however, cannot be directly used because $\Omega(x_i)$ is unknown. The simpler, improved estimators that we consider in this section are based on the fact that optimal GMM from a wider list of moments than (2.36) can be asymptotically more efficient than WG when $\Omega(x_i) \neq \sigma^2 I_{T-1}$, although not as efficient as optimal GLS. In particular, it seems natural to consider GMM estimators of the system of $T-1$ equations in orthogonal deviations (or first-differences) using the explanatory variables for all time periods as separate instruments for each equation:

$$E\left(v_i^* \otimes x_i\right) = 0. \qquad (2.38)$$

Note that the k moments in (2.36) are linear combinations of the much larger set of $kT(T-1)$ moments contained in (2.38). Also, it is convenient to write (2.38) as

$$E\left(Z_i' v_i^*\right) \equiv E\left[Z_i'(y_i^* - X_i^* \beta)\right] = 0 \qquad (2.39)$$

where $Z_i = (I_{T-1} \otimes x_i')$. With this notation, the optimal GMM estimator from (2.38) or (2.39) is given by

$$\widehat{\beta}_{GMM} = \left[\left(\sum_i X_i^{*\prime} Z_i\right) A_N \left(\sum_i Z_i' X_i^*\right)\right]^{-1} \left(\sum_i X_i^{*\prime} Z_i\right) A_N \left(\sum_i Z_i' y_i^*\right). \qquad (2.40)$$

Optimality requires that the weight matrix A_N is a consistent estimate up to a multiplicative constant of the inverse of the variance of the orthogonality conditions $E\left(Z_i' v_i^* v_i^{*\prime} Z_i\right)$.

Under Assumption A2 $E\left(Z_i' v_i^* v_i^{*\prime} Z_i\right) = \sigma^2 E\left(Z_i' Z_i\right)$, and therefore an optimal choice is $A_N = \left(\sum_i Z_i' Z_i\right)^{-1}$. In such a case the resulting estimator is numerically the same as the within-group estimator because the columns in X_i^* are linear combinations of those in Z_i.

---

[8] Appendix B provides a review of results on optimal instruments in conditional models.

More generally, an optimal choice under heteroskedasticity and serial correlation of unknown form is given by

$$A_N = \left(\sum_i Z_i' \widehat{v}_i^* \widehat{v}_i^{*\prime} Z_i \right)^{-1} \tag{2.41}$$

The resulting estimator, $\widehat{\beta}_{OGMM}$ say, will be asymptotically equivalent to WG under Assumption *A2* but strictly more efficient for large N when the assumption is violated. It will, nevertheless, be inefficient relative to $\widehat{\beta}_{UGLS}$. The relationship among the large sample variances of the three estimators is therefore

$$Var(\widehat{\beta}_{UGLS}) \leq Var(\widehat{\beta}_{OGMM}) \leq Var(\widehat{\beta}_{WG}),$$

with equality in both cases when Assumption *A2* holds.

Minimum Distance   Estimators of the previous type were considered by Chamberlain (1982, 1984) who motivated them as minimum distance (MD) estimators from a linear projection of y_i on x_i:

$$E^*(y_i \mid x_i) = \pi_0 + \Pi x_i. \tag{2.42}$$

Under the model's specification $E(y_i \mid x_i, \eta_i) = X_i\beta + \iota\eta_i$. Thus

$$\pi_0 + \Pi x_i = X_i\beta + \iota E^*(\eta_i \mid x_i) = (I_T \otimes \beta')x_i + \iota \left(\delta + \lambda' x_i \right)$$

where λ denotes the $Tk \times 1$ vector of slope coefficients in the linear projection of η_i on x_i and δ is the intercept, so that $\pi_0 = \delta\iota$ and

$$\Pi = (I_T \otimes \beta') + \iota\lambda'. \tag{2.43}$$

Chamberlain considered MD estimators of β and λ based on unrestricted OLS estimates of Π, which are equivalent to the GMM estimators given in (2.40).[9] To see this note that Π can be transformed into $A\Pi$ and $(\iota'/T)\Pi$ with the latter being unrestricted moments:

$$\Pi^* \equiv A\Pi = A \otimes \beta' \tag{2.44}$$

$$(\iota'/T)\Pi = \left(\frac{1}{T}\iota \otimes \beta \right)' + \lambda'. \tag{2.45}$$

Thus, all the information about β in Π is contained in Π^*. An unrestricted OLS estimate of Π^* is given by

---

[9]Let p be a vector of coefficients that satisfy a set of parameter restrictions $p = p(\theta)$, and let $\widehat{p}$ be an unrestricted estimator of p. An MD estimator of θ minimizes $\left[\widehat{p} - p(c)\right]' A_N \left[\widehat{p} - p(c)\right]$ for some weight matrix A_N.

$$\widehat{\Pi}^* = \sum_i y_i^* x_i' \left(\sum_i x_i x_i' \right)^{-1}, \tag{2.46}$$

and an optimal MD estimator of β minimizes the criterion

$$\left[vec(\widehat{\Pi}^* - \Pi^*) \right]' \widehat{V}^{-1} vec(\widehat{\Pi}^* - \Pi^*) \tag{2.47}$$

where $\widehat{V}$ is a consistent estimate of the large sample variance of $vec\left(\widehat{\Pi}^*\right)$.

The equivalence to GMM follows from noting that

$$vec(\widehat{\Pi}^* - \Pi^*) = vec \left[\sum_i v_i^* x_i' \left(\sum_i x_i x_i' \right)^{-1} \right] = \left(\sum_i Z_i' Z_i \right)^{-1} \sum_i Z_i' v_i^*$$

and that $\widehat{V}$ takes the form

$$\widehat{V} = \left(\sum_i Z_i' Z_i \right)^{-1} A_N \left(\sum_i Z_i' Z_i \right)^{-1}$$

Thus the MD estimator that minimizes (2.47) coincides with the WG estimator when $A_N = (\sum_i Z_i' Z_i)^{-1}$, and with $\widehat{\beta}_{OGMM}$ when A_N equals the robust choice (2.41).[10]

2.4 Likelihood Approaches

The within-group estimator can be regarded as the Gaussian maximum likelihood estimator under three different likelihood approaches—joint, conditional, and marginal—relative to the individual effects. This is a special feature of the static linear model. In other models, different likelihood approaches give rise to different estimators. Nevertheless, regardless of their maxima, the alternative likelihood functions for the static model that we discuss in this section may be of interest in their own right from a Bayesian perspective.

---

[10]If $\widehat{\Pi}^*$ were replaced by $A\widehat{\Pi}$ with

$$\widehat{\Pi} = \left(\sum_i y_i (x_i - \overline{x})' \right) \left(\sum_i (x_i - \overline{x}) (x_i - \overline{x})' \right)^{-1}.$$

that is, OLS with unrestricted intercepts in (2.42), we obtain the same equivalence with WG and, in the robust case, an equivalence with a GMM estimator that in addition to x_i uses period-specific intercepts as instruments.

2.4.1   Joint Likelihood

Under the normality assumption:

$$y_i \mid x_i, \eta_i \sim \mathcal{N}\left(X_i\beta + \eta_i\iota, \sigma^2 I_T\right), \tag{2.48}$$

the log conditional density of y_i given x_i and η_i takes the form

$$\log f\left(y_i \mid x_i, \eta_i\right) \propto -\frac{T}{2}\log\sigma^2 - \frac{1}{2\sigma^2}v_i'v_i \tag{2.49}$$

where $v_i = (y_i - X_i\beta - \eta_i\iota)$. Thus, the log likelihood of a cross-sectional sample of independent observations is a function of β, σ^2, and $\eta_1, ..., \eta_N$:

$$L\left(\beta, \sigma^2, \eta; y, x\right) = \sum_{i=1}^{N}\log f\left(y_i \mid x_i, \eta_i\right). \tag{2.50}$$

In view of our previous discussion and standard linear regression maximum likelihood (ML) estimation, joint maximization of (2.50) with respect to β, η, and σ^2 yields the WG estimator for β, the residual estimates for η given in (2.22), and the residual variance without degrees of freedom correction for σ^2:

$$\widetilde{\sigma}^2 = \frac{1}{NT}\sum_{i=1}^{N}\widehat{v}_i'\widehat{v}_i \tag{2.51}$$

where $\widehat{v}_i = \left(y_i - X_i\widehat{\beta}_{WG} - \widehat{\eta}_i\iota\right)$.

Unlike (2.25) $\widetilde{\sigma}^2$ will not be a consistent estimator of σ^2 for large N and small T panels. In effect, since $E\left(\sum_{i=1}^{N}\widehat{v}_i'\widehat{v}_i\right) = (NT - N - k)\sigma^2$, we have

$$\plim_{N\to\infty}\widetilde{\sigma}^2 = \frac{(T-1)}{T}\sigma^2.$$

Thus $\widetilde{\sigma}^2$ has a negative (cross-sectional) large sample bias given by σ^2/T. This is an example of the *incidental parameter problem* studied by Neyman and Scott (1948). The problem is that the maximum likelihood estimator need not be consistent when the likelihood depends on a subset of (incidental) parameters whose number increases with sample size. In our case, the likelihood depends on β, σ^2 and the incidental parameters $\eta_1, ..., \eta_N$. The ML estimator of β is consistent but that of σ^2 is not.

2.4.2   Conditional Likelihood

In the linear static model, $\overline{y}_i = T^{-1}\sum_{t=1}^{T}y_{it}$ is a sufficient statistic for η_i. This means that the density of y_i given x_i, η_i, and $\overline{y}_i$ does not depend on η_i

$$f\left(y_i \mid x_i, \eta_i, \overline{y}_i\right) = f\left(y_i \mid x_i, \overline{y}_i\right). \tag{2.52}$$

To see this, note that, expressing the conditional density of y_i given $\overline{y}_i$ as a ratio of the joint and marginal densities, we have

$$f\left(y_i \mid x_i, \eta_i, \overline{y}_i\right) = \frac{f\left(y_i \mid x_i, \eta_i\right)}{f\left(\overline{y}_i \mid x_i, \eta_i\right)}$$

and that under (2.48)

$$\overline{y}_i \mid x_i, \eta_i \sim \mathcal{N}\left(\overline{x}_i'\beta + \eta_i, \frac{\sigma^2}{T}\right),$$

so that

$$\log f\left(\overline{y}_i \mid x_i, \eta_i\right) \propto -\frac{1}{2}\log \sigma^2 - \frac{T}{2\sigma^2}\overline{v}_i^2. \tag{2.53}$$

Subtracting (2.53) from (2.49) we obtain:

$$\log f\left(y_i \mid x_i, \eta_i, \overline{y}_i\right) \propto -\frac{(T-1)}{2}\log \sigma^2 - \frac{1}{2\sigma^2}\sum_{t=1}^{T}\left(v_{it} - \overline{v}_i\right)^2 \tag{2.54}$$

which does not depend on η_i because it is only a function of the within-group errors.

Thus the conditional log likelihood

$$L_c\left(\beta, \sigma^2; y, x\right) = \sum_{i=1}^{N}\log f\left(y_i \mid x_i, \overline{y}_i\right) \tag{2.55}$$

is a function of β and σ^2 which can be used as an alternative basis for inference. The maximizers of (2.55) are the WG estimator of β and

$$\overline{\sigma}^2 = \frac{1}{N(T-1)}\sum_{i=1}^{N}\widehat{v}_i'\widehat{v}_i. \tag{2.56}$$

Note that contrary to (2.51), (2.56) is consistent for large N and small T, although it is not exactly unbiased as (2.25).

2.4.3 Marginal (or Integrated) Likelihood

Finally, we may consider the marginal distribution of y_i given x_i but not η_i:

$$f\left(y_i \mid x_i\right) = \int f\left(y_i \mid x_i, \eta_i\right) dF\left(\eta_i \mid x_i\right)$$

where $F\left(\eta_i \mid x_i\right)$ denotes the conditional *cdf* of η_i given x_i. One possibility, in the spirit of the MD approach discussed in the previous section, is to assume

$$\eta_i \mid x_i \sim \mathcal{N}\left(\delta + \lambda'x_i, \sigma_\eta^2\right), \tag{2.57}$$

but it is of some interest to study the form of $f\left(y_i \mid x_i\right)$ for arbitrary $F\left(\eta_i \mid x_i\right)$.

Let us consider the non-singular transformation matrix

$$H = \begin{pmatrix} T^{-1}\iota' \\ A \end{pmatrix}.$$ (2.58)

Note that

$$f(y_i \mid x_i, \eta_i) = f(Hy_i \mid x_i, \eta_i) \left| \det(H) \right|,$$ (2.59)

but since $|\det(H)| = T^{-1/2}$ is a constant it can be ignored for our purposes. Moreover, since[11]

$$Cov(y_i^*, \bar{y}_i \mid x_i, \eta_i) = E(v_i^* \bar{v}_i \mid x_i, \eta_i) = 0,$$ (2.60)

given normality we have that the conditional density of y_i factorizes into the between-group and the orthogonal deviation densities:

$$f(y_i \mid x_i, \eta_i) = f(\bar{y}_i \mid x_i, \eta_i) f(y_i^* \mid x_i, \eta_i).$$ (2.61)

Note in addition that the orthogonal deviation density is independent of η_i

$$f(y_i^* \mid x_i, \eta_i) = f(y_i^* \mid x_i),$$

and in view of (2.52) it coincides with the conditional density given $\bar{y}_i$

$$f(y_i^* \mid x_i) = f(y_i \mid x_i, \bar{y}_i).$$ (2.62)

Thus, either way we have

$$\log f(y_i \mid x_i) = \log f(y_i^* \mid x_i) + \log \int f(\bar{y}_i \mid x_i, \eta_i) \, dF(\eta_i \mid x_i).$$ (2.63)

If $F(\eta_i \mid x_i)$ is unrestricted, the second term on the right-hand side of (2.63) is uninformative about β so that the marginal ML estimators of β and σ^2 coincide with the maximizers of $\sum_{i=1}^{N} \log f(y_i^* \mid x_i)$, which are again given by the WG estimator and (2.56). This is still true when $F(\eta_i \mid x_i)$ is specified to be Gaussian with unrestricted linear projection of η_i on x_i, as in (2.57), but not when η_i is assumed to be independent of x_i (i.e. $\lambda = 0$), as we shall see in Chapter 3.

----

[11]Note that

$$E(v_i^* \bar{v}_i \mid x_i, \eta_i) = AE(v_i v_i' \mid x_i, \eta_i) \iota/T = \sigma^2 A\iota/T = 0.$$

Specifically, suppose that $F(\eta_i \mid x_i)$ is as in (2.57), then $f(\bar{y}_i \mid x_i)$ corresponds to

$$\bar{y}_i \mid x_i \sim \mathcal{N}\left(\delta + \psi' x_i, \bar{\sigma}^2\right)$$

where $\psi = \lambda + (\iota \otimes \beta / T)$ and $\bar{\sigma}^2 = \sigma_\eta^2 + \sigma^2 / T$. If λ and σ_η^2 are free parameters, ψ and $\bar{\sigma}^2$ are uninformative about β and σ^2. Note that even if (2.57) is replaced with

$$\eta_i \mid x_i \sim \mathcal{N}\left(\delta + \lambda_a' \bar{x}_i, \sigma_\eta^2\right),$$

that is, if we assume that $\lambda = \iota \otimes \lambda_a / T$,[12] the distribution of $\bar{y}_i$ given x_i remains uninformative about β and σ^2.

2.5 Nonlinear Models with Additive Effects

So far we have focused on linear regression models. Nevertheless, the arguments presented in this chapter generalize in a straightforward way to the case of conditional moment restriction models with additive effects. This class includes nonlinear regression models, and linear and nonlinear simultaneous equations models with additive effects. We first describe nonlinear regressions and linear instrumental-variable models, and conclude by considering the general case.

The crucial feature of the models in this section is that the unobservable variables are additive terms. This excludes generalized linear regression models of the form $E(y_{it} \mid x_i, \eta_i) = g(x_{it}'\beta + \eta_i)$ where $g(.)$ is some nonlinear link function (as in exponential, logit, and probit regression), and structural equations with non-additive errors, like discrete choice models with endogenous explanatory variables (panel data models with nonlinear effects are surveyed in Arellano and Honoré, 2001).

2.5.1 Nonlinear Regression

The model considered is a nonlinear version of (2.7)

$$y_{it} = g_t(x_{it}, \beta) + \eta_i + v_{it} \tag{2.64}$$

which can be stacked over time for individual i to give $y_i = g(x_i, \beta) + \iota \eta_i + v_i$. Under Assumptions *A1* and *A2*, the optimal estimator is nonlinear least-squares in orthogonal deviations or nonlinear within-groups:

$$\widehat{\beta}_{NWG} = \arg\min \sum_{i=1}^{N} [y_i - g(x_i, \beta)]' A' A [y_i - g(x_i, \beta)]. \tag{2.65}$$

If *A1* holds but *A2* does not, so that $Var(v_i^* \mid x_i) = \Omega(x_i)$, the optimal estimator is of the form

---

[12]A specification of this type was first considered by Mundlak (1978).

$$\widehat{\beta}_{NUGLS} = \arg\min \sum_{i=1}^{N} [y_i - g(x_i, \beta)]' A' \Omega^{-1}(x_i) A [y_i - g(x_i, \beta)], \quad (2.66)$$

which is a nonlinear version of the unfeasible GLS estimator given in (2.32).

2.5.2   Linear Structural Equation

In the standard fixed effects model all the "endogeneity" of x in the relationship between y and x is captured by the correlation between x and η, since x and the time-varying error v are assumed to be uncorrelated at all lags and leads. We now consider an instrumental variable fixed effects model in which x may also be correlated with v, but a vector of instruments $z_i = (z'_{i1}, ..., z'_{iT})'$ is available (possibly overlapping with some of the components of x) which may be correlated with η but not with v. The form of the model is therefore

$$y_{it} = x'_{it}\beta + \eta_i + v_{it}$$

together with

$$E(v_i \mid z_i, \eta_i) = 0. \tag{2.67}$$

In common with the standard case, the levels are uninformative about β in this model because $E(\eta_i \mid z_i)$ is an unknown unrestricted function of z_i. Thus, the basic condition is $E(v_i^* \mid z_i) = 0$ and the unfeasible optimal instrumental-variable estimator is

$$\widehat{\beta}_{UIV} = \left(\sum_{i=1}^{N} B(z_i)' X_i^* \right)^{-1} \sum_{i=1}^{N} B(z_i)' y_i^* \tag{2.68}$$

where $B(z_i)$ denotes the $(T-1) \times k$ matrix of optimal instruments given by (cf. Newey, 1993, and Appendix B):

$$B(z_i) = \Omega^{-1}(z_i) E(X_i^* \mid z_i) \tag{2.69}$$

and $\Omega(z_i) = Var(v_i^* \mid z_i)$.

Feasible approaches to optimal estimation can be based on an estimator $\widehat{B}(z_i)$ of $B(z_i)$. Alternatively, in parallel with the development in Section 2.3.3 we may consider GMM estimators based on the orthogonality conditions

$$E(v_i^* \otimes z_i) = 0. \tag{2.70}$$

The form of these estimators is the same as in (2.40) with $Z_i = (I_{T-1} \otimes z'_i)$. Using the inverse of $(\sum_i Z'_i Z_i)$ as weight matrix, we obtain the 2SLS-type estimator

$$\widehat{\beta}_{IVWG} = \left[\left(\sum_i X_i^{*'} Z_i \right) \left(\sum_i Z'_i Z_i \right)^{-1} \left(\sum_i Z'_i X_i^* \right) \right]^{-1}$$

$$\left(\sum_i X_i^{*'} Z_i\right)\left(\sum_i Z_i' Z_i\right)^{-1}\left(\sum_i Z_i' y_i^*\right). \tag{2.71}$$

If $\Omega(z_i) = \sigma^2 I_{T-1}$ and $E(X_i \mid z_i)$ is linear in z_i, then $\widehat{\beta}_{IVWG}$ and $\widehat{\beta}_{UIV}$ are asymptotically equivalent. On the other hand, if $z_{it} = x_{it}$ the statistic $\widehat{\beta}_{IVWG}$ boils down to the ordinary within-group estimator.

2.5.3 Nonlinear Simultaneous Equations

Finally, we consider a system of g nonlinear simultaneous equations with additive effects. The previous models can be regarded as special cases of this one with $g = 1$. We have:

$$\rho_t(w_i, \theta) = \eta_i + v_{it} \tag{2.72}$$

$$E(v_{it} \mid z_i, \eta_i) = 0 \ (t = 1, ..., T) \tag{2.73}$$

which can be stacked over time for individual i to give the gT-equation system $\rho(x_i, \theta) = (\iota \otimes \eta_i) + v_i$. In this model η_i denotes a $g \times 1$ vector of additive effects, and v_i is a vector of errors for different equations and time periods of dimension gT.

We consider estimation from the orthogonal-deviation conditional moment restrictions $E(v_i^* \mid z_i) = 0$ where $v_i^* = (A \otimes I_g)v_i$. The unfeasible optimal instrumental variable estimator in this case solves the estimating equations

$$\sum_{i=1}^{N} B(z_i)'(A \otimes I_g)\rho(x_i, \theta) = 0 \tag{2.74}$$

where $B(z_i)$ is now the $g(T-1) \times k$ matrix of optimal instruments

$$B(z_i) = \Omega^{-1}(z_i)E\left(\frac{\partial v_i^*}{\partial \theta'} \mid z_i\right) \tag{2.75}$$

and $\Omega(z_i) = Var(v_i^* \mid z_i)$ is a $g(T-1) \times g(T-1)$ covariance matrix. As before, feasible approaches include the use of estimated optimal instruments, and GMM estimation based on a particular choice of unconditional moment restrictions.

3

Error Components

The analysis in the previous chapter was motivated by the desire of identifying regression coefficients that are free from unobserved cross-sectional heterogeneity bias. Another major motivation for using panel data is the possibility of separating out permanent from transitory components of variation.

3.1 A Variance Decomposition

The starting point of our discussion is a simple variance-components model of the form

$$y_{it} = \mu + \eta_i + v_{it} \tag{3.1}$$

where μ is an intercept, $\eta_i \sim iid(0, \sigma_\eta^2)$, $v_{it} \sim iid(0, \sigma^2)$, and η_i and v_{it} are independent of each other. The cross-sectional variance of y_{it} in any given period is given by $(\sigma_\eta^2 + \sigma^2)$. This model tells us that a fraction $\sigma_\eta^2/(\sigma_\eta^2 + \sigma^2)$ of the total variance corresponds to differences that remain constant over time while the rest are differences that vary randomly over time and units.

Dividing total variance into two components that are either completely fixed or completely random will often be unrealistic, but this model and its extensions are at the basis of much useful econometric descriptive work. A prominent example is the study of earnings inequality and mobility (cf. Lillard and Willis, 1978). In the analysis of transitions between earnings classes, the model allows us to distinguish between aggregate or unconditional transition probabilities and individual transition probabilities given certain values of the permanent characteristics represented by η_i.

Indeed, given η_i, the ys are independent over time but with different means for different units, so that we have

$$y_i \mid \eta_i \sim id\left((\mu + \eta_i)\iota, \sigma^2 I_T\right),$$

whereas unconditionally we have

$$y_i \sim iid(\mu\iota, \Omega)$$

with

$$\Omega = \sigma^2 I_T + \sigma_\eta^2 \iota\iota'. \qquad (3.2)$$

Thus the unconditional correlation between y_{it} and y_{is} for any two periods $t \neq s$ is given by

$$Corr(y_{it}, y_{is}) = \frac{\sigma_\eta^2}{\sigma_\eta^2 + \sigma^2} = \frac{\lambda}{1+\lambda} \qquad (3.3)$$

with $\lambda = \sigma_\eta^2 / \sigma^2$.

In this model individual transition probabilities given η_i are independent of the state of origin:

$$\Pr(a \leq y_{it} \leq b \mid c \leq y_{i(t-1)} \leq d, \eta_i) = \Pr(a \leq y_{it} \leq b \mid \eta_i), \qquad (3.4)$$

but not so unconditionally:

$$\Pr(a \quad \leq \quad y_{it} \leq b \mid c \leq y_{i(t-1)} \leq d) = \qquad (3.5)$$
$$\frac{F_{t,t-1}(b,d) - F_{t,t-1}(b,c) - F_{t,t-1}(a,d) + F_{t,t-1}(a,c)}{F_{t-1}(d) - F_{t-1}(c)}$$

where $F_{t,t-1}(b,d) = \Pr(y_{it} \leq b; y_{i(t-1)} \leq d)$ and $F_{t-1}(d) = \Pr(y_{i(t-1)} \leq d)$. This is so because $F_{t,t-1}(b,d) \neq F_t(b) F_{t-1}(d)$ due to the correlation between y_{it} and $y_{i(t-1)}$ induced by the permanent effects. In effect, letting $G(.)$ be the *cdf* of η we have:

$$\begin{aligned} F_{t,t-1}(b,d) &= \int \Pr(y_{it} \leq b; y_{i(t-1)} \leq d \mid \eta) dG(\eta) \\ &= \int \Pr(y_{it} \leq b \mid \eta) \Pr(y_{i(t-1)} \leq d \mid \eta) dG(\eta). \qquad (3.6) \end{aligned}$$

Thus, decomposition (3.1) allows us to distinguish between probability statements for individuals with a given value of η from (aggregate) probability statements for groups of observationally equivalent individuals.

Estimating the Variance-Components Model One possibility is to approach estimation conditionally given η_i. That is, to estimate the realizations of the permanent effects that occur in the sample and σ^2. Natural unbiased estimates in this case would be

$$\widehat{\eta}_i = \overline{y}_i - \overline{y} \; (i = 1, ..., N) \qquad (3.7)$$

and

$$\widehat{\sigma}^2 = \frac{1}{N(T-1)} \sum_{i=1}^{N} \sum_{t=1}^{T} (y_{it} - \overline{y}_i)^2, \qquad (3.8)$$

where $\bar{y}_i = T^{-1} \sum_{t=1}^{T} y_{it}$ and $\bar{y} = N^{-1} \sum_{i=1}^{N} \bar{y}_i$. However, typically both σ_η^2 and σ^2 will be parameters of interest. To obtain an estimator of σ_η^2 note that the variance of $\bar{y}_i$ is given by

$$Var(\bar{y}_i) \equiv \bar{\sigma}^2 = \sigma_\eta^2 + \frac{\sigma^2}{T}. \tag{3.9}$$

Therefore, an unbiased estimator of σ_η^2 can be obtained as the difference between the estimated variance of $\bar{y}_i$ and $\hat{\sigma}^2/T$:

$$\hat{\sigma}_\eta^2 = \frac{1}{N} \sum_{i=1}^{N} (\bar{y}_i - \bar{y})^2 - \frac{\hat{\sigma}^2}{T}. \tag{3.10}$$

A problem with this estimator is that it is not guaranteed to be non-negative by construction.

The statistics (3.8) and (3.10) can be regarded as Gaussian ML estimates under $y_i \sim \mathcal{N}(\mu\iota, \Omega)$. To see this, note that using transformation (2.58) in general we have:

$$H y_i = \begin{pmatrix} \bar{y}_i \\ y_i^* \end{pmatrix} \sim id \left[\begin{pmatrix} \mu \\ 0 \end{pmatrix}, \begin{pmatrix} \bar{\sigma}^2 & 0 \\ 0 & \sigma^2 I_{T-1} \end{pmatrix} \right]. \tag{3.11}$$

Hence, under normality the log density of y_i can be decomposed as

$$\log f(y_i) = \log f(\bar{y}_i) + \log f(y_i^*), \tag{3.12}$$

so that the log likelihood of $(y_1, ..., y_N)$ is given by

$$L(\mu, \bar{\sigma}^2, \sigma^2) = L_B(\mu, \bar{\sigma}^2) + L_W(\sigma^2), \tag{3.13}$$

where

$$L_B(\mu, \bar{\sigma}^2) \propto -\frac{N}{2} \log \bar{\sigma}^2 - \frac{1}{2\bar{\sigma}^2} \sum_{i=1}^{N} (\bar{y}_i - \mu)^2 \tag{3.14}$$

and

$$L_W(\sigma^2) \propto -\frac{N(T-1)}{2} \log \sigma^2 - \frac{1}{2\sigma^2} \sum_{i=1}^{N} y_i^{*\prime} y_i^*. \tag{3.15}$$

Clearly the ML estimates of σ^2 and $\bar{\sigma}^2$ are given by (3.8) and the sample variance of $\bar{y}_i$, respectively.[1] Moreover, the ML estimator of σ_η^2 is given by (3.10) in view of the invariance property of maximum likelihood estimation.

Note that with large N and short T we can obtain precise estimates of σ_η^2 and σ^2 but not of the individual realizations η_i. Conversely, with small N and large T we would be able to obtain accurate estimates of η_i and σ^2 but not

---

[1]Note that $\sum_{i=1}^{N} y_i^{*\prime} y_i^* = \sum_{i=1}^{N} \sum_{t=1}^{T} (y_{it} - \bar{y}_i)^2$.

---

of σ_η^2, the intuition being that although we can estimate the individual η_i well there may be too few of them to obtain a good estimate of their variance.

For large N, σ_η^2 is just-identified when $T = 2$ in which case we have $\sigma_\eta^2 = Cov(y_{i1}, y_{i2})$.[2]

3.2 Error-Components Regression

3.2.1 The Model

Often one is interested in the analysis of error-components models given some conditioning variables. The conditioning variables may be time-varying, time-invariant or both, denoted as x_{it} and f_i, respectively. For example, we may be interested in separating out permanent and transitory components of individual earnings by labour market experience and educational categories.

This gives rise to a regression version of the previous model in which, in principle, not only μ but also σ_η^2 and σ^2 could be functions of x_{it} and f_i. Nevertheless, in the standard error-components regression model μ is period-specific and made a linear function of x_{it} and f_i, while the variance parameters are assumed not to vary with the regressors. The model is therefore

$$y_{it} = x'_{it}\beta + f'_i\gamma + u_{it} \qquad (3.16)$$

$$u_{it} = \eta_i + v_{it} \qquad (3.17)$$

together with the following assumption for the composite vector of errors $u_i = (u_{i1}, ..., u_{iT})'$:

$$u_i \mid w_i \sim iid(0, \sigma^2 I_T + \sigma_\eta^2 \iota\iota') \qquad (3.18)$$

where $w_i = (x'_{i1}, ..., x'_{iT}, f'_i)'$.

This model is similar to the one discussed in the previous chapter except in one fundamental aspect. The individual effect in the unobserved-heterogeneity model was potentially correlated with x_{it}. Indeed, this was the motivation for considering such a model in the first place. In contrast, in the error-components model η_i and v_{it} are two components of a regression error and hence both are uncorrelated with the regressors.

Formally, this model is a specialization of the unobserved-heterogeneity model of the previous chapter under Assumptions *A1* and *A2* in which in addition

$$E(\eta_i \mid w_i) = 0 \qquad (3.19)$$

$$Var(\eta_i \mid w_i) = \sigma_\eta^2. \qquad (3.20)$$

To reconcile the notation used in the two instances, note that in the unobserved heterogeneity model, the time-invariant component of the regression

---

[2]With $T = 2$, (3.10) coincides with the sample covariance between y_{i1} and y_{i2}.

$f_i'\gamma$ is subsumed under the individual effect η_i. Moreover, in the unobserved-heterogeneity model we did not specify an intercept so that $E(\eta_i)$ was not restricted, whereas for the error-components model $E(\eta_i) = 0$, and f_i will typically contain a constant term.

Note that in the error-components model β is identified in a single cross-section. The parameters that require panel data for identification in this model are the variances of the components of the error σ_η^2 and σ^2, which typically will be parameters of central interest in this context.

There are also applications of model (3.16)-(3.17) in which the main interest lies in the estimation of β and γ. In these cases it is natural to regard the error-components model as a restrictive version of the unobserved heterogeneity model of Chapter 2 with uncorrelated individual effects.

3.2.2 GLS and ML Estimation

Under the previous assumptions, OLS in levels provides unbiased and consistent but inefficient estimators of β and γ:

$$\widehat{\delta}_{OLS} = \left(\sum_{i=1}^{N} W_i'W_i\right)^{-1} \sum_{i=1}^{N} W_i'y_i \tag{3.21}$$

where $W_i = \left(X_i \vdots \iota f_i'\right)$, $X_i = (x_{i1}, ..., x_{iT})'$, and $\delta = (\beta', \gamma')'$.

Optimal estimation is achieved through GLS, also known as the Balestra–Nerlove estimator:[3]

$$\widehat{\delta}_{GLS} = \left(\sum_{i=1}^{N} W_i'\Omega^{-1}W_i\right)^{-1} \sum_{i=1}^{N} W_i'\Omega^{-1}y_i. \tag{3.22}$$

This GLS estimator is, nevertheless, unfeasible, since Ω depends on σ_η^2 and σ^2, which are unknown. Feasible GLS is obtained by replacing them by consistent estimates. Usually, the following are used:

$$\widehat{\sigma}^2 = \frac{1}{N(T-1)-k} \sum_{i=1}^{N} \sum_{t=1}^{T} \left(\widetilde{y}_{it} - \widetilde{x}_{it}'\widehat{\beta}_{WG}\right)^2 \tag{3.23}$$

$$\widehat{\sigma}_\eta^2 = \frac{1}{N} \sum_{i=1}^{N} \left(\overline{y}_i - \overline{w}_i'\widehat{\delta}_{BG}\right)^2 - \frac{\widehat{\sigma}^2}{T} \tag{3.24}$$

where $\widetilde{y}_{it} = y_{it} - \overline{y}_i$, $\widetilde{x}_{it} = x_{it} - \overline{x}_i$, and $\widehat{\delta}_{BG}$ denotes the *between-group* estimator, which is given by the OLS regression of $\overline{y}_i$ on $\overline{w}_i$:

[3]cf. Balestra and Nerlove (1966).

$$\hat{\delta}_{BG} = \left(\sum_{i=1}^{N} \overline{w}_i \overline{w}_i' \right) \sum_{i=1}^{N} \overline{w}_i \overline{y}_i. \tag{3.25}$$

Alternatively, the full set of parameters β, γ, σ^2, and σ_η^2 may be jointly estimated by maximum likelihood. As in the case without regressors, the log likelihood can be decomposed as the sum of the *between* and *within* log likelihoods. In this case we have:

$$\begin{pmatrix} \overline{y}_i \\ y_i^* \end{pmatrix} \mid w_i \sim id \left[\begin{pmatrix} \overline{x}_i'\beta + f_i'\gamma \\ X_i^*\beta \end{pmatrix}, \begin{pmatrix} \overline{\sigma}^2 & 0 \\ 0 & \sigma^2 I_{T-1} \end{pmatrix} \right], \tag{3.26}$$

so that under normality the error-components log likelihood equals:

$$L\left(\beta, \gamma, \sigma^2, \overline{\sigma}^2\right) = L_B\left(\beta, \gamma, \overline{\sigma}^2\right) + L_W\left(\beta, \sigma^2\right) \tag{3.27}$$

where

$$L_B\left(\beta, \gamma, \overline{\sigma}^2\right) \propto -\frac{N}{2} \log \overline{\sigma}^2 - \frac{1}{2\overline{\sigma}^2} \sum_{i=1}^{N} \left(\overline{y}_i - \overline{x}_i'\beta - f_i'\gamma\right)^2 \tag{3.28}$$

and

$$L_W\left(\beta, \sigma^2\right) \propto -\frac{N(T-1)}{2} \log \sigma^2 - \frac{1}{2\sigma^2} \sum_{i=1}^{N} \left(y_i^* - X_i^*\beta\right)' \left(y_i^* - X_i^*\beta\right). \tag{3.29}$$

Separate maximization of L_W and L_B give rise to within-group and between group estimation, respectively. Thus, the error-components likelihood can be regarded as enforcing the restriction that the parameter vectors β that appear in L_W and L_B coincide. This immediately suggests a (likelihood-ratio) specification test that will be further discussed below.

Moreover, in the absence of individual effects $\sigma_\eta^2 = 0$ so that $\overline{\sigma}^2 = \sigma^2/T$. Thus, the OLS estimator in levels (3.21) can be regarded as the MLE that maximizes the log-likelihood (3.27) subject to the restriction $\overline{\sigma}^2 = \sigma^2/T$. Again, this suggests a likelihood-ratio (LR) test of the existence of (uncorrelated) effects based on the comparison of the restricted and unrestricted likelihoods. Such a test will, nevertheless, be sensitive to distributional assumptions.

3.2.3   GLS, Within-Groups, and Between-Groups

We have motivated error-components regression models from a direct interest in the components themselves. Sometimes, however, correlation between individual effects and regressors can be regarded as an empirical issue. We shall address the testing of such hypothesis in the next section. Now we note the algebraic connections between within-groups, between-groups, and the Balestra–Nerlove GLS estimators.

Transforming the original system by H as in (3.26) we obtain $Hy_i = HW_i\delta + Hu_i$ or

$$
\begin{aligned}
\overline{y}_i &= \overline{x}_i'\beta + f_i'\gamma + \overline{u}_i \\
y_i^* &= X_i^*\beta + u_i^*
\end{aligned}
\tag{3.30}
$$

with

$$
\begin{pmatrix} \overline{u}_i \\ u_i^* \end{pmatrix} \mid w_i \sim iid \left[0, \begin{pmatrix} \overline{\sigma}^2 & 0 \\ 0 & \sigma^2 I_{T-1} \end{pmatrix} \right].
$$

The usefulness of this transformation is that the complete system is divided into two conditionally independent sub-systems. Namely, $T - 1$ within-group equations which are free from individual effects, and one average equation which is not. Therefore, in terms of the transformed model, $\widehat{\delta}_{GLS}$ can be written as a weighted least-squares estimator of the form:

$$
\widehat{\delta}_{GLS} = \left[\sum_{i=1}^{N} \left(W_i^{*\prime} W_i^* + \phi^2 \overline{w}_i \overline{w}_i' \right) \right]^{-1} \sum_{i=1}^{N} \left(W_i^{*\prime} y_i^* + \phi^2 \overline{w}_i \overline{y}_i \right)
\tag{3.31}
$$

where ϕ^2 is the ratio of the within to the between error variances $\phi^2 = \sigma^2/\overline{\sigma}^2$, $W_i^* = AW_i$, and $\overline{w}_i = T^{-1}W_i'\iota$. Thus $\widehat{\delta}_{GLS}$ can be regarded as a matrix-weighted average of the within-group and between-group estimators (cf. Maddala, 1971). The statistic (3.31) is identical to (3.22).[4] For feasible GLS, ϕ^2 is replaced by the ratio of the within to the between sample residual variances $\widehat{\phi}^2 = \widehat{\sigma}^2/\widehat{\overline{\sigma}}^2$. For maximum likelihood, ϕ^2 corresponds to the ratio of residual variances evaluated at the MLE itself.[5]

3.3 Testing for Correlated Unobserved Heterogeneity

Sometimes correlated unobserved heterogeneity is a basic property of the model of interest. An example is a "λ-constant" labour supply or demand equation where η_i is determined by the marginal utility of initial wealth, which according to the underlying life-cycle model will depend on wages or prices in all periods (cf. MaCurdy, 1981; Browning, Deaton, and Irish, 1985). Another example is when a regressor is a lagged dependent variable, as in the autoregressive models discussed in Part II. In cases like this, testing for lack of correlation between

---

[4]When $\phi^2 = T$ (or $\sigma_\eta^2 = 0$) (3.31) boils down to the OLS in levels estimator (3.21), whereas if $\sigma_\eta^2 \to \infty$ then $\phi^2 \to 0$ and $\widehat{\delta}_{GLS}$ tends to within-groups.

[5]Although estimates of σ^2 and $\overline{\sigma}^2$ will be non-negative by construction (and hence also those of ϕ^2), estimates of σ_η^2 may be negative. The ML estimator that enforces the constraint $\sigma_\eta^2 \geq 0$ may exhibit a boundary solution. This problem was discussed by Maddala (1971).

regressors and individual effects is not warranted since we wish the model to have this property.

On other occasions, correlation between regressors and individual effects can be regarded as an empirical issue. In these cases testing for correlated un-observed heterogeneity can be a useful *specification test* for regression models estimated in levels. Researchers may have a preference for models in levels because estimates in levels are in general more precise than estimates in devia-tions (dramatically so when the time series variation in the regressors relative to the cross-sectional variation is small), or because of an interest in regressors that lack time series variation.

3.3.1   Specification Tests

We have already suggested a specification test of correlated effects from a likeli-hood ratio perspective. This was a test of equality of the β coefficients appear-ing in the WG and BG likelihoods. Similarly, from a least-squares perspective, we may consider the system

$$\overline{y}_i = \overline{x}_i'b + f_i'c + \varepsilon_i \tag{3.32}$$

$$y_i^* = X_i^*\beta + u_i^*, \tag{3.33}$$

where b, c, and ε_i are such that $E^*(\varepsilon_i \mid \overline{x}_i, f_i) = 0$, and formulate the problem as a (Wald) test of the null hypothesis[6]

$$H_0: \quad \beta = b. \tag{3.34}$$

The least-squares perspective is of interest because it can easily accommo-date robust generalizations to heteroskedasticity and serial correlation as we shall see below.

Under the unobserved-heterogeneity model

$$E(\overline{y}_i \mid w_i) = \overline{x}_i'\beta + f_i'\gamma + E(\eta_i \mid w_i),$$

so that (3.32) can be regarded as a specification of the alternative hypothesis of the form

$$H_1: \quad E(\eta_i \mid w_i) = \overline{x}_i'\lambda_1 + f_i'\lambda_2 \tag{3.35}$$

with $b = \beta + \lambda_1$ and $c = \gamma + \lambda_2$. H_0 is, therefore, equivalent to $\lambda_1 = 0$. Note that H_0 does not specify that $\lambda_2 = 0$, which is not testable.

Under (3.35) and the additional assumption $Var(\eta_i \mid w_i) = \sigma_\eta^2$, the error covariance matrix of the system (3.32)-(3.33) is given by $Var(\varepsilon_i \mid w_i) = \overline{\sigma}^2$,

---

[6]Indeed under the assumptions of the error-components model $b = \beta$, $c = \gamma$, and $\varepsilon_i = \overline{u}_i$.

$Cov\,(\varepsilon_i, u_i^* \mid w_i) = 0$, and $Var\,(u_i^* \mid w_i) = \sigma^2 I_{T-1}$. Thus the optimal LS estimates of $(b', c')'$ and β are the BG and the WG estimators, respectively. Explicit expressions for the BG estimator of b and its estimated variance matrix are:

$$\hat{b}_{BG} = \left(\overline{X}' M \overline{X}\right)^{-1} \overline{X}' M \overline{y} \tag{3.36}$$

$$\hat{V}_{BG} \equiv \widehat{Var}\left(\hat{b}_{BG}\right) = \hat{\sigma}^2 \left(\overline{X}' M \overline{X}\right)^{-1} \tag{3.37}$$

where $M = I - F\,(F'F)^{-1}\,F'$, $F = (f_1, ..., f_N)'$, $\overline{X} = (\overline{x}_1, ..., \overline{x}_N)'$, and $\overline{y} = (\overline{y}_1, ..., \overline{y}_N)'$. Likewise, the estimated variance matrix of the WG estimator is

$$\hat{V}_{WG} \equiv \widehat{Var}\left(\hat{\beta}_{WG}\right) = \hat{\sigma}^2 \left(\sum_{i=1}^{N} X_i^{*'} X_i^*\right)^{-1} \tag{3.38}$$

Moreover, since $Cov\left(\hat{b}_{BG}, \hat{\beta}_{WG}\right) = 0$, the Wald test of (3.34) is given by

$$h = \left(\hat{b}_{BG} - \hat{\beta}_{WG}\right)' \left(\hat{V}_{WG} + \hat{V}_{BG}\right)^{-1} \left(\hat{b}_{BG} - \hat{\beta}_{WG}\right). \tag{3.39}$$

Under H_0, the statistic h will have a χ^2 distribution with k degrees of freedom in large samples. Clearly, h will be sensitive to the nature of the variables included in f_i. For example, H_0 might be rejected when f_i only contains a constant term, but not when a larger set of time-invariant regressors is included.

Hausman (1978) originally motivated the testing of correlated effects as a comparison between WG and the Balestra–Nerlove GLS estimator, suggesting a statistic of the form

$$h = \left(\hat{\beta}_{GLS} - \hat{\beta}_{WG}\right)' \left(\hat{V}_{WG} - \hat{V}_{GLS}\right)^{-1} \left(\hat{\beta}_{GLS} - \hat{\beta}_{WG}\right), \tag{3.40}$$

where

$$\hat{V}_{GLS} = \hat{\sigma}^2 (X^{*'} X^* + \hat{\phi}^2 \overline{X}' M \overline{X})^{-1}. \tag{3.41}$$

Under H_0 both estimators are consistent, so we would expect the difference $\hat{\beta}_{GLS} - \hat{\beta}_{WG}$ to be small. Moreover, since $\hat{\beta}_{GLS}$ is efficient, the variance of the difference must be given by the difference of variances. Otherwise, we could find a linear combination of the two estimators that would be more efficient than GLS. Under H_1 the WG estimator remains consistent but GLS does not, so their difference and the test statistic will tend to be large. A statistic of the form given in (3.40) is known as a Hausman test statistic. As shown by Hausman and Taylor (1981), (3.40) is in fact the same statistic as (3.39). Thus h can be regarded both as a Hausman test or as a Wald test of the restriction $\lambda_1 = 0$ from OLS estimates of the model under the alternative (Arellano, 1993).

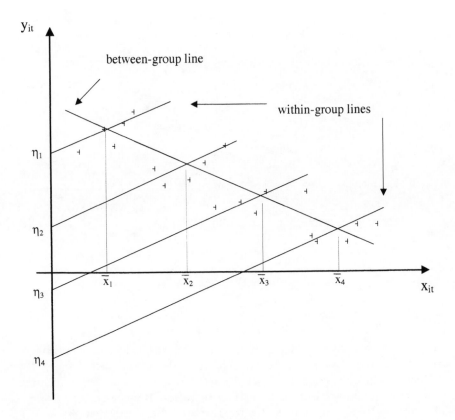

Figure 3.1: Within-group and between-group lines

Fixed Effects *versus* Random Effects These specification tests are sometimes described as tests of random effects against fixed effects. However, according to the previous discussion, for typical econometric panels, we shall not be testing the nature of the sampling process but the dependence between individual effects and regressors. Thus, for our purposes individual effects may be regarded as being random without loss of generality. Provided one has an interest in partial regression coefficients holding effects constant, what matters is whether the effects are independent of the observed regressors or not.[7]

---

[7]More generally, the econometrics literature has tended to regard statistical models with incidental parameters (Neyman and Scott, 1948) as semi-parametric random effects models in which the conditional distribution of the effects given some conditioning variables is left unspecified (Chamberlain, 1992a, 1992b, and discussion in Lancaster, 2000).

Figure 3.1 provides a simple illustration for the scatter diagram of a panel data set with $N = 4$ and $T = 5$. In this example there is a marked difference between the positive slope of the within-group lines and the negative one of the between-group regression. This situation is the result of the strong negative association between the individual intercepts and the individual averages of the regressors.

3.3.2 Robust Alternatives

Robust Wald Testing If the errors are heteroskedastic and/or serially correlated, the previous formulae for the large sample variances of the WG, BG, and GLS estimators are not valid. Moreover, WG and GLS cannot be ranked in terms of efficiency so that the variance of the difference between the two does not coincide with the difference of variances.

Following the least-squares Wald approach, Arellano (1993) discussed a generalized test which is robust to heteroskedasticity and autocorrelation of arbitrary forms. To describe this procedure, it is convenient to write system (3.32)-(3.33) in the following matrix form

$$
\begin{pmatrix} \bar{y}_i \\ y_i^* \end{pmatrix} = \begin{pmatrix} \bar{x}_i' & f_i' & \bar{x}_i' \\ 0 & 0 & X_i^* \end{pmatrix} \begin{pmatrix} b - \beta \\ c \\ \beta \end{pmatrix} + \begin{pmatrix} \varepsilon_i \\ u_i^* \end{pmatrix} \tag{3.42}
$$

or

$$
y_i^\dagger = W_i^\dagger \psi + u_i^\dagger.
$$

In this format, OLS estimation of ψ directly provides the difference $\widehat{b}_{BG} - \widehat{\beta}_{WG}$ together with $\widehat{c}_{BG}$ and $\widehat{\beta}_{WG}$:

$$
\widehat{\psi} = \begin{pmatrix} \widehat{b}_{BG} - \widehat{\beta}_{WG} \\ \widehat{c}_{BG} \\ \widehat{\beta}_{WG} \end{pmatrix} = \left(\sum_{i=1}^{N} W_i^{\dagger\prime} W_i^\dagger \right)^{-1} \sum_{i=1}^{N} W_i^{\dagger\prime} y_i^\dagger. \tag{3.43}
$$

A robust estimate of the asymptotic variance of $\widehat{\psi}$ can be obtained using White's formulae (cf. White, 1984):

$$
\widehat{Var}\left(\widehat{\psi} \right) = \left(\sum_{i=1}^{N} W_i^{\dagger\prime} W_i^\dagger \right)^{-1} \left(\sum_{i=1}^{N} W_i^{\dagger\prime} \widehat{u}_i^\dagger \widehat{u}_i^{\dagger\prime} W_i^\dagger \right) \left(\sum_{i=1}^{N} W_i^{\dagger\prime} W_i^\dagger \right)^{-1}
$$

$$
= \begin{pmatrix} \widehat{V}_{dd} & \widehat{V}_{dc} & \widehat{V}_{d\beta} \\ \widehat{V}_{cd} & \widehat{V}_{cc} & \widehat{V}_{c\beta} \\ \widehat{V}_{\beta d} & \widehat{V}_{\beta c} & \widehat{V}_{\beta\beta} \end{pmatrix} \tag{3.44}
$$

where $\widehat{u}_i^\dagger = y_i^\dagger - W_i^\dagger \widehat{\psi}$ and $d = b - \beta$. Hence, a generalized Wald test of the null (3.34) that is robust to heteroskedasticity and autocorrelation is given by

$$
h^\dagger = \left(\widehat{b}_{BG} - \widehat{\beta}_{WG} \right)' \widehat{V}_{dd}^{-1} \left(\widehat{b}_{BG} - \widehat{\beta}_{WG} \right). \tag{3.45}
$$

GMM Estimation and Testing   Under the null of uncorrelated effects we may consider GMM estimation based on the orthogonality conditions[8]

$$E\left[x_i\left(\overline{y}_i - \overline{x}_i'\beta - f_i'\gamma\right)\right] = 0 \tag{3.46}$$

$$E\left[f_i\left(\overline{y}_i - \overline{x}_i'\beta - f_i'\gamma\right)\right] = 0 \tag{3.47}$$

$$E\left[(y_i^* - X_i^*\beta) \otimes x_i\right] = 0. \tag{3.48}$$

In parallel with the development in Section 2.3.3, the resulting estimates of β and γ will be asymptotically equivalent to Balestra–Nerlove GLS with classical errors, but strictly more efficient when heteroskedasticity or autocorrelation is present. However, under the alternative of correlated effects, any GMM estimate that relies on the moments (3.46) will be inconsistent for β. Thus, we may test for correlated effects by considering an incremental test of the over identifying restrictions (3.46). Note that under the alternative, GMM estimates based on (3.47)-(3.48) will be consistent for β but not necessarily for γ.

Optimal GMM estimates in this context minimize a criterion of the form

$$s(\delta) = \left[\sum_{i=1}^{N}(y_i - W_i\delta)H'Z_i\right]\left(\sum_{i=1}^{N}Z_i'H\widehat{u}_i\widehat{u}_i'H'Z_i\right)^{-1}\left[\sum_{i=1}^{N}Z_i'H(y_i - W_i\delta)\right] \tag{3.49}$$

where $H\widehat{u}_i$ are some one-step consistent residuals. Under uncorrelated effects the instrument matrix Z_i takes the form

$$Z_i = \begin{pmatrix} x_i' & f_i' & 0 \\ 0 & 0 & I_{T-1} \otimes x_i' \end{pmatrix}, \tag{3.50}$$

whereas under correlated effects we shall use

$$Z_i = \begin{pmatrix} f_i' & 0 \\ 0 & I_{T-1} \otimes x_i' \end{pmatrix}. \tag{3.51}$$

3.4   Models with Information in Levels

Sometimes it is of central interest to measure the effect of a time-invariant explanatory variable controlling for unobserved heterogeneity. Returns to schooling holding unobserved ability constant is a prominent example. In those cases,

---

[8]We could also add:
$$E\left[(y_i^* - X_i^*\beta) \otimes f_i\right] = 0,$$
in which case, the entire set of moments can be expressed in terms of the original equation system as:
$$E\left[\left(y_i - X_i\beta - \iota f_i'\gamma\right) \otimes w_i\right] = 0.$$
When f_i contains a constant term only, this amounts to including a set of time dummies in the instrument set.

as explained in Chapter 2, panel data is not directly useful. Hausman and Taylor (1981) argued, however, that panel data might still be useful in an indirect way if the model contained time-varying explanatory variables that were uncorrelated with the effects.

Suppose there are subsets of the time-invariant and time-varying explanatory variables, f_{1i} and $x_{1i} = (x'_{1i1}, ..., x'_{1iT})'$ respectively, that can be assumed a priori to be uncorrelated with the effects. In such case, the following subset of the orthogonality conditions (3.46)-(3.48) hold

$$E\left[x_{1i}\left(\overline{y}_i - \overline{x}'_i\beta - f'_i\gamma\right)\right] = 0 \tag{3.52}$$

$$E\left[f_{1i}\left(\overline{y}_i - \overline{x}'_i\beta - f'_i\gamma\right)\right] = 0 \tag{3.53}$$

$$E\left[(y_i^* - X_i^*\beta) \otimes x_i\right] = 0. \tag{3.54}$$

The parameter vector β will be identified from the moments for the errors in deviations (3.54). The basic point noted by Hausman and Taylor is that the coefficients γ may also be identified using the variables x_{1i} and f_{1i} as instruments for the errors in levels, provided the rank condition is satisfied.

Given identification, the coefficients β and γ can be estimated by GMM. With classical errors, optimal GMM estimation based on the orthogonality conditions (3.52)-(3.54) leads to

$$\widehat{\delta}_{HT} = \left[\left(\sum_{i=1}^{N} W_i^{*\prime} W_i^*\right) + \phi^2 \left(\sum_{i=1}^{N} \overline{w}_i m_i'\right) \left(\sum_{i=1}^{N} m_i m_i'\right)^{-1} \left(\sum_{i=1}^{N} m_i \overline{w}_i'\right)\right]^{-1}$$
$$\left[\left(\sum_{i=1}^{N} W_i^{*\prime} y_i^*\right) + \phi^2 \left(\sum_{i=1}^{N} \overline{w}_i m_i'\right) \left(\sum_{i=1}^{N} m_i m_i'\right)^{-1} \left(\sum_{i=1}^{N} m_i \overline{y}_i\right)\right] \tag{3.55}$$

where $m_i = (x'_{1i}, f'_{1i})'$. Note that with $m_i = (x'_i, f'_i)'$, (3.55) coincides with the Balestra–Nerlove GLS estimator (3.31) because the variables in $\overline{w}_i$ are linear combinations of those in $(x'_i, f'_i)'$.

Hausman and Taylor did in fact consider (3.55) with $m_i = (\overline{x}'_{1i}, f'_{1i})'$. Additional estimators of this type were considered by other authors. Bhargava and Sargan (1983) and Amemiya and MaCurdy (1986) suggested that a weaker identification condition and further efficiency could be achieved by using as instruments the full set of lags and leads of the x_{1it} variables instead of their time means, as described in our presentation. Moreover, Bhargava and Sargan (1983) and Breusch, Mizon, and Schmidt (1989) suggested to use deviations from time means of correlated time-varying regressors as additional instruments on the assumption of constant correlation with the effects. Finally, Arellano and Bover (1995) presented a GMM formulation for models containing instruments for errors in levels, and derived the information bound for these models.

The notion that a time-varying variable that is uncorrelated with an individual effect can be used at the same time as an instrument for itself and for a correlated time-invariant variable is potentially appealing. Nevertheless, the impact of these models in applied work has been limited, due to the difficulty in finding exogenous variables that can be convincingly regarded a priori as being uncorrelated with the individual effects. For example, Chowdhury and Nickell (1985) attempted to estimate returns to education using union status, sickness, and past unemployment variables as candidates for possible time-varying variables uncorrelated with the effect, but concluded that the instruments were either invalid or ineffective within their PSID sample.

3.5 Estimating the Error Component Distributions

If the motivation for using an error-components model is to study transition probabilities or first passage times,[9] the emphasis on the variances seems misplaced since knowledge of the distributions is required in order to evaluate probabilities. Empirical work on earnings mobility often assumed a normal distribution for the components of log earnings errors, but the distributions can also be nonparametrically estimated using deconvolution techniques. Horowitz and Markatou (1996) proposed estimators along these lines which we describe next.[10]

Let us consider the error-components model (3.16)-(3.17):

$$y_{it} = x_{it}'\beta + f_i'\gamma + u_{it}$$
$$u_{it} = \eta_i + v_{it},$$

together with the assumption that v_{it} is *iid* and independent of η_i, and both are continuous random variables.

Let $h_u(\tau)$, $h_\Delta(\tau)$, $h_\eta(\tau)$, and $h_v(\tau)$ denote the characteristic functions (*cf*) of u, Δu, η, and v, respectively. We then have

$$h_u(\tau) = E\left(e^{i\tau(\eta+v)}\right) = h_\eta(\tau)h_v(\tau) \tag{3.56}$$

and

$$h_\Delta(\tau) = E\left(e^{i\tau\Delta v}\right) = |h_v(\tau)|^2 \tag{3.57}$$

where $i = \sqrt{-1}$ (when not used as a subscript for individuals) and $|\vartheta|$ denotes the modulus of the complex variable ϑ. Under the assumption that v has a symmetric distribution (so that $h_v(\tau) > 0$ and real for all τ), we have

$$h_v(\tau) = h_\Delta(\tau)^{1/2} \tag{3.58}$$

[9]For a given integer $\theta > 0$, the probability that the first passage time for threshold y^* exceeds θ is $\pi(\theta, y^*) = \Pr(y_{i1} < y^*, ..., y_{i\theta} < y^*)$.

[10]In addition, Bayesian flexible estimators of error component distributions have been considered by Chamberlain and Hirano (1999), Geweke and Keane (2000), and Hirano (2002).

and

$$h_\eta(\tau) = \frac{h_u(\tau)}{h_\Delta(\tau)^{1/2}}. \tag{3.59}$$

Now, using the inversion formulae for characteristic functions, the densities of v and η can be obtained from their *cf*s as:

$$f_v(r) = \frac{1}{2\pi} \int_{-\infty}^{\infty} e^{-ir\tau} h_\Delta(\tau)^{1/2} d\tau \tag{3.60}$$

and

$$f_\eta(r) = \frac{1}{2\pi} \int_{-\infty}^{\infty} e^{-ir\tau} \frac{h_u(\tau)}{h_\Delta(\tau)^{1/2}} d\tau. \tag{3.61}$$

Turning to inference, under suitable regularity conditions, $h_u(\tau)$ and $h_\Delta(\tau)$ are consistently estimated by the empirical *cf*s of consistent residuals $\hat{u}$ and $\Delta\hat{u}$:

$$\widehat{h}_u(\tau) = \frac{1}{NT} \sum_{j=1}^{N} \sum_{t=1}^{T} \exp\left(i\tau\hat{u}_{jt}\right) \tag{3.62}$$

$$\widehat{h}_\Delta(\tau) = \frac{1}{N(T-1)} \sum_{j=1}^{N} \sum_{t=2}^{T} \exp\left(i\tau\Delta\hat{u}_{jt}\right). \tag{3.63}$$

However, the densities $f_v(r)$ and $f_\eta(r)$ cannot be estimated by replacing $h_u(\tau)$ and $h_\Delta(\tau)$ by their empirical counterparts in (3.60) and (3.61), because the corresponding integrals do not exist in general. To avoid this problem, Horowitz and Markatou convoluted v and η with a suitable continuous random variable that becomes degenerate as $N \to \infty$.[11] Let us consider the variables

$$v^\dagger = v + \lambda_{vN}\zeta \tag{3.64}$$

$$\eta^\dagger = \eta + \lambda_{\eta N}\zeta \tag{3.65}$$

where ζ is a random variable with known, bounded, real *cf* $g(\tau)$, and $\{\lambda_{vN}\}$ and $\{\lambda_{\eta N}\}$ are sequences of positive constants such that $\lambda_{vN} \to 0$ and $\lambda_{\eta N} \to 0$ as $N \to \infty$. Thus, the *cf* of $v^\dagger$ is given by $h_v(\tau)g(\lambda_{vN}\tau)$ and the *cf* of $\eta^\dagger$ is $h_\eta(\tau)g(\lambda_{\eta N}\tau)$.

The idea is to use the inversion formulae to estimate the *pdf*s of $v^\dagger$ and $\eta^\dagger$, on the grounds that since λ_{vN} and $\lambda_{\eta N}$ tend to zero the resulting estimators

---

[11]This procedure is similar to introducing a kernel smoothing of the empirical distributions of $\hat{u}$ and $\Delta\hat{u}$.

converge to the *pdf*s of v and η. Therefore, the estimators proposed by Horowitz and Markatou are of the form

$$\widehat{f}_v(r) = \frac{1}{2\pi} \int_{-\infty}^{\infty} e^{-ir\tau} \left| \widehat{h}_\Delta(\tau) \right|^{1/2} g\left(\lambda_{vN}\tau\right) d\tau \tag{3.66}$$

$$\widehat{f}_\eta(r) = \frac{1}{2\pi} \int_{-\infty}^{\infty} e^{-ir\tau} \frac{\widehat{h}_u(\tau)}{\left| \widehat{h}_\Delta(\tau) \right|^{1/2}} g\left(\lambda_{\eta N}\tau\right) d\tau. \tag{3.67}$$

They showed that these estimators are consistent but converge very slowly, something that is, nevertheless, in the nature of the approach. Horowitz and Markatou also considered a small-sample bias correction, and extensions to serially correlated and asymmetric v (see also Horowitz, 1998, 4.2). Finally, they estimated conditional first passage times for PSID earnings, showing that assuming normality leads to substantial overestimation of the probability that an individual with low earnings will become a high earner in future.

A Graphical Test of Normality of Individual Effects   The estimated characteristic function of the individual effects can be used to perform an informal graphical diagnostic of normality. If η is normally distributed

$$\log h_\eta\left(\tau\right) = -\frac{1}{2}\sigma_\eta^2\tau^2. \tag{3.68}$$

On the other hand, an unrestricted estimate of $\log h_\eta\left(\tau\right)$ is given by

$$\log \widehat{h}_\eta\left(\tau\right) = \log \widehat{h}_u(\tau) - \frac{1}{2}\log\left| \widehat{h}_\Delta(\tau) \right| \tag{3.69}$$

where $\widehat{h}_u(\tau)$ and $\widehat{h}_\Delta(\tau)$ are the empirical *cf*s (3.62) and (3.63).

Thus, Horowitz and Markatou suggested to plot $\log \widehat{h}_\eta\left(\tau\right)$ against $-\tau^2$ as a graphical test of normality. If the distribution of η is normal the plot will be a scatter around a straight line. These authors found that in their PSID earnings data, possible departures from normality of η were small. They did find, however, evidence of non-normality in the distribution of v. Its tails were thicker than those of the normal distribution but thinner than those of a Cauchy distribution.

4

Error in Variables

4.1 An Introduction to the Standard Regression Model with Errors in Variables

Let us consider a cross-sectional regression model

$$y_i = \alpha + x_i^\dagger \beta + v_i. \tag{4.1}$$

Suppose we actually observe y_i and x_i, which is a noisy measure of $x_i^\dagger$ subject to an additive measurement error ε_i

$$x_i = x_i^\dagger + \varepsilon_i. \tag{4.2}$$

We assume that all the unobservables $x_i^\dagger$, v_i, and ε_i are mutually independent with variances $\sigma_\dagger^2$, σ_v^2, and σ_ε^2. Since v_i is independent of $x_i^\dagger$, β is given by the population regression coefficient of y_i on $x_i^\dagger$:

$$\beta = \frac{Cov(y_i, x_i^\dagger)}{Var(x_i^\dagger)}, \tag{4.3}$$

but since $x_i^\dagger$ is unobservable we cannot use a sample counterpart of this expression as an estimator of β.

What do we obtain by regressing y_i on x_i in the population? The result is

$$\frac{Cov(y_i, x_i)}{Var(x_i)} = \frac{Cov(y_i, x_i^\dagger + \varepsilon_i)}{\sigma_\dagger^2 + \sigma_\varepsilon^2} = \frac{Cov(y_i, x_i^\dagger)}{\sigma_\dagger^2 + \sigma_\varepsilon^2} = \frac{\beta}{1 + \lambda} \tag{4.4}$$

where $\lambda = \sigma_\varepsilon^2/\sigma_\dagger^2$. Note that since λ is non-negative by construction, the population regression coefficient of y_i on x_i will always be smaller than β in absolute value as long as $\sigma_\varepsilon^2 > 0$.

This type of model is relevant in at least two conceptually different situations. One corresponds to instances of actual measurement errors due to misreporting, rounding-off errors, etc. The other arises when the variable of economic interest is a latent variable which does not correspond exactly to the one that is available in the data.

In either case, the worry is that the variable to which agents respond does not coincide with the one that is entered as a regressor in the model. The result is that the unobservable component in the relationship between y_i and x_i will contain a multiple of the measurement error in addition to the error term in the original relationship:

$$y_i = \alpha + x_i\beta + u_i \tag{4.5}$$

$$u_i = v_i - \beta\varepsilon_i. \tag{4.6}$$

Clearly, the observed regressor x_i will be correlated with u_i even if the latent variable $x_i^\dagger$ is not.

This problem is often of practical significance, specially in regression analysis with micro data, since the resulting biases may be large. Note that the magnitude of the bias does not depend on the absolute magnitude of the measurement error variance but on the "noise to signal" ratio λ. For example, if $\lambda = 1$, so that 50 per cent of the total variance observed in x_i is due to measurement error—which is not an uncommon situation—the population regression coefficient of y_i on x_i will be half the value of β.

As for solutions, suppose we have the means of assessing the extent of the measurement error, so that λ or σ_ε^2 are known or can be estimated. Then β can be determined as

$$\beta = (1+\lambda)\frac{Cov(y_i,x_i)}{Var(x_i)} = \frac{Cov(y_i,x_i)}{Var(x_i) - \sigma_\varepsilon^2}. \tag{4.7}$$

More generally, in a model with k regressors and a conformable vector of coefficients β

$$y_i = x_i'\beta + (v_i - \varepsilon_i'\beta) \tag{4.8}$$

with $E(\varepsilon_i\varepsilon_i') = \Omega_\varepsilon$, $E(x_i^\dagger x_i^{\dagger\prime}) = \Omega_\dagger$ and $\Lambda = \Omega_\dagger^{-1}\Omega_\varepsilon$:

$$\beta = (I_k + \Lambda)\left[E(x_i x_i')\right]^{-1} E(x_i y_i) = \left[E(x_i x_i') - \Omega_\varepsilon\right]^{-1} E(x_i y_i). \tag{4.9}$$

In this notation, x_i will include a constant term, and possibly other regressors without measurement error. This situation will be reflected by the occurrence of zeros in the corresponding elements of Ω_ε.

The expression (4.9) suggests an estimator of the form

$$\widetilde{\beta} = \left(\frac{1}{N}\sum_{i=1}^N x_i x_i' - \widetilde{\Omega}_\varepsilon^{-1}\right)\frac{1}{N}\sum_{i=1}^N x_i y_i. \tag{4.10}$$

where $\widetilde{\Omega}_\varepsilon$ denotes a consistent estimate of Ω_ε.

Alternatively, if we have a second noisy measure of $x_i^\dagger$

$$z_i = x_i^\dagger + \zeta_i \qquad (4.11)$$

such that the measurement error ζ_i is independent of ε_i and the other unobservables, it can be used as an instrumental variable. In effect, for scalar x_i we have

$$\frac{Cov(z_i, y_i)}{Cov(z_i, x_i)} = \frac{Cov(x_i^\dagger + \zeta_i, y_i)}{Cov(x_i^\dagger + \zeta_i, x_i^\dagger + \varepsilon_i)} = \frac{Cov(y_i, x_i^\dagger)}{Var(x_i^\dagger)} = \beta. \qquad (4.12)$$

Moreover, since also

$$\frac{Cov(x_i, y_i)}{Cov(x_i, z_i)} = \beta, \qquad (4.13)$$

there is one overidentifying restriction in this problem.

In some way the instrumental variable solution is not different from the previous one. Indirectly, the availability of two noisy measures is used to identify the systematic and measurement error variances. Note that since

$$Var \begin{pmatrix} x_i \\ z_i \end{pmatrix} = \begin{pmatrix} \sigma_\dagger^2 + \sigma_\varepsilon^2 & \sigma_\dagger^2 \\ \sigma_\dagger^2 & \sigma_\dagger^2 + \sigma_\zeta^2 \end{pmatrix} \qquad (4.14)$$

we can determine the variances of the unobservables as

$$\sigma_\dagger^2 = Cov(z_i, x_i) \qquad (4.15)$$

$$\sigma_\varepsilon^2 = Var(x_i) - Cov(z_i, x_i) \qquad (4.16)$$

$$\sigma_\zeta^2 = Var(z_i) - Cov(z_i, x_i). \qquad (4.17)$$

In econometrics the instrumental variable approach is the most widely used technique. Thus, the response to measurement error bias in linear regression problems is akin to the response to simultaneity bias. This similarity, however, no longer holds in the nonlinear regression context. The problem is that in a nonlinear regression the measurement error is no longer additively separable from the true value of the regressor (see Hausman, Newey, and Powell, 1995, for discussion and references on nonlinear regression models with errors in variables).

4.2 Measurement Error Bias and Unobserved Heterogeneity Bias

Let us consider a cross-sectional model that combines measurement error and unobserved heterogeneity

$$y_i = x_i^\dagger \beta + \eta_i + v_i \qquad (4.18)$$

$$x_i = x_i^\dagger + \varepsilon_i,$$

where all unobservables are independent, except $x_i^\dagger$ and η_i. The population regression coefficient of y_i on x_i is given by

$$\frac{Cov(y_i, x_i)}{Var(x_i)} = \beta + \frac{Cov(\eta_i + v_i - \beta\varepsilon_i, x_i)}{Var(x_i)} = \beta - \left(\frac{\sigma_\varepsilon^2}{\sigma_\dagger^2 + \sigma_\varepsilon^2}\right)\beta + \left(\frac{Cov(\eta_i, x_i^\dagger)}{\sigma_\dagger^2 + \sigma_\varepsilon^2}\right).$$

$$(4.19)$$

Note that there are two components to the bias. The first one is due to measurement error and depends on σ_ε^2. The second is due to unobserved heterogeneity and depends on $Cov(\eta_i, x_i^\dagger)$. Sometimes these two biases tend to offset each other. For example, if $\beta > 0$ and $Cov(\eta_i, x_i^\dagger) > 0$, the measurement error bias will be negative while the unobserved heterogeneity bias will be positive. A full offsetting would only occur if $Cov(\eta_i, x_i^\dagger) = \sigma_\varepsilon^2\beta$, something that could only happen by chance.

Measurement Error Bias in First-Differences   Suppose we have panel data with $T = 2$ and consider a regression in first-differences as a way of removing unobserved heterogeneity bias. In such a case we obtain

$$\frac{Cov(\Delta y_{i2}, \Delta x_{i2})}{Var(\Delta x_{i2})} = \frac{\beta}{1 + \lambda_\Delta} \tag{4.20}$$

where $\lambda_\Delta = Var(\Delta\varepsilon_{i2})/Var(\Delta x_{i2}^\dagger)$.

The main point to make here is that first-differencing may exacerbate the measurement error bias. The reason is as follows. If ε_{it} is an *iid* error then $Var(\Delta\varepsilon_{i2}) = 2\sigma_\varepsilon^2$. If $x_{it}^\dagger$ is also *iid* then $\lambda_\Delta = \lambda$, and the measurement error bias in levels and first-differences will be of the same magnitude. However, if $x_{it}^\dagger$ is a stationary time series with positive serial correlation

$$Var(\Delta x_{i2}^\dagger) = 2\left[\sigma_\dagger^2 - Cov(x_{i1}^\dagger, x_{i2}^\dagger)\right] < 2\sigma_\dagger^2 \tag{4.21}$$

and therefore $\lambda_\Delta > \lambda$.[1]

A related example of this situation in data with a group structure arises in the analysis of the returns to schooling with data on twin siblings (Taubman, 1976a, 1976b; Goldberger, 1978; Ashenfelter and Krueger, 1994). Regressions in differences remove genetic ability bias but may exacerbate measurement error bias in schooling if the siblings' measurement errors are independent but their true schooling attainments are highly correlated (Griliches, 1977, 1979).

Under the same circumstances, the within-group measurement error bias with $T > 2$ will be smaller than that in first-differences but higher than the measurement error bias in levels (cf. Griliches and Hausman, 1986).

---

[1]Note that, as explained in Chapter 3, the cross-sectional covariance between $x_{i1}^\dagger$ and $x_{i2}^\dagger$ will also be positive in the presence of heterogeneity, even if the individual time series are not serially correlated.

Therefore, the finding of significantly different results in regressions in first-differences and orthogonal deviations may be an indication of the presence of measurement error.

4.3 Instrumental Variable Estimation with Panel Data

The availability of panel data helps to solve the problem of measurement error bias by providing internal instruments as long as we are willing to restrict the serial dependence in the measurement error.

In a model without unobserved heterogeneity the following orthogonality conditions are valid provided the measurement error is white noise and $T \geq 2$:

$$E\left[\begin{pmatrix} 1 \\ x_{i1} \\ \vdots \\ x_{i(t-1)} \\ x_{i(t+1)} \\ \vdots \\ x_{iT} \end{pmatrix} (y_{it} - \alpha - x_{it}\beta)\right] = 0 \ (t = 1, ..., T). \tag{4.22}$$

Note that this situation is compatible with the presence of serial correlation in the disturbance term in the relationship between y and x. This is so because the disturbance is made of two components:

$$u_{it} = v_{it} - \varepsilon_{it}\beta$$

and only the second is required to be white noise for the validity of the moment conditions above.

Also note that identification of β from the previous moments requires that x_{it} is predictable from its past and future values. Thus, the rank condition for identification would fail if the latent variable $x_{it}^\dagger$ was also white noise.

In a model with unobserved heterogeneity and a white noise measurement error, we can rely on the following moments for the errors in first-differences provided $T \geq 3$:[2]

---

[2]In this discussion we use first-differences to remove individual effects. Note that the use of forward orthogonal deviations would preclude the use of future values of x as instruments.

$$E[\begin{pmatrix} x_{i1} \\ \vdots \\ x_{i(t-2)} \\ x_{i(t+1)} \\ \vdots \\ x_{iT} \end{pmatrix} (\Delta y_{it} - \Delta x_{it}\beta)] = 0 \ (t = 2, ..., T). \qquad (4.23)$$

Moments of this type and GMM estimators based on them were proposed by Griliches and Hausman (1986). See also Wansbeek and Meijer (2000), and Wansbeek (2001) for further discussion and some extensions.

With $T = 3$ we would have the following two orthogonality conditions:

$$E\left[x_{i3}\left(\Delta y_{i2} - \Delta x_{i2}\beta\right)\right] = 0 \qquad (4.24)$$

$$E\left[x_{i1}\left(\Delta y_{i3} - \Delta x_{i3}\beta\right)\right] = 0. \qquad (4.25)$$

As in the previous case, if $x_{it}^\dagger$ were white noise the rank condition for identification would not be satisfied. Also, if $x_{it}^\dagger$ was a random walk then $Cov(x_{i1}, \Delta x_{i3}) = 0$ but $Cov(x_{i3}, \Delta x_{i2}) \neq 0$. Note that these instrumental variable methods can be expected to be useful in the same circumstances under which differencing exacerbates measurement error bias. Namely, when there is more time series dependence in $x_{it}^\dagger$ than in ε_{it}.

If measured persistence in $x_{it}^\dagger$ is exclusively due to unobserved heterogeneity, however, the situation is not different from the homogeneous white noise case and the rank condition will still fail. Specifically, suppose that

$$x_{it}^\dagger = \mu_i + \xi_{it} \qquad (4.26)$$

where ξ_{it} is *iid* over i and t, and independent of μ_i. Then $Cov(x_{i1}, \Delta x_{i3}) = Cov(x_{i3}, \Delta x_{i2}) = 0$, with the result that β is unidentifiable from (4.24) and (4.25). This situation was discussed by Chamberlain (1984, 1985) who noted the observational equivalence between the measurement error and the fixed effects models when the process for $x_{it}^\dagger$ is as in (4.26).

Finally, note that the assumptions about the measurement error properties can be relaxed somewhat provided the panel is sufficiently long and there is suitable dependence in the latent regressor. For example, ε_{it} could be allowed to be a first-order moving average process in which case the valid instruments in the first-difference equation for period t would be

$$\left(x_{i1}, ..., x_{i(t-3)}, x_{i(t+2)}, ..., x_{iT}\right). \qquad (4.27)$$

4.4 Illustration: Measuring Economies of Scale in Firm Money Demand

As an illustration of the previous discussion, we report some estimates from Bover and Watson (2000) concerning economies of scale in a firm money demand equation of the type discussed in Chapter 2.

The equations estimated by Bover and Watson are of the general form given in (2.5):

$$\log m_{it} = c(t) \log s_{it} + b(t) + \eta_i + v_{it}. \tag{4.28}$$

The scale coefficient $c(t)$ is specified as a second-order polynomial in t to allow for changes in economies of scale over the sample period. The year dummies $b(t)$ capture changes in relative interest rates together with other aggregate effects. The individual effect is meant to represent permanent differences across firms in the production of transaction services (so that $\eta = -\log a$), and v contains measurement errors in cash holdings and sales. We would expect a non-negative correlation between sales and a, implying $Cov(\log s, \eta) \leq 0$ and a downward unobserved heterogeneity bias in economies of scale.

Table 4.1
Firm Money Demand Estimates
Sample period 1986–1996

	OLS Levels	OLS Orthogonal deviations	OLS 1st-diff.	GMM 1st-diff.	GMM 1st-diff. m. error	GMM Levels m. error
Log sales	.72 (30.)	.56 (16.)	.45 (12.)	.49 (16.)	.99 (7.5)	.75 (35.)
Log sales ×trend	−.02 (3.2)	−.03 (9.7)	−.03 (4.9)	−.03 (5.3)	−.03 (5.0)	−.03 (4.0)
Log sales ×trend²	.001 (1.2)	.002 (6.6)	.001 (1.9)	.001 (2.0)	.001 (2.3)	.001 (1.4)
Sargan (p-value)				.12	.39	.00

All estimates include year dummies, and those in levels also include industry dummies. t-ratios in brackets robust to heteroskedasticity & serial correlation. N=5649. Source: Bover and Watson (2000).

All the estimates in Table 4.1 are obtained from an unbalanced panel of 5649 Spanish firms with at least four consecutive annual observations during the period 1986−1996.[3]

The comparison between OLS in levels and orthogonal deviations (columns 1 and 2) is consistent with a positive unobserved heterogeneity bias (the opposite to what we expected), but the smaller sales effect obtained by OLS in first-differences (column 3) suggests that measurement error bias may be important.

Column 4 shows two-step robust GMM estimates based on the moments $E(\log s_{it}\Delta v_{is}) = 0$ for all t and s (in addition to time dummies). These estimates are of the form given in (2.40) with weight matrix (2.41). In the absence of measurement error, we would expect them to be consistent for the same parameters as OLS in orthogonal deviations and first-differences. In fact, in the case of Table 4.1 the last two differ, the GMM sales coefficient lies between the two, and the test statistic of overidentifying restrictions (Sargan) is marginal.

Column 5 shows GMM estimates based on

$$E(\log s_{it}\Delta v_{is}) = 0 \quad (t = 1, ..., s - 2, s + 1, .., T; s = 1, ..., T), \qquad (4.29)$$

thus allowing for both correlated firm effects and serially independent multiplicative measurement errors in sales. Interestingly, now the leading sales coefficient is much higher and close to unity, and the Sargan test has a p-value close to 40 per cent.

Finally, column 6 shows GMM estimates based on

$$E(\log s_{it}v_{is}) = 0 \quad (t = 1, ..., s - 1, s + 1, .., T; s = 1, ..., T). \qquad (4.30)$$

In this case, as with the other estimates in levels, firm effects in (4.28) are replaced by industry effects. Therefore, the estimates in column 6 allow for serially uncorrelated measurement error in sales but not for correlated effects. The leading sales effect in this case is close to OLS in levels, suggesting that in levels the measurement error bias is not as important as in the estimation in differences. The Sargan test provides a sound rejection, which can be interpreted as a rejection of the null of lack of correlation between sales and firm effects, allowing for measurement error.

What is interesting about this example is that a comparison between estimates in levels and deviations without consideration of the possibility of measurement error (e.g. restricted to compare columns 1 and 2, or 1 and 3, as in Hausman-type testing), would lead to the conclusion of correlated effects, but with biases going in entirely the wrong direction.

---

[3]The use of an unbalanced panel requires the introduction of some modifications in the formulae for the estimators, which we do not consider here (see, for example, Arellano and Bond, 1991).

Part II

Time Series Models with Error Components

5

Covariance Structures for Dynamic Error Components

5.1 Introduction

The models and methods discussed in this and the next chapter are motivated by an interest in the time series properties of panel data sets. As in Part I, the emphasis will be on short panels. Such interest may arise for a variety of reasons. We may be interested in separating out permanent from transitory components of variation as in earnings mobility studies. In another type of application, we may be able to test theories or identify parameters of policy interest from the mapping between a time series model and a model of individual behaviour. Examples include Hall and Mishkin's test of the permanent income hypothesis (Hall and Mishkin, 1982)—that we discuss below—and Abowd and Card's study of earnings and hours of work data in the context of intertemporal labour supply models (Abowd and Card, 1989). Finally, we may be interested in a predictive distribution for use in some optimization problem under uncertainty. For example, Deaton (1991) uses a predictive distribution of future earnings given past earnings to derive optimal consumption paths for consumers who maximize life-cycle expected utility. A decision-theoretic discussion of this problem is presented by Chamberlain (2000).

A natural extension of the basic error-components model considered in Chapter 3 is to allow for serial correlation in the time-varying component. This is commonly achieved by specifying a simple homogeneous time series process (e.g. moving average or autoregressive). We have

$$y_{it} = \eta_i + v_{it}$$

and the covariance matrix of the $T \times 1$ vector y_i is given by:

$$\Omega = \sigma^2 V + \sigma_\eta^2 \iota \iota' \tag{5.1}$$

where V is the $T \times T$ autocovariance matrix of v_{it}. In the basic case considered in (3.2), $V = I_T$. We shall later discuss the specification and inference for models of this type. The rest of this introduction is devoted to an informal discussion of the problem of distinguishing between unobserved heterogeneity and individual dynamics in short panels.

Distinguishing Unobserved Heterogeneity from Genuine Dynamics Let us consider the identification problem that arises in short panels by considering first a panel with $T = 2$. In time series analysis, given a single time series of size T $\{y_1, ..., y_T\}$ a first-order autocovariance is calculated as an average of the $T - 1$ products of observations one period apart: $(T - 1)^{-1} \sum_{t=2}^{T} y_t y_{t-1}$. With panel data of size $T = 2$, we have N time series with two observations each. In such a situation calculating individual *time series autocovariances* is not possible because the time series averages would have just one observation. We can nevertheless calculate a *cross-sectional first-order autocovariance* for the specific two periods available in the panel. This will take the form of an average of the N products of the two observations for each individual: $N^{-1} \sum_{i=1}^{N} y_{i1} y_{i2}$. Thus, when we consider population moments in this context they are to be regarded as population counterparts of cross-sectional moments of the previous type. As for example,

$$E\left(y_{i1}y_{i2}\right) = \underset{N \to \infty}{\text{plim}} \frac{1}{N} \sum_{i=1}^{N} y_{i1} y_{i2}. \tag{5.2}$$

In Chapter 3 we saw that the standard error-components model with white noise v_{it} was identified with $T = 2$ since

$$Var\left(y_{i1}\right) = Var\left(y_{i2}\right) = \sigma_\eta^2 + \sigma_v^2 \tag{5.3}$$

$$Cov\left(y_{i1}, y_{i2}\right) = \sigma_\eta^2. \tag{5.4}$$

In this model all the observed correlation between first and second period data is due to heterogeneity, since for a given individual the sequence of ys is a random white noise process around his specific level η_i. The point to note here is that this *pure heterogeneity model* is observationally equivalent to a *homogeneous model with serial correlation*. For example, if the model is

$$y_{it} = \eta + v_{it} \tag{5.5}$$

$$v_{it} = \alpha v_{i(t-1)} + \varepsilon_{it}, \tag{5.6}$$

where η is a constant, $\varepsilon_{it} \sim iid\left(0, \sigma_\varepsilon^2\right)$, $v_{i1} \sim iid\left(0, \sigma_v^2\right)$, and $\sigma_v^2 = \sigma_\varepsilon^2 / \left(1 - \alpha^2\right)$, we have

$$Var\left(y_{i1}\right) = Var\left(y_{i2}\right) = \sigma_v^2 \tag{5.7}$$

$$Cov\left(y_{i1}, y_{i2}\right) = \alpha\sigma_v^2. \tag{5.8}$$

In the heterogeneity model the observed autocorrelation ρ_1 is given by

$$\rho_1 = \frac{\lambda}{(1+\lambda)} \tag{5.9}$$

with $\lambda = \sigma_\eta^2/\sigma_v^2$, whereas in the homogeneous AR(1) model we have

$$\rho_1 = \alpha. \tag{5.10}$$

If, for example, the variance of η_i is four times the variance of v_{it} in the heterogeneity model, we get $\rho_1 = 4/5 = 0.8$, exactly the same observed correlation as we would get with a homogeneous AR(1) model with $\alpha = 0.8$. So there is no way to distinguish empirically between the two models from the autocovariance matrix when $T = 2$, as long as $\alpha \geq 0$.

With $T = 3$ the previous two models are distinguishable and non-nested since the heterogeneity model implies

$$Cov\left(y_{i1}, y_{i3}\right) = \sigma_\eta^2 \tag{5.11}$$

whereas for the AR(1)

$$Cov\left(y_{i1}, y_{i3}\right) = \alpha^2\sigma_v^2. \tag{5.12}$$

Now the combined model with heterogeneous level and homogeneous AR(1) serial correlation (which allows the intercept η in (5.5) to be individual specific with variance σ_η^2) is just identified with

$$Var\left(y_{i1}\right) = Var\left(y_{i2}\right) = Var\left(y_{i3}\right) = \sigma_\eta^2 + \sigma_v^2 \tag{5.13}$$

$$Cov\left(y_{i1}, y_{i2}\right) = Cov\left(y_{i2}, y_{i3}\right) = \sigma_\eta^2 + \alpha\sigma_v^2 \tag{5.14}$$

$$Cov\left(y_{i1}, y_{i3}\right) = \sigma_\eta^2 + \alpha^2\sigma_v^2. \tag{5.15}$$

Pursuing the previous argument, note that with $T = 3$ the AR(1) model with heterogeneous mean will be indistinguishable from a homogeneous AR(2) model. These simple examples suggest that a nonparametric test of heterogeneity will only be possible for large T and N, and in the absence of structural breaks.

Note that with $T = 2$ the "reduced form" autocovariance matrix contains three free coefficients (two variances and one covariance). Since the model that combines AR(1) errors and heterogeneity also has three parameters α, σ_η^2, and σ_v^2, the order condition for identification is satisfied with equality, but not the rank condition. This is so because the variance equation for the second period will be either redundant or incompatible.

In general, persistence measured from cross-sectional autocorrelation coefficients will combine two different sources. In the AR(1) model with heterogeneous mean we have

$$\rho_1 = \frac{\sigma_\eta^2 + \alpha\sigma_v^2}{\sigma_\eta^2 + \sigma_v^2} = \alpha + \frac{(1-\alpha)\sigma_\eta^2}{\sigma_\eta^2 + \sigma_v^2} = \alpha + \frac{(1-\alpha)\lambda}{(1+\lambda)}. \tag{5.16}$$

which particularizes to (5.9) or (5.10) when either α or λ are equal to zero, respectively.

Often with micro data $\rho_1 \simeq 1$. Nevertheless, a value of ρ_1 close to one may be compatible with many different values of α and λ. For example, fitting the AR(1) model with heterogeneous mean to annual employment from a short balance account-based panel of firms we obtained $\rho_1 = 0.995$, $\alpha = 0.8$, and $\lambda = 36$ (see Section 6.7).

The estimation of autoregressive models with individual effects will be discussed in detail in Chapter 6. In the remainder of this chapter we consider time effects, moving average models, and inference from covariance structures. Autoregressive models will also be briefly considered in this chapter as an illustration of the advantages of using transformed covariance structures.

The previous discussion could have been conducted using first-order moving average instead of autoregressive processes.[1] One advantage of MA over AR processes is that they imply linear restrictions in the autocovariance matrix (e.g. with $T = 3$ the pure MA(1) process implies $Cov\,(y_{i1}, y_{i3}) = 0$). The advantages of autoregressive representations are in the possibilities of incorporating certain non-stationary features (like unit roots or nonstationary initial conditions), and the relationship to regression and instrumental-variable settings.

5.2   Time Effects

Often a time series analysis of individual time series will only be meaningful after conditioning on common features. For example, in the empirical consumption model of Hall and Mishkin considered below, the time series properties of consumption and income were investigated after conditioning on trends and demographic characteristics of the household. In other instances, it may be important to remove business cycle or seasonal effects in order to avoid confusion between aggregate and individual specific dynamics. One might consider specifying a regression of y_{it} on some aggregate variables z_t (like GDP growth, the unemployment rate, inflation, or functions of time)

$$y_{it} = \gamma' z_t + y_{it}^I \tag{5.17}$$

---

[1] Except for the fact that a pure MA(1) process restricts the range of possible values of ρ_1.

together with a time series model for the individual-specific component y_{it}^I.
Alternatively, the aggregate component could be specified as a latent common
stochastic process y_t^a:

$$y_{it} = y_t^a + y_{it}^I. \tag{5.18}$$

One would then specify time series models for both y_t^a and y_{it}^I. If $y_t^a \sim$
$iid\left(0, \sigma_a^2\right)$ and y_{it}^I follows the basic error-components model, we obtain the
two-way error-components model considered by Wallace and Hussain (1969)
and Amemiya (1971):

$$y_{it} = y_t^a + \eta_i + v_{it}, \tag{5.19}$$

whose covariance matrix is given by

$$Var(y) = \sigma_v^2 I_{NT} + \sigma_\eta^2 \left(I_N \otimes \iota_T \iota_T'\right) + \sigma_a^2 \left(\iota_N \iota_N' \otimes I_T\right). \tag{5.20}$$

where $y = (y_1', ..., y_N')'$, and ι_T and ι_N denote vectors of ones of dimensions T
and N.[2]

Stochastic modelling of both y_t^a and η_i requires large T and N. In panels
with small N and large T the individual effects are treated as parameters. Tiao
and Ali (1971) presented an early likelihood analysis of a regression version of
this type of model in which v_{it} was a white noise error and y_t^a followed an
ARMA(1,1) process.[3]

Time Dummies in Short Panels Conversely, with short micro panels,
the number of time series observations is too small to attempt a stochastic
modelling of y_t^a. On the other hand, the cross-sectional sample size is large so
that the realizations of y_t^a that occur in the sample can be treated as unknown
period specific parameters to be estimated. To this end we may specify a set
of T time dummies:

$$y_{it} = y^{a\prime} d_t + y_{it}^I \tag{5.21}$$

where $y^a = (y_1^a, ..., y_T^a)'$ and d_t is a $T \times 1$ vector with one in the t-th position
and zero elsewhere.

Note that any aggregate variable z_t will be a linear combination of the
time dummies. Thus, if a full set of time dummies is included any aggregate
variable will be perfectly co-linear with them and hence redundant. If one has
a substantive interest in the effects of macro variables, time dummies would not
be employed. Indeed, the specification for the macro variables can be regarded
as a model for the time dummies. If the substantive interest is in the individual
dynamics and the data is sufficiently informative, however, time dummies afford
a robust control for common aggregate effects in short panels.

---

[2]See Hsiao (1986) and Baltagi (1995) for discussions on estimation of these models, and
additional references.

[3]The dynamic factor models used in econometric applications with large T panels can also
be regarded as generalizations of models of this type. Examples include the factor models
for stock markets of King, Sentana, and Wadhwani (1994), and the disaggregated business
cycle models of Forni and Reichlin (1998).

Individual-Specific Trends   In the basic error-components model there is a heterogeneous constant level of the process. This can be generalized to consider a heterogeneous trend. In the case of a linear trend we have

$$y_{it} = \eta_{0i} + \eta_{1i}t + v_{it} \tag{5.22}$$

or in vector notation

$$y_i = S\eta_i + v_i \tag{5.23}$$

where $\eta_i = (\eta_{0i}, \eta_{1i})'$ and S denotes the $T \times 2$ matrix

$$S = \begin{pmatrix} 1 & 1 \\ 1 & 2 \\ \vdots & \vdots \\ 1 & T \end{pmatrix}.$$

Letting $Var(\eta_i) = \Omega_\eta$, and assuming that $v_{it} \sim iid(0, \sigma^2)$ and independent of η_i, the $T \times T$ covariance matrix of y_i is given by

$$\Omega = S\Omega_\eta S' + \sigma^2 I_T. \tag{5.24}$$

A necessary condition for identification of Ω_η and σ^2 is that $T \geq 3$. To illustrate the situation, let us consider for $T = 3$ the covariance matrix of the variables y_{i1}, Δy_{i2}, and $\Delta^2 y_{i3}$ (where $\Delta^2 y_{i3} = \Delta y_{i3} - \Delta y_{i2}$):

$$y_{i1} = \eta_{0i} + \eta_{1i} + v_{i1} \tag{5.25}$$

$$\Delta y_{i2} = \eta_{1i} + (v_{i2} - v_{i1}) \tag{5.26}$$

$$\Delta^2 y_{i3} = v_{i3} - 2v_{i2} + v_{i1} \tag{5.27}$$

which provides a non-singular transformation of the original covariance matrix Ω. The two covariance matrices contain the same information, but the transformation simplifies the relationship between the model's parameters and the variances and covariances of the data:

$$Var \begin{pmatrix} y_{i1} \\ \Delta y_{i2} \\ \Delta^2 y_{i3} \end{pmatrix} = \begin{pmatrix} \sigma_{00} + \sigma_{11} + 2\sigma_{01} + \sigma^2 & \sigma_{11} + \sigma_{01} - \sigma^2 & \sigma^2 \\ & \sigma_{11} + 2\sigma^2 & -3\sigma^2 \\ & & 6\sigma^2 \end{pmatrix}. \tag{5.28}$$

Thus, σ^2 is determined from the variance and covariances in the last column. Given σ^2, σ_{11} can be determined from $Var(\Delta y_{i2})$. Then σ_{01} is determined from $Cov(y_{i1}, \Delta y_{i2})$, and finally σ_{00} is determined from $Var(y_{i1})$.[4]

Models for the covariance structure of earnings with individual specific trends were considered by Lillard and Weiss (1979) and Hause (1980).

---

[4]With $T = 2$, the variances of η_{0i}, η_{1i}, and v_{it} are just identified if η_{0i} and η_{1i} are assumed to be uncorrelated.

Individual-Specific Responses to Aggregate Variables   The previous case can be extended to consider individual-specific responses to aggregate variables (like business cycle movements) of the form

$$y_{it} = \eta_i' z_t + v_{it} \qquad (5.29)$$

where z_t denotes a vector of observable aggregate variables, and η_i is a vector of individual specific effects of z_t on y_{it}. Note that for $S = (z_1, ..., z_T)'$ and $Var(\eta_i) = \Omega_\eta$, the variance matrix of y_i is of the same form as (5.24). Identification in this case will require that z_t has sufficient variation and the dimension of η_i is not too large relative to T.

Model (5.29) could also describe a *stochastic seasonal pattern* by letting z_t represent a vector of seasonal dummies. A model of this kind was considered by Alvarez (1999) for the analysis of quarterly earnings.

Time Effects Interacted with Individual Effects   Let us now consider a model of the form

$$y_{it} = \eta_i \delta_t + v_{it}. \qquad (5.30)$$

This model can be regarded as specifying an aggregate shock δ_t that has individual-specific effects, or a permanent characteristic η_i that has changing effects over time. The difference with the previous model is that z_t in (5.29) was known whereas δ_t in (5.30) is not. Therefore, in a short panel $\delta = (\delta_1, ..., \delta_T)'$ will be treated as a vector of parameters to be estimated.

Assuming that $v_{it} \sim iid(0, \sigma^2)$ and independent of η_i, the data covariance matrix in this case takes the form

$$\Omega = \sigma_\eta^2 \delta \delta' + \sigma^2 I_T. \qquad (5.31)$$

This is the structure of the traditional one-factor model of factor analysis. Some scale normalization is required in order to determine δ. Using $\delta' \delta = 1$, it follows that $\sigma_\eta^2 + \sigma^2$ is the largest eigenvalue of Ω and δ is the corresponding eigenvector. Moreover, the remaining $T - 1$ eigenvalues of Ω are equal to σ^2.

Let us illustrate the identification of this type of model by considering a case in which $T = 3$ and the v_{it} are allowed to have period-specific variances σ_t^2. With the normalization $\delta_1 = 1$, the covariance matrix is given by

$$Var \begin{pmatrix} y_{i1} \\ y_{i2} \\ y_{i3} \end{pmatrix} = \begin{pmatrix} \sigma_\eta^2 + \sigma_1^2 & \sigma_\eta^2 \delta_2 & \sigma_\eta^2 \delta_3 \\ & \sigma_\eta^2 \delta_2^2 + \sigma_2^2 & \sigma_\eta^2 \delta_2 \delta_3 \\ & & \sigma_\eta^2 \delta_3^2 + \sigma_3^2 \end{pmatrix}. \qquad (5.32)$$

In this case, subject to compatibility, the parameters are just identified and given by

$$\delta_2 = \frac{Cov(y_{i2}, y_{i3})}{Cov(y_{i1}, y_{i3})} \qquad (5.33)$$

$$\delta_3 = \frac{Cov(y_{i2}, y_{i3})}{Cov(y_{i1}, y_{i2})} \tag{5.34}$$

$$\sigma_\eta^2 = \frac{Cov(y_{i1}, y_{i2})Cov(y_{i1}, y_{i3})}{Cov(y_{i2}, y_{i3})} \tag{5.35}$$

$$\sigma_t^2 = Var(y_{it}) - \sigma_\eta^2 \delta_t^2 \ (t = 1, 2, 3). \tag{5.36}$$

Note that (5.33) and (5.34) can be interpreted as instrumental variable estimating parameters from autoregressive equations. This is a specially useful perspective when v_{it} itself follows an autoregressive process. Models of this type will be discussed in the next chapter.

5.3   Moving Average Autocovariances

Stationary Models   We begin by considering stationary models. Covariance stationarity requires that for all t and j, $Cov\left(y_{it}, y_{i(t-j)}\right)$ does not depend on t:

$$Cov\left(y_{it}, y_{i(t-j)}\right) = \gamma_j. \tag{5.37}$$

Thus, under stationarity, the $T \times T$ autocovariance matrix of a scalar variable y_{it} depends at most on only T different coefficients $\gamma_0, ..., \gamma_{T-1}$, which implies that it satisfies $T(T+1)/2 - T$ restrictions.

A stationary moving-average structure of order q MA(q) with individual effects will further restrict the coefficients γ_j for $j > q$ to take the same value (corresponding to the variance of the individual effect):

$$\gamma_{q+1} = ... = \gamma_{T-1}. \tag{5.38}$$

The absence of individual effects will be signalled by the additional restriction that the previous coefficients are equal to zero

$$\gamma_{q+1} = ... = \gamma_{T-1} = 0. \tag{5.39}$$

Therefore, given stationarity, an MA($T-2$) process (with individual effects) or an MA($T-1$) process (without them) will be observationally equivalent saturated models.

A moving average process may also imply inequality restrictions on the elements of the covariance matrix. As an example, suppose that

$$y_{it} = \eta_i + v_{it}$$

where v_{it} is an invertible MA(1) process of the form

$$v_{it} = \varepsilon_{it} + \phi\varepsilon_{i(t-1)} \tag{5.40}$$

with $|\phi| \le 1$ and $\varepsilon_{it} \sim iid(0, \sigma_\varepsilon^2)$, for all t. We then have

$$\gamma_0 = \sigma_\eta^2 + \sigma_\varepsilon^2(1 + \phi^2) \qquad (5.41)$$

$$\gamma_1 = \sigma_\eta^2 + \sigma_\varepsilon^2 \phi \qquad (5.42)$$

$$\gamma_2 = ... = \gamma_{T-1} = \sigma_\eta^2. \qquad (5.43)$$

Therefore, the γ_js will satisfy the inequality constraints:[5]

$$\gamma_0 \geq 0 \qquad (5.44)$$

$$\gamma_j \geq 0 \ (j = 2, ..., T - 1) \qquad (5.45)$$

$$\left| \frac{\gamma_1 - \gamma_j}{\gamma_0 - \gamma_j} \right| \leq \frac{1}{2} \ (j = 2, ..., T - 1). \qquad (5.46)$$

Nonstationary Models Nonstationarity, in the sense of failure of condition (5.37), may arise for a variety of reasons. Examples include the individual-specific trends and responses to aggregate variables considered above,[6] or nonstationary initial conditions (as discussed for autoregressive models in the next chapter). Moreover, nonstationarity may also arise as a result of unit roots in autoregressive processes, time-varying error variances (possibly due to life-cycle or aggregate effects), or ARMA models with coefficients that vary over time (MaCurdy, 1982b).

Provided $q < T - 1$, a nonstationary MA(q) process without permanent effects will satisfy the $(T - q)(T - q - 1)/2$ restrictions

$$Cov(y_{it}, y_{i(t-j)}) = 0 \text{ for } j > q. \qquad (5.47)$$

In such a model, the elements in the main diagonal of the autocovariance matrix and those in the first q subdiagonals will be free coefficients, except for the symmetry and non-negativity restrictions. Similarly, in a nonstationary MA(q) process with permanent effects the zero elements in the autocovariance matrix will be replaced by a constant coefficient.

---

[5]The last inequality restriction arises from the fact that the first-order autocorrelation of the MA(1) component, given by

$$\frac{\gamma_1 - \gamma_j}{\gamma_0 - \gamma_j} = \frac{\phi}{1 + \phi^2},$$

cannot exceed $1/2$ in absolute value for any real number ϕ.

[6]Note, however, that from the point of view of the time series process of a given individual, model (5.22) introduces a deterministic trend, whereas model (5.29) is compatible with a stationary process for y_{it} provided z_t is stationary itself. Thus, the immediate reason why (5.29) is "nonstationary" in our terminology is because we are conditioning on the realizations of z_t.

An MA process with *nonstationary variances* provides a tighter specification leading to a nonstationary moving average autocovariance matrix. One possibility is to consider the following specification:

$$y_{it} = \eta_i + v_{it}$$

$$v_{it} = \sigma_t v_{it}^\dagger \tag{5.48}$$

where $v_{it}^\dagger$ is a stationary MA process with $iid(0,1)$ errors. In this way we can allow for arbitrary heteroskedasticity over time and at the same time specify a stationary serial correlation pattern for v_{it} (Arellano, 1985). This is so because $Cov(v_{it}, v_{is}) = \sigma_t \sigma_s Cov\left(v_{it}^\dagger, v_{is}^\dagger\right)$ and thus $Corr(v_{it}, v_{is}) = Corr\left(v_{it}^\dagger, v_{is}^\dagger\right)$ for any value of $|t - s|$. This is not the case if we consider instead an MA process where the variance of the white noise error is varying over time.

Multivariate Models   The previous considerations can be generalized to a multivariate context. Let y_{it} denote an $m \times 1$ random vector. Then the autocovariance matrix of the vector $y_i = (y'_{i1}, ..., y'_{iT})'$ is of order mT. Under stationarity, for any t and j the $m \times m$ block $Cov\left(y_{it}, y_{i(t-j)}\right)$ does not depend on t:

$$Cov\left(y_{it}, y_{i(t-j)}\right) = \Gamma_j. \tag{5.49}$$

A stationary vector-MA(q) process with individual effects introduces the restrictions

$$\Gamma_{q+1} = ... = \Gamma_{T-1}. \tag{5.50}$$

Moreover, if no variable contains individual-specific intercepts then also

$$\Gamma_{q+1} = ... = \Gamma_{T-1} = 0. \tag{5.51}$$

Similar remarks can be made for nonstationary vector-MA specifications.

Abowd and Card (1989) presented an empirical analysis of changes in the logs of annual earnings and hours from three different panels (actually of residuals from regressions of those variables on time dummies and potential experience). For each data set they found evidence supporting the restrictions implied by a nonstationary MA(2) bivariate process without individual effects.[7] Abowd and Card also considered a three-components model with one common factor, which can be written as

$$\Delta y_{it} = \begin{pmatrix} \mu \\ 1 \end{pmatrix} \Delta z_{it} + \Delta u_{it} + \varepsilon_{it},$$

where Δy_{it} is a 2×1 vector of growth rates in earnings and hours of work, Δz_{it} is a scalar MA(2) common component, and u_{it} and ε_{it} are bivariate white

---

[7]Recall that individual effects in the changes of the variables would correspond to individual-specific trends in their levels.

noise processes, accounting for measurement errors and permanent shocks, respectively. This was a rationalization of their bivariate MA representation that
was suitable for mapping to life-cycle labour supply models.

The permanent income model of Hall and Mishkin (1982) was also a bivariate model of changes in income and consumption, which contained a shared
component and moving average transitory errors. We shall use this model as
an illustration in Section 5.5.

Covariance Matrices of Levels and First-Differences   Abowd and
Card (1989) and Hall and Mishkin (1982) did not consider the covariance structure of the levels of their variables. They focused on the implications of the
time series properties of changes in the variables for life-cycle labour supply
and consumption models.

To examine the relationship between the covariance structures in levels and
first-differences, let us consider the covariance matrix of the transformed series

$$
Var \begin{pmatrix} y_{i1} \\ \Delta y_{i2} \\ \vdots \\ \Delta y_{iT} \end{pmatrix} = \Omega^* = \begin{pmatrix} \omega_{11}^* & \omega_{12}^* & \cdots & \omega_{1T}^* \\ \omega_{12}^* & & & \\ \vdots & & \Omega_\Delta & \\ \omega_{1T}^* & & & \end{pmatrix}. \tag{5.52}
$$

The matrix Ω^* is a non-singular transformation of the covariance matrix in
levels (so that knowledge of one implies knowledge of the other), and Ω_Δ is the
covariance matrix in first-differences. Therefore, a model of Ω_Δ is equivalent
to a model of the covariance matrix in levels that leaves the coefficients ω_{1t}^*
$(t = 1, ..., T)$ unrestricted. This equivalence requires that both Ω^* and Ω_Δ are
finite. If Ω_Δ is finite but y_{it} contains an additive individual effect with infinite
variance, it will be appropriate to conduct covariance analysis in first-differences
but not in levels.

When the variance matrix of the levels is finite, the terms ω_{1t}^* may be
informative about the structural parameters in Ω_Δ. If y_{it} follows an MA(q)
process with individual effects, Δy_{it} will be an MA($q + 1$) process without
individual effects. In such a case even if initial conditions are assumed to be
nonstationary we would expect

$$
\omega_{1t}^* = 0 \text{ for } t > q + 2. \tag{5.53}
$$

Enforcing these restrictions will in general lead to more efficient estimates of
parameters in the structure for Ω_Δ.

5.4   Estimating Covariance Structures

The previous models all specify a structure on a data covariance matrix. It is
of some interest to approach identification and inference with reference to a covariance structure, especially when the interest is in estimating the parameters

in the structure as opposed to a substantive interest in the probability distribution of the data. In some cases, restrictions on higher-order moments may add identification content, but it is still often useful to know when a parameter of interest in a time series model may or may not be identified from the data covariance matrix alone.

5.4.1 GMM/MD Estimation

Abstracting from mean components for simplicity, suppose the covariance matrix of a $p \times 1$ time series y_i is a function of a $k \times 1$ parameter vector θ given by

$$E(y_i y_i') = \Omega(\theta). \tag{5.54}$$

If y_i is a scalar time series its dimension will coincide with T, but in the multivariate context $p = mT$.

Vectorizing the expression and eliminating redundant elements (due to symmetry) we obtain a vector of moments of order $r = (p+1)p/2$:

$$vech E\left[y_i y_i' - \Omega(\theta)\right] = E\left[s_i - \omega(\theta)\right], \tag{5.55}$$

where the *vech* operator stacks by rows the lower triangle of a square matrix.[8]

If $r > k$ and $H(\theta) = \partial\omega(\theta)/\partial\theta'$ has full column rank, the model is over identified. In that case a standard optimal GMM or MD estimator solves:

$$\widehat{\theta} = \arg\min_c \left[\bar{s} - \omega(c)\right]' \widehat{V}^{-1} \left[\bar{s} - \omega(c)\right] \tag{5.56}$$

where $\bar{s}$ is the sample mean vector of s_i:

$$\bar{s} = \frac{1}{N} \sum_{i=1}^{N} s_i \tag{5.57}$$

and $\widehat{V}$ is some consistent estimator of $V = Var(s_i)$.[9] A natural choice is the sample covariance matrix of s_i:

$$\widehat{V} = \frac{1}{N} \sum_{i=1}^{N} s_i s_i' - \bar{s}\bar{s}'. \tag{5.58}$$

The first-order conditions from the optimization problem are

$$-H(c)' \widehat{V}^{-1} \left[\bar{s} - \omega(c)\right] = 0. \tag{5.59}$$

---

[8] If we were interested in considering mean restrictions of the form $E(y_i) = \mu(\theta)$ jointly with covariance restrictions, we could proceed in the same way after redefining the vectors s_i and $\omega(\theta)$ as $s_i = (y_i', [vech(y_i y_i')]')'$ and $\omega(\theta) = (\mu(\theta)', [vech\Omega(\theta)]')'$, respectively.

[9] Since $\bar{s}$ is a sample average, (5.56) is both an MD and a GMM objective function.

The two standard useful results for large sample inference are, first, asymptotic normality of the scaled estimation error

$$\left[\frac{1}{N} H(\widehat{\theta})' \widehat{V}^{-1} H(\widehat{\theta}) \right]^{-1/2} \left(\widehat{\theta} - \theta \right) \xrightarrow{d} \mathcal{N}(0, I) \tag{5.60}$$

and, second, the asymptotic chi-square distribution of the minimized estimation criterion (*test statistic of overidentifying restrictions*)[10]

$$S = N \left[\overline{s} - \omega(\widehat{\theta}) \right]' \widehat{V}^{-1} \left[\overline{s} - \omega(\widehat{\theta}) \right] \xrightarrow{d} \chi^2_{r-k}. \tag{5.61}$$

The estimation and testing of covariance structures from panel data has been considered amongst others by Jöreskog and Sörbom (1977), MaCurdy (1982b), Chamberlain (1982), Abowd and Card (1989), and Arellano (1990). See Aigner, Hsiao, Kapteyn, and Wansbeek (1984) for a comprehensive survey and references on latent variable modelling in econometrics.

Example: Fitting a Homogeneous MA(1) model with T=3 In such a case $r = 6$ and $k = 2$ with $\theta = (\gamma_0, \gamma_1)$ and

$$\Omega = \begin{pmatrix} \gamma_0 & \gamma_1 & 0 \\ \gamma_1 & \gamma_0 & \gamma_1 \\ 0 & \gamma_1 & \gamma_0 \end{pmatrix}. \tag{5.62}$$

We could alternatively parameterize Ω using $(\sigma_\varepsilon^2, \phi)$ instead of (γ_0, γ_1) as in (5.41)-(5.42) with $\sigma_\eta^2 = 0$, but the restrictions in terms of the latter are linear and there is a one-to-one mapping between the two once we restrict ourselves to invertible solutions. Thus we have

$$s_i = \left(\begin{array}{cccccc} y_{i1}^2 & y_{i2}y_{i1} & y_{i2}^2 & y_{i3}y_{i1} & y_{i3}y_{i2} & y_{i3}^2 \end{array} \right)' \tag{5.63}$$

and

$$\omega(\theta) = \begin{pmatrix} \gamma_0 \\ \gamma_1 \\ \gamma_0 \\ 0 \\ \gamma_1 \\ \gamma_0 \end{pmatrix} = \begin{pmatrix} 1 & 0 \\ 0 & 1 \\ 1 & 0 \\ 0 & 0 \\ 0 & 1 \\ 1 & 0 \end{pmatrix} \begin{pmatrix} \gamma_0 \\ \gamma_1 \end{pmatrix} = H\theta. \tag{5.64}$$

Since the restrictions are linear, an explicit expression for the GMM estimator is available:

$$\widehat{\theta} = \left(H' \widehat{V}^{-1} H \right)^{-1} H' \widehat{V}^{-1} \overline{s}. \tag{5.65}$$

Thus, $\widehat{\theta}$ can be obtained as a GLS regression of $\overline{s}$ on H using $\widehat{V}$ as weight matrix. Note that this estimator will not impose the inequality restrictions $\gamma_0 \geq 0$ and $\mid \gamma_1/\gamma_0 \mid \leq 1/2$, which may be an especially undesirable feature in some applications.

---

[10] A review of the theory of the generalized method of moments is in Appendix A.

5.4.2   Using Transformations of the Original Moments

Sometimes using a (possibly parameter-dependent) transformation of the original moments may lead to a simpler estimation problem. One simplification arises when the transformed moments are linear in the parameters whereas the original moments are nonlinear. Another simplification is when a subset of the transformed moments are unrestricted, so that one can concentrate on smaller sets of moments and parameters without loss of efficiency.

The general idea is to replace the original moments (5.55) with the transformed moments

$$E\left\{A(\theta)\left[s_i - \omega(\theta)\right]\right\} = 0 \tag{5.66}$$

where $A(\theta)$ is a non-singular transformation matrix, and consider a GMM estimator based on (5.66):

$$\widetilde{\theta} = \arg\min_c \left[\bar{s} - \omega(c)\right]' A(c)' \widehat{V^*}^{-1} A(c) \left[\bar{s} - \omega(c)\right]. \tag{5.67}$$

As long as plim $\widehat{V^*} = A(\theta) V A(\theta)'$, the GMM estimator based on the transformed moments (5.67) will be asymptotically equivalent to the one based on the original moments (5.56). The result follows from inspection of the corresponding optimal GMM asymptotic covariance matrices, after noting that the expected gradient of the transformed moments evaluated at the true parameter values is given by[11]

$$E\left\{\frac{\partial}{\partial\theta'} A(\theta)\left[s_i - \omega(\theta)\right]\right\} = -A(\theta)H(\theta). \tag{5.68}$$

Example: An AR(1) Model with Individual Effects   As an example, let us consider the stationary AR(1) model with individual effects described in Section 5.1. This model implies the nonlinear restrictions

$$\omega_{st} = \sigma_\eta^2 + \alpha^{s-t}\sigma_v^2 \text{ for } s \le t. \tag{5.69}$$

The point to note is that these restrictions can be equivalently written as

$$\omega_{st} = \begin{cases} \psi + \alpha\omega_{s(t-1)} & \text{for } s < t \\ \sigma_0^2 & \text{for } s = t \end{cases} \tag{5.70}$$

where $\sigma_0^2 = \sigma_\eta^2 + \sigma_v^2$ and $\psi = (1-\alpha)\sigma_\eta^2$. Thus, for $\theta = (\alpha, \sigma_0^2, \psi)$, we consider the transformed moments that use

---

[11]Note that the derivatives are

$$\frac{\partial}{\partial c'} A(c)\left[s_i - \omega(c)\right] = -A(c)H(c) + \left[I_r \otimes (s_i - \omega(c))\right]' \frac{\partial}{\partial c'} vecA(c)$$

and that the expected value of the second term at $c = \theta$ vanishes.

$$A(\theta) = I - \alpha\Phi \tag{5.71}$$

where I is an identity matrix, and Φ is a $0 - 1$ matrix that maps the vector $\omega(\theta)$ of elements ω_{st} into a vector with elements equal to $\omega_{s(t-1)}$ for $s < t$ and equal to zero for $s = t$ (cf. Arellano, 1990).

The resulting $T(T + 1)/2$ transformed orthogonality conditions are linear in θ and can be written as:

$$E\left[y_{is}(y_{it} - \alpha y_{i(t-1)}) - \psi\right] = 0 \text{ for } s < t \text{ and } t = 2, ..., T \tag{5.72}$$

$$E\left(y_{it}^2 - \sigma_0^2\right) = 0 \text{ for } t = 1, ..., T. \tag{5.73}$$

Thus, in this example the estimator (5.67) is linear whereas the one based on the original moments is not. The disadvantage of (5.67) is that a preliminary consistent estimate of θ is required to obtain a consistent estimate of $V^* = A(\theta)VA(\theta)'$.

For later reference notice that by suitable differencing of the $(T - 1)T/2$ moments in (5.72), they can be expressed as the $(T - 2)(T - 1)/2$ moments:

$$E\left[y_{is}(\Delta y_{it} - \alpha\Delta y_{i(t-1)})\right] = 0 \text{ for } s < t - 1 \text{ and } t = 3, ..., T, \tag{5.74}$$

together with the $(T - 2)$ moments:

$$E\left[\Delta y_{i(t-1)}(y_{it} - \alpha y_{i(t-1)})\right] = 0 \text{ for } t = 3, ..., T, \tag{5.75}$$

and the single moment

$$E\left[y_{i1}(y_{i2} - \alpha y_{i1}) - \psi\right] = 0. \tag{5.76}$$

The last set of moments illustrates another potential benefit of transformation. Namely, since (5.76) is an unrestricted moment, optimal GMM estimates of α and σ_0^2 based on (5.73)-(5.75)—with the exclusion of (5.76)—are asymptotically efficient.[12]

5.4.3 Relationship between GMM and Pseudo ML

If $y_i \sim iid\mathcal{N}\left[0, \Omega(\theta)\right]$, the maximum likelihood estimator of θ solves[13]

$$\widehat{\theta}_{PML} = \arg\min_{c}\left[\log\det\Omega(c) + \frac{1}{N}\sum_{i=1}^{N}y_i'\Omega^{-1}(c)y_i\right]. \tag{5.77}$$

If the distribution of y_i is not assumed to be normal, $\widehat{\theta}_{PML}$ can be regarded as a Gaussian pseudo maximum likelihood estimator (PML).

---

[12]The irrelevance of unrestricted moments is discussed in section A.8.

[13]In a model with heterogeneous level and homogeneous autocorrelation of the form $y_i = \eta_i\iota + v_i$, unconditional joint normality of y_i can be regarded as the result of both conditional normality given η_i, namely $y_i \mid \eta_i \sim \mathcal{N}(\eta_i\iota, \sigma^2 V)$, and normality of the η_i: $\eta_i \sim \mathcal{N}(0, \sigma_\eta^2)$, so that $\Omega = \sigma_\eta^2\iota\iota' + \sigma^2 V$.

Defining the selection matrix $\mathcal{D} = \partial vec\Omega / \partial(vech\Omega)'$, the first-order conditions for this problem are

$$-H(c)' \left[\mathcal{D}' \left(\Omega^{-1}(c) \otimes \Omega^{-1}(c) \right) \mathcal{D} \right] [\bar{s} - \omega(c)] = 0, \qquad (5.78)$$

which are of the same form as those for the GMM problem above given in (5.59).[14]

Under normality, fourth-order moments are functions of second-order moments. Specifically, the elements of $E(s_i s_i')$ are of the form:

$$E\left(y_{it} y_{is} y_{it'} y_{is'}\right) = \omega_{ts}\omega_{t's'} + \omega_{tt'}\omega_{ss'} + \omega_{ts'}\omega_{st'}, \qquad (5.79)$$

and indeed it can be shown that[15]

$$V^{-1} = \frac{1}{2}\mathcal{D}' \left(\Omega^{-1}(\theta) \otimes \Omega^{-1}(\theta) \right) \mathcal{D}. \qquad (5.80)$$

Thus, under normality an alternative optimal GMM estimator could use some consistent estimate of $\mathcal{D}' \left(\Omega^{-1}(\theta) \otimes \Omega^{-1}(\theta) \right) \mathcal{D}$ as weight matrix. Such estimator does not coincide with $\widehat{\theta}_{PML}$ because in the latter the weight matrix is continuously updated as a function of c in (5.78), but the two can be proved to be asymptotically equivalent with or without normality. Under non-normality, they remain consistent and asymptotically normal but they are inefficient for large N relative to the GMM estimator that uses $\widehat{V}^{-1}$ as weight matrix.

A PML or Gaussian-weight-GMM estimator may still be preferable even under non-normality on the grounds of better finite sample properties (which may be the case if fourth-order moments are large relative to N), but in such case it is important to base inference on a distributional result that is robust to non-normality. A result of this type takes the form:

$$\left[\frac{1}{N} \mathcal{H}^{-1} H(\widehat{\theta}_{PML})' \widehat{W}^{-1} \widehat{V} \widehat{W}^{-1} H(\widehat{\theta}_{PML}) \mathcal{H}^{-1} \right]^{-1/2} \left(\widehat{\theta}_{PML} - \theta \right) \xrightarrow{d} \mathcal{N}(0, I)$$
$$(5.81)$$

where

$$\widehat{W}^{-1} = \mathcal{D}' \left(\Omega^{-1}(\widehat{\theta}_{PML}) \otimes \Omega^{-1}(\widehat{\theta}_{PML}) \right) \mathcal{D} \qquad (5.82)$$

and

$$\mathcal{H} = H(\widehat{\theta}_{PML})' \widehat{W}^{-1} H(\widehat{\theta}_{PML}). \qquad (5.83)$$

---

[14]This and similar results follow from the rules for the differentials of the inverse and log determinant:
$$d \log \det \Omega = tr(\Omega^{-1} d\Omega)$$
$$d\Omega^{-1} = -\Omega^{-1}(d\Omega)\Omega^{-1},$$
and the properties of the *vec* operator (stacking by rows):
$$[vec(A)]' vec(B) = tr(A'B)$$
$$vec(ABC) = (A \otimes C')vec(B).$$
For proofs and additional results see Magnus and Neudecker (1988).

[15]See, for example, Richard (1975).

Continuously Updated GMM Estimation An inconvenience of GMM estimation relative to PML is lack of invariance to parameter-dependent transformations of the moment conditions. An alternative method that provides both asymptotic efficiency under non-normality and invariance is the continuously updated GMM estimator suggested by Hansen, Heaton, and Yaron (1996). In our case it takes the form:

$$\widehat{\theta}_{cu} = \arg \min_c \left[\bar{s} - \omega(c)\right]' \left(\frac{1}{N} \sum_{i=1}^{N} (s_i - \omega(c))(s_i - \omega(c))'\right)^{-1} \left[\bar{s} - \omega(c)\right].$$
(5.84)

This estimator will be clearly invariant to transformations of the moments such as those considered in (5.66).

An estimator that is closely related to continuously updated GMM is the following alternative PML:

$$\widehat{\theta}_{CPML} = \arg \min_c \log \det \left(\frac{1}{N} \sum_{i=1}^{N} (s_i - \omega(c))(s_i - \omega(c))'\right).$$
(5.85)

This statistic is an unlikely candidate for maximum likelihood estimation since it would require the vector s_i (which consists of squares and cross-products of the original variables) to be jointly normally distributed. It is, nevertheless, asymptotically equivalent to optimal GMM regardless of non-normality of the original variables or their squares. The corresponding first-order conditions are

$$-H(c)' \left(\frac{1}{N} \sum_{i=1}^{N} (s_i - \omega(c))(s_i - \omega(c))'\right)^{-1} \left[\bar{s} - \omega(c)\right] = 0,$$
(5.86)

which can be regarded as a robust counterpart to (5.78). Note that the first-order conditions from (5.84), in addition to (5.86), will include a second term containing derivatives with respect to the weight matrix. Since this extra term will only vanish asymptotically, $\widehat{\theta}_{cu}$ and $\widehat{\theta}_{CPML}$ are asymptotically equivalent but numerically different estimators.

5.4.4 Testing Covariance Restrictions

Testing Nested Restrictions Using Incremental Sargan Tests The test statistic of overidentifying restrictions (5.61) can be used as an overall test of specification against the unrestricted data covariance matrix. Sometimes, however, we are interested in testing additional constraints within a particular covariance structure. For example, we may wish to test for the absence of random effects in a stationary moving average model, or to test for a stationary moving average against a nonstationary one.[16] Testing of nested restrictions of this kind can be accomplished using incremental statistics of overidentifying restrictions.[17]

Let us express the additional constraints under test by the condition

$$\theta = g(\psi) \tag{5.87}$$

where ψ is another set of parameters of order $s \times 1$ ($s < k$) and each element of g is a twice differentiable function. Then the GMM/MD estimator of ψ is

$$\widehat{\psi} = \arg\min_{a} \{\overline{s} - \omega[g(a)]\}' \widehat{V}^{-1} \{\overline{s} - \omega[g(a)]\} \tag{5.88}$$

so that the estimator of θ subject to the restrictions (5.87) is $\widehat{\theta}_R = g(\widehat{\psi})$. Moreover, for the corresponding test statistic of overidentifying restrictions we have

$$S_R = N \left[\overline{s} - \omega(\widehat{\theta}_R)\right]' \widehat{V}^{-1} \left[\overline{s} - \omega(\widehat{\theta}_R)\right] \xrightarrow{d} \chi^2_{r-s}. \tag{5.89}$$

Finally, the incremental Sargan or LR-type test statistic S_Δ has a limiting chi-square distribution with $k - s$ degrees of freedom:

$$S_\Delta = S_R - S \xrightarrow{d} \chi^2_{k-s}, \tag{5.90}$$

and is independent of S in their joint asymptotic distribution. A proof of this result can be found in Chamberlain (1982, Proposition 8′).[18] Thus, large values of S_Δ will lead to rejection of the restrictions (5.87).

Fragility of LR Tests of Covariance Restrictions to Non-Normality

A Gaussian LR test statistic or a Sargan test statistic based on a Gaussian weight matrix like (5.82) will not have a limiting chi-square distribution unless (5.79) holds, regardless of the validity of the restrictions. In fact, under non-normality both statistics have the same asymptotic distribution. This is given by a linear combination of independent χ^2 variables with one degree of freedom (cf. Arellano, 1985). Although this distribution can be numerically evaluated, a simpler procedure is to rely on the test statistics that are robust to non-normality.

An illustration of this point is in the work of Abowd and Card (1989, p. 426), who showed how overlooking non-normality leads to spurious rejections of covariance structures for PSID earnings and hours of work.

---

[16]These examples also involve inequality restrictions. When using two-sided tests of the type described below they are ignored, which in some cases may cause a substantial loss of power.

[17]Asymptotic tests of non-nested covariance restrictions can be developed along the lines of Vuong (1989) using Schwarz adjusted Gaussian LR Statistics, or Schwarz adjusted empirical likelihood LR statistics.

[18]See also section A.8 in the Appendix for a review of incremental Sargan tests in a related context.

5.5   Illustration: Testing the Permanent Income Hypothesis

Hall and Mishkin (1982) used food consumption and labour income from a PSID sample of $N = 2309$ US households over $T = 7$ years to test the predictions of a simple permanent income model of consumption behaviour. We use their work as an empirical illustration of dynamic panel covariance structures.

Hall and Mishkin specified individual means of income and consumption changes as linear regressions on age, age squared, time, and changes in the number of children and adults living in the household.[19] Thus, they were implicitly allowing for unobserved intercept heterogeneity in the levels of the variables, but only for observed heterogeneity in their changes. Deviations from the individual means of income and consumption, denoted $\bar{y}_{it}$ and $\bar{c}_{it}$ respectively, were specified as follows.

Specification of the Income Process   Hall and Mishkin assumed that income errors $\bar{y}_{it}$ were the result of two different types of shocks, permanent and transitory:

$$\bar{y}_{it} = y_{it}^L + y_{it}^S. \tag{5.91}$$

They also assumed that agents were able to distinguish one type of shock from the other and respond to them accordingly.

The permanent component y_{it}^L was specified as a random walk

$$y_{it}^L = y_{i(t-1)}^L + \varepsilon_{it}, \tag{5.92}$$

and the transitory component y_{it}^S as a stationary moving average process

$$y_{it}^S = \eta_{it} + \rho_1 \eta_{i(t-1)} + \rho_2 \eta_{i(t-2)}. \tag{5.93}$$

A significant limitation acknowledged by Hall and Mishkin is the lack of a measurement error component in observed income. That is, a component to which agents' consumption does not respond at all. This is specially important in this case since there is evidence that measurement error in PSID income is large. Identification in the presence of such a component, however, would require the use of additional indicators of permanent income.[20]

The previous process has an equivalent representation in which the first difference of $\bar{y}_{it}$ follows a third-order moving average process. For simplicity,

---

[19]Removing means as functions of the number of family members prior to the analysis amounts to taking these household composition variables as being strictly exogenous. A point to which we shall return in Chapter 8.

[20]Altonji and Siow (1987) tested the life-cycle consumption model allowing for measurement error in income. To do so they relied on independent measures of determinants of income such as wage rates, layoffs, quits, promotions, and hours unemployed.

let us consider the relationship between the two representations in the case of $\rho_1 = \rho_2 = 0$ (so that $\Delta \bar{y}_{it}$ follows an MA(1) process):

$$\Delta \bar{y}_{it} = \varepsilon_{it} + \left(\eta_{it} - \eta_{i(t-1)} \right). \tag{5.94}$$

This implies $Var(\Delta \bar{y}_{it}) = \sigma_\varepsilon^2 + 2\sigma_\eta^2$, $Cov(\Delta \bar{y}_{it}, \Delta \bar{y}_{i(t-1)}) = -\sigma_\eta^2$, and $Cov(\Delta \bar{y}_{it}, \Delta \bar{y}_{i(t-j)}) = 0$ for $j > 1$. Now write

$$\Delta \bar{y}_{it} = \zeta_{it} + \psi \zeta_{i(t-1)}, \tag{5.95}$$

so that we have $Var(\Delta \bar{y}_{it}) = \left(1 + \psi^2\right) \sigma_\zeta^2$, $Cov(\Delta \bar{y}_{it}, \Delta \bar{y}_{i(t-1)}) = \psi \sigma_\zeta^2$, and $Cov(\Delta \bar{y}_{it}, \Delta \bar{y}_{i(t-j)}) = 0$ for $j > 1$. Clearly, ψ needs to be negative. Matching coefficients from the two representations we obtain $\sigma_\varepsilon^2 = (1 + \psi)^2 \sigma_\zeta^2$ and $\sigma_\eta^2 = -\psi\sigma_\zeta^2$.[21]

Specification of the Consumption Process Turning to the consumption function, Hall and Mishkin specified mean deviations in consumption changes as responding one-to-one to permanent income shocks and by a fraction β to transitory shocks. The magnitude of β will depend on the persistence in transitory shocks (measured by ρ_1 and ρ_2) and on real interest rates. It will also depend on age, but the analysis was simplified by treating it as a constant. This model can be formally derived from an optimization problem with quadratic utility (an unattractive specification of attitudes towards risk), and constant interest rates that are equal to the subjective discount factor. Since only food consumption is observed, an adjustment was made by assuming a constant marginal propensity to consume food, denoted by α. With these assumptions we have

$$\Delta \bar{c}_{it} = \alpha \varepsilon_{it} + \alpha \beta \eta_{it}. \tag{5.96}$$

In addition, Hall and Mishkin introduced a stationary measurement error in the level of consumption (or transitory consumption that is independent of income shocks) with an MA(2) specification:

$$c_{it}^S = v_{it} + \lambda_1 v_{i(t-1)} + \lambda_2 v_{i(t-2)}. \tag{5.97}$$

---

[21] The implication is that

$$(1 + \psi)^2 / \psi = -\phi$$
$$\sigma_\zeta^2 = \sigma_\varepsilon^2 / (1 + \psi)^2$$

where $\phi = \sigma_\varepsilon^2 / \sigma_\eta^2$ is the ratio of the variance of the permanent component to the transitory component. The invertible solution for ψ equals

$$\psi = -1 - \frac{1}{2} \left[\phi - \left(\phi^2 + 4\phi \right)^{1/2} \right].$$

The Resulting Bivariate Covariance Structure   Therefore, the model that is taken to the data consists of a joint specification for mean deviations in consumption and income changes as follows:

$$\Delta \bar{c}_{it} = \alpha \varepsilon_{it} + \alpha \beta \eta_{it} + v_{it} - (1 - \lambda_1) \, v_{i(t-1)} - (\lambda_1 - \lambda_2) \, v_{i(t-2)} - \lambda_2 v_{i(t-3)} \quad (5.98)$$

$$\Delta \bar{y}_{it} = \varepsilon_{it} + \eta_{it} - (1 - \rho_1) \, \eta_{i(t-1)} - (\rho_1 - \rho_2) \, \eta_{i(t-2)} - \rho_2 \eta_{i(t-3)}. \quad (5.99)$$

The three innovations in the model are assumed to be mutually independent with constant variances σ_ε^2, σ_η^2, and σ_v^2 (i.e. no heterogeneity in individual risk). Thus, the model contains nine unknown coefficients:

$$\theta = \begin{pmatrix} \alpha & \beta & \lambda_1 & \lambda_2 & \rho_1 & \rho_2 & \sigma_\varepsilon^2 & \sigma_\eta^2 & \sigma_v^2 \end{pmatrix}'.$$

The model specifies a covariance structure for the 12×1 vector:

$$w_i = \begin{pmatrix} \Delta \bar{c}_{i2} & \Delta \bar{c}_{i3} & \cdots & \Delta \bar{c}_{i7} & \Delta \bar{y}_{i2} & \Delta \bar{y}_{i3} & \cdots & \Delta \bar{y}_{i7} \end{pmatrix}'$$

$$E\left(w_i w_i'\right) = \Omega(\theta).$$

Let us look in some detail at the form of various elements in $\Omega(\theta)$. We have

$$Var(\Delta \bar{y}_{it}) = \sigma_\varepsilon^2 + 2 \left(1 - \rho_1 - \rho_1 \rho_2 + \rho_1^2 + \rho_2^2\right) \sigma_\eta^2 \quad (t = 2, ..., 7) \quad (5.100)$$

$$Cov(\Delta \bar{y}_{it}, \Delta \bar{y}_{i(t-1)}) = -\left[(1 - \rho_1) - (1 - \rho_1 + \rho_2) \, (\rho_1 - \rho_2)\right] \sigma_\eta^2 \quad (5.101)$$

and also

$$Cov(\Delta \bar{c}_{it}, \Delta \bar{y}_{it}) = \alpha \sigma_\varepsilon^2 + \alpha \beta \sigma_\eta^2 \quad (t = 2, ..., 7) \quad (5.102)$$

$$Cov(\Delta \bar{c}_{it}, \Delta \bar{y}_{i(t-1)}) = 0 \quad (5.103)$$

$$Cov(\Delta \bar{c}_{i(t-1)}, \Delta \bar{y}_{it}) = -\alpha \beta \, (1 - \rho_1) \, \sigma_\eta^2. \quad (5.104)$$

A fundamental restriction of the model is lack of correlation between current consumption changes and lagged income changes, as captured by terms like (5.103). The model, nevertheless, predicts correlation between current consumption changes and current and future income changes, as seen from (5.102) and (5.104).

Instrumental Variable Interpretation   Identification of β can also be given an instrumental variable interpretation. To see this in a simple way, let us consider a stripped down version of the model with $\alpha = 1$ and $\rho_1 = \rho_2 = 0$. In such a case

$$\beta = \frac{Cov(\Delta\bar{y}_{i(t+1)}, \Delta\bar{c}_{it})}{Cov(\Delta\bar{y}_{i(t+1)}, \Delta\bar{y}_{it})}. \tag{5.105}$$

Thus, future changes in income are used as an instrumental variable in identifying a linear relationship between current consumption and income changes. The relationship is given by

$$\Delta\bar{c}_{it} = \beta\Delta\bar{y}_{it} + \left[(1 - \beta)\varepsilon_{it} + \beta\eta_{i(t-1)} + \Delta c_{it}^S\right] \tag{5.106}$$

Note that the instrumental variable $\Delta\bar{y}_{i(t+1)} = \varepsilon_{i(t+1)} + \eta_{i(t+1)} - \eta_{it}$ is uncorrelated to the equation's error but correlated to $\Delta\bar{y}_{it}$ as long as $\sigma_\eta^2 > 0$ (i.e. provided there is a transitory income component).

Empirical Results   Hall and Mishkin estimated their model by Gaussian PML. In the calculation of standard errors no adjustment was made for possible non-normality. Since PSID income exhibits non-normal kurtosis, their inferences—in particular the rejection of the permanent income hypothesis (PIH)—may have been affected by this fact.[22] They estimated $\hat{\beta} = 0.3$, which given their estimates of ρ_1 and ρ_2 ($\hat{\rho}_1 = 0.3$, $\hat{\rho}_2 = 0.1$) turned out to be consistent with the model only for unrealistic values of real interest rates (above 30 per cent). Moreover, they estimated the marginal propensity to consume food as $\hat{\alpha} = 0.1$, and the moving average parameters for transitory consumption as $\hat{\lambda}_1 = 0.2$ and $\hat{\lambda}_2 = 0.1$. The variance of the permanent income shocks was twice as large as that of the transitory shocks: $\hat{\sigma}_\varepsilon^2 = 3.4$ and $\hat{\sigma}_\eta^2 = 1.5$.

Finally, they tested the covariance structure focusing on the fundamental restriction of lack of correlation between current changes in consumption and lagged changes in income. They found a negative covariance which was significantly different from zero. They did not consider overall tests of overidentifying restrictions.[23] As a result of this finding they considered an extended version of the model in which a fraction of consumers spent their current income ("Keynesian" consumers).

Alternative Income Processes   Testing of the PIH crucially hinges on the way observed income is broken down into anticipated and unanticipated

---

[22]Note that they modelled the levels of income and consumption (as opposed to their logs), which would be expected to be unconditionally asymmetric and non-normal. Their assumption was in fact the more plausible one of conditional normality given the set of regressors used in subtracting individual means from the variables.

[23]Mariger and Shaw (1993) tested Hall and Mishkin's income process and found evidence that the process was not time-invariant.

components. Abstracting from family composition and age terms, Hall and Mishkin's model for income can be written as[24]

$$y_{it} = bt + y_{i0}^L + \left(\varepsilon_{it} + \varepsilon_{i(t-1)} + ... + \varepsilon_{i1}\right) + \left(\eta_{it} + \rho_1 \eta_{i(t-1)} + \rho_2 \eta_{i(t-2)}\right). \quad (5.107)$$

Therefore, at $t-1$ an individual's income forecast for period t will be given by

$$P_{t-1}\left(y_{it}\right) = bt + y_{i0}^L + \left(\varepsilon_{i(t-1)} + ... + \varepsilon_{i1}\right) + \left(\rho_1 \eta_{i(t-1)} + \rho_2 \eta_{i(t-2)}\right). \quad (5.108)$$

Short panel data allows us to identify b, $Var\left(y_{i0}^L\right)$, σ_ε^2, ρ_1, ρ_2, and σ_η^2 under the assumption that for a given individual permanent and transitory shocks are uncorrelated, and both types of shock are uncorrelated across individuals.

The previous model specifies heterogeneous initial conditions, but homogeneous income growth captured by b. In an alternative model, one could allow for a heterogeneous trend as well (i.e. a time-invariant individual effect in the equation for income changes). The model would be

$$y_{it} = b_i t + y_{i0}^L + \left(\varepsilon_{it} + \varepsilon_{i(t-1)} + ... + \varepsilon_{i1}\right) + \left(\eta_{it} + \rho_1 \eta_{i(t-1)} + \rho_2 \eta_{i(t-2)}\right).$$
$$(5.109)$$

We could assume a bivariate distribution for $\left(b_i, y_{i0}^L\right)$ as in model (5.22). If such heterogeneity is present, Hall and Mishkin's estimates of σ_ε^2 will be biased, hence misrepresenting the extent of permanent innovations in the model. Typically, the result will be that the econometrician assumes that agents' income forecasts are worse than in fact they are. The reason being that agents construct forecasts using individual specific income growth rates, whereas the econometrician uses an average growth rate. These two models are likely to produce different answers to the question of how much uncertainty is present in the income growth process.

Another aspect that has received much attention in this literature refers to the possibility of correlation between shocks for different individuals. If common shocks are not captured entirely by time dummies there will be a cross-sectional correlation between anticipated income and innovations—as found by Hall and Mishkin—which would not occur in the case of time series correlations (Deaton, 1991, 1244–1246, elaborates formally on this point). This situation has fostered an interest in long T panels or pseudo panels for testing life-cycle consumption models (e.g. Browning, Deaton, and Irish, 1985).

The previous comments reflect the fragility of tests of the PIH to statistical assumptions about income processes. It is unlikely that decisive progress can be made on these issues purely on the basis of univariate time series models for income even if T is reasonably large. Major income shocks arise as a result of

---

[24]If there is an individual specific intercept, it will be subsumed in y_{i0}^L. Hall and Mishkin specified a linear trend for income changes. This implies a quadratic trend in levels, but here it is omitted for simplicity.

job loses, job changes, etc. There may be large variations in the (subjective) probabilities of these events across households and for a given household over time. To some extent, such probabilities depend on observable characteristics like type of contract or job tenure. In these cases progress can be expected from using individual information other than income history in constructing predictive income distributions.

Relationship to Error-Components Models   Hall and Mishkin's model can be regarded as a bivariate error-components model. Let s_i be the 12×1 vector of observed changes in consumption and labour income: $\Delta s_i = (\Delta c_i' \ \Delta y_i')'$, say. The model in terms of the original variables can be written as

$$\Delta s_i = (I_2 \otimes X_i)\gamma + w_i \tag{5.110}$$

$$E(w_i \mid X_i) = 0 \tag{5.111}$$

$$E(w_i w_i' \mid X_i) = \Omega(\theta) \tag{5.112}$$

where X_i is the matrix of regressors used in specifying individual means (trend, and age and family composition variables), and as before $w_i = (\Delta \tilde{c}_i' \ \Delta \tilde{y}_i')'$.

Note that the parameters of interest in Hall and Mishkin's study were not the regression coefficients γ, but the coefficients θ parameterizing the restrictions in the residual covariance matrix.

6

Autoregressive Models with Individual Effects

In this chapter we discuss the specification and estimation of autoregressive models with individual specific intercepts. To simplify the presentation we focus on first-order processes, since the main insights generalize in a straightforward but tedious way to higher-order and multivariate cases.

We begin by considering the properties of the within-group estimator. In contrast with the fixed effects model of Part I, WG has a small T bias which does not disappear as N becomes large.

Next, we consider instrumental variable estimators that are consistent for panels with small T and large N. These estimators use lagged observations as instruments for errors in first-differences.

In the next three sections we study the role in short panels of assumptions about initial conditions, homoskedasticity, and whether the parameter space includes the possibility of unit roots or not. The various versions of the model that we consider imply specific covariance structures with nonlinear restrictions. Thus, given covariance identification, they can all be estimated by minimum distance or PML methods. We also discuss, however, alternative representations of the restrictions that can be obtained by transformation along the lines suggested in the previous chapter. These representations are useful as a way of clarifying the efficiency properties of the IV estimators, and for suggesting alternative GMM estimators of autoregressive parameters.

Finally, the last section provides a detailed discussion of various aspects of inference with VAR panel data models in the context of an empirical illustration using firm level data on employment and wages.

In the development below we assume that y_{i0} is observed, so that for each individual we have $T + 1$ observations. This is just a matter of convention, but one that helps to simplify the presentation.

6.1   Assumptions

We assume that $\{(y_{i0}, y_{i1}, ..., y_{iT}, \eta_i), i = 1, ..., N\}$ is a random sample with finite first- and second-order moments, and that

$$y_{it} = \alpha y_{i(t-1)} + \eta_i + v_{it} \quad (t = 1, ..., T) \quad |\alpha| < 1 \qquad (6.1)$$

together with

Assumption B1:

$$E\left(v_{it} \mid y_i^{t-1}, \eta_i\right) = 0$$

where $y_i^{t-1} = (y_{i0}, y_{i1}, ..., y_{i(t-1)})'$. We observe y_i^T but not the individual intercept η_i, which can be regarded as a missing time-invariant variable with $E(\eta_i) = \eta$ and $Var(\eta_i) = \sigma_\eta^2$.[1]

   B1 is the fundamental assumption specifying the conditional mean of the variable y_{it} given its past and a value of η_i. An implication of the assumption is that the errors v_{it} are conditionally serially uncorrelated. Namely, for $j > 0$ we have

$$E\left(v_{it} v_{i(t-j)} \mid y_i^{t-1}, \eta_i\right) = 0 \qquad (6.2)$$

and therefore by the law of iterated expectations $E\left(v_{it} v_{i(t-j)}\right) = 0$ as well.

   Another implication of *B1* is lack of correlation between η_i and v_{it} for all t. For fixed T it is, nevertheless, possible to imagine an alternative autoregressive data generating process such that η_i and v_{it} are correlated. This suggests the possibility of considering the conditional mean assumption

$$E\left(v_{it} \mid y_i^{t-1}\right) = 0 \qquad (6.3)$$

instead of *B1*, as a less restrictive condition. However, mean independence of v_{it} with respect to $\{y_{i(t-1)}, ..., y_{i(t-J)}\}$ implies lack of correlation between v_{it} and η_i in the limit as $J \to \infty$. This is so because

$$\eta_i = (1 - \alpha) \plim_{J \to \infty} \frac{1}{J} \sum_{j=1}^{J} y_{i(t-j)}. \qquad (6.4)$$

Thus, for a process that started at $-\infty$ we would have orthogonality between η_i and v_{it}, and more generally any correlation between individual effects and shocks will tend to vanish as t increases.

   Homoskedasticity   Assumption *B1* also implies that $E\left(v_{it}\right) = 0$ cross-sectionally for any t, but does not restrict the variance of v_{it}. That is, the

---

[1]Given *B1*, assuming that the joint distribution of y_i^T has finite first- and second-order moments implies that η_i also has finite mean and variance.

conditional variance may be some period-specific non-negative function of y_i^{t-1} and η_i

$$E\left(v_{it}^2 \mid y_i^{t-1}, \eta_i\right) = \varphi_t\left(y_i^{t-1}, \eta_i\right),\tag{6.5}$$

and the unconditional variance may change with t

$$E\left(v_{it}^2\right) = E\left[\varphi_t\left(y_i^{t-1}, \eta_i\right)\right] = \sigma_t^2.\tag{6.6}$$

Thus, we may consider two different homoskedasticity assumptions. One is an assumption of *conditional homoskedasticity*:

Assumption B2:

$$E\left(v_{it}^2 \mid y_i^{t-1}, \eta_i\right) = \sigma_t^2,$$

while the other is an assumption of *time series homoskedasticity*:

Assumption B3:

$$E\left(v_{it}^2\right) = \sigma^2.$$

Note that *B2* and *B3* may hold in conjunction, but any of them may also occur in the absence of the other.

Assumption *B3* is also compatible with a model having individual-specific error variances of the form $E\left(v_{it}^2 \mid \eta_i\right) = \sigma_i^2$. Moreover, since we may not wish to think of σ_i^2 as being exclusively a function of η_i, the latter could be replaced in the model's conditioning set by a larger vector of individual-specific components, leaving the argument unaffected.

Stationarity Finally, let us consider conditions for stationarity. Having assumed that the autoregressive coefficient lies inside the unit circle, $\mid \alpha \mid < 1$, guarantees that the process is stable but not necessarily stationary. Stationarity also requires that the process started in the distant past or, equivalently, that the distribution of initial observations coincides with the steady state distribution of the process.

Solving equation (6.1) recursively we obtain

$$y_{it} = \left(\sum_{s=0}^{t-1} \alpha^s\right)\eta_i + \alpha^t y_{i0} + \sum_{s=0}^{t-1}\alpha^s v_{i(t-s)}.\tag{6.7}$$

Furthermore, *B1* implies

$$E\left(y_{it} \mid \eta_i\right) = \left(\sum_{s=0}^{t-1}\alpha^s\right)\eta_i + \alpha^t E\left(y_{i0}\mid \eta_i\right),\tag{6.8}$$

which for $\mid \alpha \mid < 1$ and large t tends to $\mu_i = \eta_i/(1-\alpha)$. We shall refer to μ_i as the *steady state mean* for individual i. Thus, stationarity in mean requires the assumption

Assumption B4:

$$E\left(y_{i0} \mid \eta_i\right) = \frac{\eta_i}{(1-\alpha)}$$

in which case all $E\left(y_{it} \mid \eta_i\right)$ are time-invariant and coincide with the steady state mean.

Similarly, under *B1-B3*, for $j \geq 0$ we have

$$Cov\left(y_{it}, y_{i(t-j)} \mid \eta_i\right) = \alpha^{2t-j}Var\left(y_{i0} \mid \eta_i\right) + \alpha^j \left(\sum_{s=0}^{t-j-1} \alpha^{2s}\right)\sigma^2, \quad (6.9)$$

which for $\mid \alpha \mid < 1$ and large t tends to the *steady state j-th autocovariance* for individual i given by $\alpha^j\sigma^2/(1-\alpha^2)$. Thus, under homoskedasticity, covariance stationarity requires

Assumption B5:

$$Var\left(y_{i0} \mid \eta_i\right) = \frac{\sigma^2}{(1-\alpha^2)}$$

in which case all $Cov\left(y_{it}, y_{i(t-j)} \mid \eta_i\right)$ are time-invariant and coincide with the steady state autocovariances.

6.2   The Within-Group Estimator

In this section we consider the WG estimator of the autoregressive model. Following Chapter 2, this is given by the slope coefficient in an OLS regression of y on lagged y and a full set of individual dummy variables, or equivalently by the OLS estimate in deviations from time means or orthogonal deviations.

Letting $y_i = (y_{i1}, ..., y_{iT})'$ and $y_{i(-1)} = (y_{i0}, ..., y_{i(T-1)})'$, the WG estimator for α is

$$\widehat{\alpha}_{WG} = \frac{\sum_{i=1}^{N} y'_{i(-1)}Qy_i}{\sum_{i=1}^{N} y'_{i(-1)}Qy_{i(-1)}} \quad (6.10)$$

where Q is the WG operator of order T.

The autoregressive equation (6.1) is of the same form as the fixed effects model (2.7) with $x_{it} = y_{i(t-1)}$, but it does not satisfy the strict exogeneity assumption *A1* of Chapter 2 because v_{it} is correlated with future values of the regressor. Indeed, for any value of T

$$E\left(y'_{i(-1)}Qv_i\right) = \sum_{t=1}^{T} E\left[y_{i(t-1)}\left(v_{it} - \bar{v}_i\right)\right] \neq 0 \quad (6.11)$$

since $y_{i(t-1)}$ is correlated with the average error $\bar{v}_i$ through the terms $v_{i1}...v_{i(t-1)}$. As a consequence, $\widehat{\alpha}_{WG}$ is inconsistent for fixed T as N tends to infinity. The bias will nevertheless tend to zero as T increases since $\text{plim}_{T \to \infty} \bar{v}_i = 0$. Thus, in common with standard time series autoregression, least-squares estimation is biased but consistent as T tends to infinity (Hurwicz, 1950). The problem is that when T is small biases may be very large regardless of the value of N. The properties of these biases were studied in the Monte Carlo work of Nerlove (1967, 1971) and the analytical calculations of Nickell (1981).

The Nickell Bias Let us study the form of these biases when there are individual-specific intercepts. This is important in order to have information about the environments in which WG can be expected to perform well.

For fixed T as N tends to infinity, the bias is given by

$$\plim_{N\to\infty} (\widehat{\alpha}_{WG} - \alpha) = \frac{E\left(y'_{i(-1)}Qv_i\right)}{E\left(y'_{i(-1)}Qy_{i(-1)}\right)}. \tag{6.12}$$

Under assumptions $B1$ and $B3$ it can be shown that[2]

$$E\left(y'_{i(-1)}Qv_i\right) = -\sigma^2 h_T(\alpha) \tag{6.13}$$

where

$$h_T(\alpha) = \frac{1}{(1-\alpha)}\left[1 - \frac{1}{T}\left(\frac{1-\alpha^T}{1-\alpha}\right)\right]. \tag{6.14}$$

Moreover, if $B4$ and $B5$ also hold, the denominator of (6.12) satisfies

$$E\left(y'_{i(-1)}Qy_{i(-1)}\right) = \frac{\sigma^2(T-1)}{(1-\alpha^2)}\left(1 - \frac{2\alpha h_T(\alpha)}{(T-1)}\right). \tag{6.15}$$

Thus, the specific form of the bias depends, through the denominator, on the assumption about initial conditions.

The form of the bias as given by Nickell (1981) is therefore:

$$\plim_{N\to\infty} (\widehat{\alpha}_{WG} - \alpha) = -\frac{(1-\alpha^2)h_T(\alpha)}{(T-1)}\left(1 - \frac{2\alpha h_T(\alpha)}{(T-1)}\right)^{-1}. \tag{6.16}$$

The WG bias is of order $1/T$, so that it vanishes as $T \to \infty$, but it may be important for small values of T.

When $T = 2$ the bias under stationarity is given by

$$\plim_{N\to\infty} (\widehat{\alpha}_{WG} - \alpha) = -\frac{(1+\alpha)}{2}, \tag{6.17}$$

which coincides with the bias of OLS in first-differences.

The following table shows the Nickell bias for several values of α and T.

[2]See, for example, Alvarez and Arellano (1998).

Table 6.1
WG Bias under Strict Stationarity

$T\backslash\alpha$	0.05	0.5	0.95
2	−0.52	−0.75	−0.97
3	−0.35	−0.54	−0.73
10	−0.11	−0.16	−0.26
15	−0.07	−0.11	−0.17

If $\alpha > 0$ the bias is always negative, and massive with the very small values of T. It becomes smaller in absolute value as T increases, but even when $T = 15$ the bias is still substantial (e.g. 22 per cent with $\alpha = 0.5$).

The Bias Under Nonstationarity   To illustrate the effect of initial conditions upon the bias, let us consider various situations for $T = 2$. In such a case WG coincides with OLS in first-differences. In the absence of specific assumptions about the distribution of $y_{i0} \mid \eta_i$, we have the following expression for the bias:

$$b \equiv \plim_{N\to\infty} (\widehat{\alpha}_{WG} - \alpha) = \frac{Cov\left(\Delta y_{i1}, \Delta v_{i2}\right)}{Var\left(\Delta y_{i1}\right)}$$

$$= -\frac{\sigma_1^2}{(1-\alpha)^2 Var(y_{i0}) + \sigma_\eta^2 + \sigma_1^2 - 2(1-\alpha)Cov(y_{i0}, \eta_i)}. \qquad (6.18)$$

Under *B4* (mean stationarity) $Cov(y_{i0}, \eta_i) = \sigma_\eta^2/(1-\alpha)$ and $Var[E(y_{i0} \mid \eta_i)] = \sigma_\eta^2/(1-\alpha)^2$, so that the bias becomes

$$b = -\frac{\sigma_1^2}{(1-\alpha)^2 \sigma_0^2 + \sigma_1^2}, \qquad (6.19)$$

where $\sigma_0^2 = E[Var(y_{i0} \mid \eta_i)]$.[3] If *B3* and *B5* also hold, then $\sigma_1^2 = \sigma^2$ and $\sigma_0^2 = \sigma^2/(1-\alpha^2)$, and we obtain the bias given in (6.17). On the other hand, if $Var(y_{i0}) = Cov(y_{i0}, \eta_i) = 0$ (i.e. a fixed start of the process) we get

$$b = -\frac{1}{(\sigma_\eta^2/\sigma_1^2) + 1}. \qquad (6.20)$$

This bias goes to zero as $(\sigma_\eta^2/\sigma_1^2) \to \infty$ (a point noted by Chamberlain, 2000). In fact as long as there is lack of mean stationarity we shall have $b \to 0$ as $(\sigma_\eta^2/\sigma_1^2) \to \infty$. This result suggests that even for very small values of T, a combination of nonstationary initial conditions and large individual effect variances could make WG to be approximately unbiased.

[3]We have used the variance decomposition $Var(y_{i0}) = Var[E(y_{i0} \mid \eta_i)] + E[Var(y_{i0} \mid \eta_i)]$.

Likelihood Conditional on η_i In general, the likelihood for one individual conditional on η_i can be sequentially factorized as

$$f(y_i^T \mid \eta_i) = f(y_{i0} \mid \eta_i) \prod_{t=1}^{T} f(y_{it} \mid y_i^{t-1}, \eta_i). \qquad (6.21)$$

If we assume that $y_{it} \mid y_i^{t-1}, \eta_i$ is normally distributed with conditional
mean and variance given by assumptions *B1*, *B2*, and *B3*, so that

$$y_{it} \mid y_i^{t-1}, \eta_i \sim \mathcal{N}\left(\alpha y_{i(t-1)} + \eta_i, \sigma^2\right), \qquad (6.22)$$

the log-likelihood conditional on η_i and y_{i0} is given by

$$\ell_i = \log \prod_{t=1}^{T} f(y_{it} \mid y_i^{t-1}, \eta_i)$$

$$\propto -\frac{T}{2} \log \sigma^2 - \frac{1}{2\sigma^2} \sum_{t=1}^{T} \left(y_{it} - \alpha y_{i(t-1)} - \eta_i\right)^2. \qquad (6.23)$$

Clearly, the maximizer of $\sum_{i=1}^{N} \ell_i$ with respect to α, σ^2, and $\eta_1, ..., \eta_N$ gives
rise to the WG estimator, which is therefore the Gaussian MLE of α (conditional
on y_{i0}) estimated jointly with the individual-specific intercepts. Given the
large-N-fixed-T inconsistency of WG, this can be regarded as another example
of Neyman and Scott's incidental parameter problem introduced in Chapter 2.

Despite the small T inconsistency of WG, it is still possible to obtain "fixed
effects" consistent ML estimates by considering the likelihood conditioned on
ML estimates of the individual effects ("approximate conditional likelihood").
Estimates of this kind will be discussed in Section 6.4.

Asymptotic Distribution of WG as N/T **Tends to a Constant** Even
if the WG estimator is consistent as $T \to \infty$, its asymptotic distribution may
contain an asymptotic bias term when $N \to \infty$, depending on the relative rates
of increase of T and N.

Under assumptions *B1–B5* together with (6.22), it can be shown that as
both N and T tend to infinity, provided $N/T \to k < \infty$ and $N/T^3 \to 0$ we
have

$$\sqrt{NT} \left[\widehat{\alpha}_{WG} - \left(\alpha - \frac{1}{T}(1+\alpha)\right)\right] \xrightarrow{d} \mathcal{N}\left(0, 1 - \alpha^2\right). \qquad (6.24)$$

If $\lim(N/T) = 0$ (which includes N fixed) there is no asymptotic bias, but
if $\lim(N/T) > 0$, the bias term in (6.24) cannot be neglected. The asymptotic
bias will contain additional terms for lower relative rates of increase of T. For
example, if $\lim(N/T^3) \neq 0$ but $\lim(N/T^5) = 0$, the bias will include a T^2 term.

These results have been found by Alvarez and Arellano (1998) and Hahn
and Kuersteiner (2002). Nickell (1981) noted that the term $-T^{-1}(1+\alpha)$ could

be used as a simple approximation to the WG bias "for reasonably large values" of T.

6.3   Instrumental Variable Estimation

The WG estimator is inconsistent for fixed T because taking differences or deviations to eliminate the effects creates a negative correlation between lagged ys and errors in the transformed equation. However, values of y lagged two periods or more are valid instruments in the equations in first-differences (or forward orthogonal deviations). Specifically, an implication of *B1* is that the following $(T-1)T/2$ linear IV moment restrictions hold:

$$E\left[y_i^{t-2}\left(\Delta y_{it} - \alpha \Delta y_{i(t-1)}\right)\right] = 0 \ (t = 2, ..., T). \tag{6.25}$$

This gives rise to a system of $T-1$ equations with cross-equation restrictions and different instruments valid for different equations, which can be estimated by linear GMM.

Simple IV estimators of this type were first proposed by Anderson and Hsiao (1981, 1982). Their proposal was to consider a single moment of the form

$$E\left[\sum_{t=2}^{T} y_{i(t-2)}\left(\Delta y_{it} - \alpha \Delta y_{i(t-1)}\right)\right] = 0, \tag{6.26}$$

or alternatively

$$E\left[\sum_{t=3}^{T} \Delta y_{i(t-2)}\left(\Delta y_{it} - \alpha \Delta y_{i(t-1)}\right)\right] = 0. \tag{6.27}$$

Since (6.26) and (6.27) are linear combinations of (6.25), for large N and fixed T, the Anderson–Hsiao IV estimates will be asymptotically inefficient relative to GMM based on (6.25). IV estimates based on a constant number of moments, however, will remain well defined and will be consistent regardless of whether T or N or both tend to infinity.

GMM estimators that used all the available lags at each period as instruments for the equations in first-differences were proposed by Holtz-Eakin, Newey, and Rosen (1988) and Arellano and Bond (1991).

A GMM estimator based on the IV moment conditions (6.25) takes the form

$$\hat{\alpha}_{GMM} = \left[\left(\Delta y'_{-1} Z\right) V_N^{-1} \left(Z' \Delta y_{-1}\right)\right]^{-1} \left(\Delta y'_{-1} Z\right) V_N^{-1} \left(Z' \Delta y\right) \tag{6.28}$$

where $Z'\Delta y = \sum_{i=1}^{N} Z'_i \Delta y_i$, $Z'\Delta y_{-1} = \sum_{i=1}^{N} Z'_i \Delta y_{i(-1)}$, $\Delta y_i = (\Delta y_{i2}, ..., \Delta y_{iT})'$, $\Delta y_{i(-1)} = (\Delta y_{i1}, ..., \Delta y_{i(T-1)})'$, and

$$Z_i = \begin{pmatrix} y_{i0} & 0 & 0 & \cdots & 0 & \cdots & 0 \\ 0 & y_{i0} & y_{i1} & & 0 & & 0 \\ \vdots & & & \ddots & & & \vdots \\ 0 & 0 & 0 & \cdots & y_{i0} & \cdots & y_{i(T-2)} \end{pmatrix}. \tag{6.29}$$

According to standard GMM theory, an optimal choice of the inverse weight matrix V_N is a consistent estimate of the covariance matrix of the orthogonality conditions $E(Z_i' \Delta v_i \Delta v_i' Z_i)$. Under conditional and time series homoskedasticity (assumptions *B1*, *B2*, and *B3*):[4]

$$E(Z_i' \Delta v_i \Delta v_i' Z_i) = \sigma^2 E(Z_i' DD' Z_i) \tag{6.30}$$

where D is the $(T-1) \times T$ first-difference matrix operator. Thus, a one-step GMM estimator uses

$$\widehat{V} = \sum_{i=1}^{N} Z_i' DD' Z_i, \tag{6.31}$$

whereas a two-step GMM estimator uses the robust choice

$$\widetilde{V} = \sum_{i=1}^{N} Z_i' \Delta \widehat{v}_i \Delta \widehat{v}_i' Z_i, \tag{6.32}$$

where $\Delta \widehat{v}_i$ are one-step GMM residuals.

A heteroskedasticity-robust estimate of the asymptotic variance of one-step GMM can be calculated as

$$\widehat{Var}(\widehat{a}_{GMM1}) = \mathcal{M}^{-1} \left[\left(\Delta y_{-1}' Z \right) \widehat{V}^{-1} \widetilde{V} \widehat{V}^{-1} \left(Z' \Delta y_{-1} \right) \right] \mathcal{M}^{-1} \tag{6.33}$$

where $\mathcal{M} = \left(\Delta y_{-1}' Z \right) \widehat{V}^{-1} \left(Z' \Delta y_{-1} \right)$. Furthermore, an estimate of the asymptotic variance of two-step GMM is given by

$$\widehat{Var}(\widehat{a}_{GMM2}) = \left[\left(\Delta y_{-1}' Z \right) \widetilde{V}^{-1} \left(Z' \Delta y_{-1} \right) \right]^{-1}. \tag{6.34}$$

Sargan test statistics of the overidentifying restrictions can also be obtained from the minimized two-step GMM criterion as follows:

$$S = \left(\Delta \widetilde{v}' Z \right) \widetilde{V}^{-1} \left(Z' \Delta \widetilde{v} \right). \tag{6.35}$$

In our case, S will have a limiting chi-square distribution with $[(T-1)T/2] - 1$ degrees of freedom. These statistics are widely used as useful specification diagnostics.

As we shall see below, (6.25) are not the only restrictions on the data second-order moments implied by the conditional mean independence and homoskedasticity Assumptions *B1–B3*, but they are the only ones that are valid in the absence of homoskedasticity or lack of correlation between η_i and v_{it}.

---

[4]Note that under *B1–B3* a typical block of $E(Z_i' \Delta v_i \Delta v_i' Z_i)$ satisfies

$$E\left(\Delta v_{it} \Delta v_{i(t-j)} y_i^{t-2} y_i^{t-j-2\prime} \right) = E\left(\Delta v_{it} \Delta v_{i(t-j)} \right) E\left(y_i^{t-2} y_i^{t-j-2\prime} \right).$$

Neither of these estimators, however, achieves asymptotic efficiency, not even relative to the information bound corresponding to the weaker conditional moment restriction (6.3). The reason is that the use of nonlinear functions of the lagged dependent variables as additional instruments might result in efficiency improvements. This would be the case in the presence of conditional heteroskedasticity or nonlinear dependence between the individual effects and the y_{it} variables. This problem will be addressed in Chapter 8 in the context of more general models with sequential moment conditions.

Asymptotic Distribution of GMM as T/N Tends to a Constant
WG is consistent as T tends to infinity, but is inconsistent for fixed T and large N. On the other hand, GMM estimators based on (6.25) are consistent for fixed T but the number of orthogonality conditions increases with T. In panels in which the value of T is not negligible relative to N (such as the PSID household panel in the US, or the balance sheet-based company panels that are available in many countries), the knowledge of the asymptotic behaviour of the estimators as both T and N tend to infinity may be useful in assessing alternative methods.

Alvarez and Arellano (1998) showed that under *B1–B5*, as both N and T tend to infinity, provided $T/N \to c < \infty$, one-step GMM is consistent and asymptotically normal with

$$\sqrt{NT}\left[\widehat{\alpha}_{GMM1} - \left(\alpha - \frac{1}{N}(1+\alpha)\right)\right] \xrightarrow{d} \mathcal{N}\left(0, 1-\alpha^2\right). \qquad (6.36)$$

The consistency result for GMM1 contrasts with those available for structural equations, where 2SLS is known to be inconsistent when the ratio of number of instruments to sample size tends to a positive constant (e.g. Bekker, 1994). Here the number of instruments, which is given by $T(T-1)/2$, increases very fast and yet consistency is obtained. The intuition for this result is that in our context as T tends to infinity the "endogeneity bias" tends to zero, and so closeness of GMM1 to OLS in deviations (i.e. within-groups) becomes a desirable property.

Result (6.36), in conjunction with (6.24), provides an interesting comparison between GMM1 and WG. When $T/N \to 0$ the fixed T results for GMM1 remain valid, but WG, although consistent, has an asymptotic bias in its asymptotic distribution (which only disappears if $N/T \to 0$). However, when T/N tends to a positive constant, both WG and GMM1 exhibit negative biases in their asymptotic distributions. Moreover, for $T < N$ the GMM1 asymptotic bias is always smaller than the WG bias (GMM1 is only well defined for $(T-1) \le N$).

The Crude GMM Estimator in First-Differences   Alvarez and Arellano (1998) also showed that the crude GMM estimator (CIV) that neglects the autocorrelation in the first-differenced errors (i.e. one-step GMM in first-differences with weight matrix equal to $(Z'Z)^{-1}$) is inconsistent as $T/N \to c > 0$, despite being consistent for fixed T. The result is:

$$\widehat{\alpha}_{CIV} \xrightarrow{p} \alpha - \frac{(1+\alpha)}{2}\left(\frac{c}{2-(1+\alpha)(2-c)/2}\right). \qquad (6.37)$$

The intuition for this result is that the "endogeneity bias" of OLS in first-differences (unlike the one for WG) does not tend to zero as $T \to \infty$. Thus, for fixed T both GMM1 and CIV are consistent, whereas as T increases the former remains consistent but the latter is inconsistent. Moreover, notice that the bias may be qualitatively relevant. The fixed-T large-N GMM theory would just describe the CIV estimator as being asymptotically less efficient than GMM1 as a consequence of using a non-optimal choice of weight matrix.

6.4 Initial Conditions and Heteroskedasticity

In this section we examine the role of assumptions about initial conditions and heteroskedasticity in the estimation of AR models from short panels. We consider three different types of covariance structures. Type 1 relies on stationarity assumptions (*B1* and *B3–B5*). Type 2 is the covariance structure assuming an unrestricted joint distribution of y_{i0} and η_i, and time series homoskedasticity (*B1* and *B3*). Finally, Type 3 is the least restrictive covariance structure which allows for both unrestricted initial conditions and time series heteroskedasticity (Assumption *B1* only).[5] The choice of auxiliary assumptions is important since there is a sharp trade-off between robustness and efficiency in this context.

6.4.1 Estimation under Stationarity

Under assumptions *B1*, *B3*, *B4*, and *B5* the first- and second-order moments of y_i^T are functions of the four parameters α, σ^2, σ_μ^2, and μ of the form

$$E\left(y_{it} - \mu\right) = 0 \ (t = 0, 1, ..., T) \qquad (6.38)$$

$$E\left(y_{it}y_{is} - \omega_{ts} - \mu^2\right) = 0 \ (t = 0, 1, ..., T; s = 0, 1, ..., t), \qquad (6.39)$$

where $\mu = E(\mu_i)$, $\sigma_\mu^2 = Var(\mu_i)$, and ω_{ts} is the (t, s)-th element of the covariance matrix of y_i^T given by

$$\omega_{ts} = \sigma_\mu^2 + \alpha^{|t-s|}\frac{\sigma^2}{(1-\alpha^2)}. \qquad (6.40)$$

---

[5]In the next section we shall discuss one further covariance structure that relies on mean stationarity but allows for nonstationary variances.

Method of Moments Estimation The parameters can be estimated by nonlinear GMM using (6.38) and (6.39). In Chapter 5 we used this model (with $\mu = 0$) to illustrate how moments that are nonlinear in the parameters can be converted into linear moment equations by transformation and reparameterization. Assuming that y_{i0} is observed and μ is unknown, these moments can be restated as:

$$E\left[y_i^{t-2}\left(\Delta y_{it} - \alpha \Delta y_{i(t-1)}\right)\right] = 0 \ (t = 2, ..., T) \qquad (6.41a)$$

$$E\left[\Delta y_{i(t-1)}\left(y_{it} - \alpha y_{i(t-1)}\right)\right] = 0 \ (t = 2, ..., T) \qquad (6.41b)$$

$$E\left(y_{it} - \mu\right) = 0 \ (t = 0, 1, ..., T) \qquad (6.41c)$$

$$E\left(y_{it}^2 - \varphi^2\right) = 0 \ (t = 0, 1, ..., T) \qquad (6.41d)$$

$$E\left[y_{i0}\left(y_{i1} - \alpha y_{i0}\right) - \psi\right] = 0 \qquad (6.41e)$$

where $\varphi^2 = \mu^2 + \sigma_\mu^2 + \sigma^2/(1 - \alpha^2)$ and $\psi = (1 - \alpha)(\sigma_\mu^2 + \mu^2)$. Thus, α, μ, φ^2, and ψ can be estimated by linear GMM using (6.41a)-(6.41e). Original parameters can be recovered by undoing the reparameterization. The two sets of GMM estimates will be asymptotically equivalent for optimal choices of the weight matrices.

The orthogonality conditions (6.41a) coincide with those in (6.25) and are reproduced here for convenience. The moments (6.41b) also have a straightforward instrumental variable interpretation: they state that $\Delta y_{i(t-1)}$ has zero mean and is orthogonal to $\eta_i + v_{it}$; (6.41c) and (6.41d) state the unconditional stationarity of the first and second moments, respectively, and (6.41e) is an unrestricted moment that determines the variance of the individual effect.

Marginal PML Estimation under Stationarity The integrated likelihood marginal on μ_i is given by

$$f(y_i^T) = \int f(y_i^T \mid \mu_i) dG(\mu_i) = \int \prod_{t=1}^{T} f(y_{it} \mid y_i^{t-1}, \mu_i) f(y_{i0} \mid \mu_i) dG(\mu_i) \quad (6.42)$$

where $G(\mu_i)$ is the cumulative distribution function of μ_i.

The normal log likelihood conditional on y_{i0} and μ_i was given in (6.23). If in addition to (6.22) we assume that $y_{i0} \mid \mu_i$ is normally distributed with mean and variance given by assumptions $B4$ and $B5$, so that

$$y_{i0} \mid \mu_i \sim \mathcal{N}\left(\mu_i, \frac{\sigma^2}{1 - \alpha^2}\right), \qquad (6.43)$$

and also

$$\mu_i \sim \mathcal{N}\left(\mu, \sigma_\mu^2\right), \qquad (6.44)$$

the log of $f(y_i^T)$ takes the form

$$\log f(y_i^T) \propto -\frac{1}{2} \log \det \Omega - \frac{1}{2} \left(y_i^T - \mu\iota\right)' \Omega^{-1} \left(y_i^T - \mu\iota\right), \tag{6.45}$$

where ι denotes a $(T+1) \times 1$ vector of ones, and Ω is a covariance matrix of order $T+1$ with elements ω_{ts} given in (6.40). So we can write:

$$\Omega = \sigma_\mu^2 \iota\iota' + \sigma^2 V \tag{6.46}$$

where the (t, s)-th element of V is $\alpha^{|t-s|}/(1 - \alpha^2)$.

When the log density of y_i^T is given by (6.45), the statistic that maximizes $\sum_{i=1}^N \log f(y_i^T)$ is the ML estimator, which is asymptotically equivalent to optimal GMM. Otherwise it is just a PML estimator that remains consistent as long as the moment conditions (6.41a)-(6.41e) are satisfied, but it is less efficient asymptotically than optimal GMM (see discussion in Chapter 5).[6]

Lack of joint normality of y_i^T may result from a variety of circumstances. For example, the presence of conditional heteroskedasticity (failure of Assumption B2), together with conditionally normal y_{it}s and normal μ_is, would cause the unconditional distribution of the y_{it}s to be non-normal.[7] Furthermore, a non-normal distribution of y_i^T will result in general from non-normality of either μ_i, the shocks v_{it}, or the distribution of initial conditions.

Conditional PML under Stationarity Joint ML estimation of the common parameters and the realizations of the effects may lead to inconsistent estimates when T is small. Examples include the joint MLE of the error variance in the static regression model (Section 2.4.1) and the WG estimator of the autoregressive parameter (Section 6.2). In some cases, consistent estimates can be obtained by maximizing a conditional likelihood given sufficient statistics for the effects (Andersen, 1970). An example is the conditional likelihood interpretation of WG in the static regression model (Section 2.4.2).

When a sufficient statistic for the effects is not available, it may still be possible to obtain consistent estimates based on the conditional likelihood given ML estimates of the effects, as long as the effects and the common parameters are orthogonal (i.e. their scores are uncorrelated), or have been orthogonalized by transformation (Cox and Reid, 1987).

We now turn to examine conditional PML estimation[8] of the AR model under stationarity given estimates of the effects (regarded as functions of the common parameters). The log density of y_i^T given μ_i is given by

---

[6] We do not consider implications for higher-order moments that might provide efficiency increases under non-normality. Efficiency increases of this kind were considered by MaCurdy (1982a), and are discussed here in Section B.6 of the Appendix.

[7] Conversely, if (y_i^T, η_i) were jointly normally distributed, all conditional variances of the form $Var(y_{it} \mid y_i^{t-1}, \eta_i)$ would be constant.

[8] Or "approximate conditional PML" estimation, if we reserve the term "conditional PML" for a likelihood conditioned on a sufficient statistic.

$$\ell_i \equiv \log f(y_i^T \mid \mu_i) \tag{6.47}$$

$$\propto -\frac{(T+1)}{2}\log\sigma^2 - \frac{1}{2}\log\det V - \frac{1}{2\sigma^2}\left(y_i^T - \mu_i\iota\right)' V^{-1}\left(y_i^T - \mu_i\iota\right).$$

Moreover, the first derivative with respect to μ_i is

$$\frac{\partial\ell_i}{\partial\mu_i} = \frac{1}{\sigma^2}\iota' V^{-1}\left(y_i^T - \mu_i\iota\right). \tag{6.48}$$

Hence, the MLE of μ_i for given α is

$$\widehat{\mu}_i = \left(\iota' V^{-1}\iota\right)^{-1}\iota' V^{-1}y_i^T. \tag{6.49}$$

As noted by Lancaster (2002), for this model the score for μ_i (6.48) is uncorrelated to the score statistics for α and σ^2. This can be seen from the expected values of the corresponding cross-terms in the hessian, both of which vanish:

$$E\left(\frac{\partial^2\ell_i}{\partial\mu_i\partial\alpha}\mid\mu_i\right) = \frac{1}{\sigma^2}\iota'\frac{\partial V^{-1}}{\partial\alpha}E\left(y_i^T - \mu_i\iota\mid\mu_i\right) = 0 \tag{6.50a}$$

$$E\left(\frac{\partial^2\ell_i}{\partial\mu_i\partial\sigma^2}\mid\mu_i\right) = -\frac{1}{\sigma^4}\iota' V^{-1}E\left(y_i^T - \mu_i\iota\mid\mu_i\right) = 0. \tag{6.50b}$$

Information orthogonality between μ_i and (α,σ^2) suggests that it may be possible to obtain consistent estimates of α and σ^2 by maximizing the likelihood conditioned on $\widehat{\mu}_i$. This can be easily obtained by considering the following non-singular transformation matrix of order $T+1$:

$$\mathcal{H} = \begin{pmatrix} \left(\iota' V^{-1}\iota\right)^{-1}\iota' V^{-1} \\ D \end{pmatrix} \tag{6.51}$$

which transforms y_i^T to $(\widehat{\mu}_i, Dy_i^T)$, where D denotes the $T \times (T+1)$ first-difference matrix operator. Since $y_i^T \mid \mu_i$ is normal, so is $\mathcal{H}y_i^T \mid \mu_i$. Moreover,

$$Var\left(\mathcal{H}y_i^T \mid \mu_i\right) = \sigma^2 \begin{pmatrix} \left(\iota' V^{-1}\iota\right)^{-1} & 0 \\ 0 & DVD' \end{pmatrix} \tag{6.52}$$

so that $\widehat{\mu}_i$ and Dy_i^T are conditionally independent. Therefore,

$$f(y_i^T \mid \mu_i) = f(\mathcal{H}y_i^T \mid \mu_i)\left|\det(\mathcal{H})\right| = f(\widehat{\mu}_i \mid \mu_i)f(Dy_i^T \mid \mu_i) = f(\widehat{\mu}_i \mid \mu_i)f(Dy_i^T). \tag{6.53}$$

This is so because Dy_i^T is independent of μ_i and the fact that for any non-singular matrix V, $|\det(\mathcal{H})| = 1.$[9]

[9]To see this, let $q' = \left(\iota' V^{-1}\iota\right)^{-1}\iota' V^{-1}$ so that

$$\det(\mathcal{H}\mathcal{H}') = q'[I - D'(DD')^{-1}D]q\det(DD') = (T+1)^{-1}q'\iota\iota'q\det(DD').$$

Moreover, since $q'\iota = 1$ and $\det(DD') = (T+1)$ it follows that $\det(\mathcal{H}\mathcal{H}') = 1$.

The implication is that the likelihood conditional on $\widehat{\mu}_i$ does not depend on μ_i and coincides with the likelihood for the data in first-differences:[10]

$$f(y_i^T \mid \widehat{\mu}_i, \mu_i) = \frac{f(y_i^T \mid \mu_i)}{f(\widehat{\mu}_i \mid \mu_i)} = f(Dy_i^T). \tag{6.54}$$

The log likelihood in first-differences for one individual is given by

$$\log f(Dy_i^T) \propto -\frac{T}{2} \log \sigma^2 - \frac{1}{2} \log \det(DVD') - \frac{1}{2\sigma^2} y_i^{T\prime} D'(DVD')^{-1} Dy_i^T. \tag{6.55}$$

Thus, an (approximate) conditional MLE for this problem is the maximizer of $\sum_{i=1}^{N} \log f(Dy_i^T)$. To the extent that the restrictions in the covariance matrix of Dy_i^T are satisfied, this estimator will be consistent and asymptotically normal for fixed T.[11]

Comparing Conditional and Marginal PML   The comparison with marginal PML can be made using the factorization:

$$\begin{aligned} \log f(y_i^T) &= \log f(Dy_i^T) + \log \int f(\widehat{\mu}_i \mid \mu_i) dG(\mu_i) \\ &\equiv \log f(Dy_i^T) + \log f(\widehat{\mu}_i), \end{aligned} \tag{6.56}$$

which comes from expression (6.53) and $f(y_i^T) = \int f(y_i^T \mid \mu_i) dG(\mu_i)$. Thus, the log density of the data in levels is the sum of the log density of the data in first-differences and the log density of the MLE of the effects.

Estimates based on the first-differences of the data do not exploit the lack of correlation between $\widehat{\mu}_i$ and Dy_i^T, which only depends on the boundedness of second-order moments for y_i^T (see also the discussion in Section 5.3).

The first two unconditional moments of $\widehat{\mu}_i$ are $E(\widehat{\mu}_i) = \mu$ and $Var(\widehat{\mu}_i) = \sigma_\mu^2 + \sigma^2(\iota'V^{-1}\iota)^{-1} = \sigma_{\widehat{\mu}}^2$, say. If μ_i is normally distributed so is $\widehat{\mu}_i$, in which case the relationship between the marginal and the conditional score statistics for α can be written as

$$\frac{\partial \log f(y_i^T)}{\partial \alpha} = \frac{\partial \log f(Dy_i^T)}{\partial \alpha} + \frac{1}{\sigma_{\widehat{\mu}}^2} (\widehat{\mu}_i - \mu) \frac{\partial \widehat{\mu}_i}{\partial \alpha}. \tag{6.57}$$

Since the two scores will tend to coincide for large values of $\sigma_{\widehat{\mu}}^2$, the additional information about α contained in the marginal likelihood will tend to vanish as the variance of the effects σ_μ^2 becomes large. In principle, the efficiency gain

---

[10] A similar result was given by Kiefer (1980) in the context of a regression model with fixed effects and unrestricted error autocovariance matrix.

[11] Estimates for stationary autoregressive models using first-differences have been considered by Kruiniger (1998), Hsiao, Pesaran, and Tahmiscioglu (2002), and Lancaster (2002).

from using the marginal likelihood can be empirically assessed, since whether the effects have infinite variance or not is something that can be explored by analysing the distribution of the data in levels.

From a GMM perspective, even if Δy_{it} is normally distributed but μ_i is not, as long as the μ_i are independent draws from some distribution with bounded variance, PML (or GMM) estimates based on the first-differences alone will never be more efficient than the optimal GMM estimator based on the full covariance structure for the data in levels.

6.4.2   Unrestricted Initial Conditions

In the time series context whether a stationary AR model is estimated conditional on the first observation or not does not matter for robustness or asymptotic efficiency. We obtain different estimates in each case but both have similar properties when T is large.

With short panels the situation is fundamentally different. An estimator of α obtained under the assumption that $y_{i0} \mid \mu_i$ follows the stationary unconditional distribution of the process will be inconsistent when the assumption is false.[12] This is therefore an instance of a trade-off between robustness and efficiency, since in short panels the assumption of stationary initial conditions may be very informative about α.

The question to ask is whether initial conditions at the start of the sample are representative of the steady state behaviour of the model or not. In the analysis of country panel data, Barro and Sala-i-Martin (1995) described some examples—like data sets that start at the end of a war or other major historical event—in which one would not expect initial conditions to be distributed according to the steady state distribution of the process. In the case of micro panels, the starting point of the sample may be much closer to the start of the process for some units than others. For example, for young workers or new firms initial conditions may be less related to steady state conditions than for older ones (see Hause, 1980, p. 1021).

An AR(1) Model with Unrestricted Initial Conditions   Taking these considerations into account, a more robust specification would be one in which the distribution of y_{i0} given μ_i (or η_i) is left unrestricted.[13] In particular, we drop assumptions *B4* and *B5* and let $E(y_{i0} \mid \mu_i)$ and $Var(y_{i0} \mid \mu_i)$ be arbitrary functions of μ_i, while retaining the basic stable specification of equation (6.1).

---

[12]Although we emphasize models with individual-specific intercepts, this would also be true for homogeneous models estimated from short panels.

[13]Note that the moving average models of Chapter 5 assumed stationary initial conditions by specifying $y_{i0} = \mu_i + v_{i0}$.

To analyse this case it is convenient to introduce the following notation for the linear projection of y_{i0} on μ_i:

$$y_{i0} = \delta_0 + \delta\mu_i + \varepsilon_{i0} \tag{6.58}$$

where ε_{i0} is the linear projection error. By construction $E(\varepsilon_{i0}) = 0$ and $Cov(\varepsilon_{i0}, \mu_i) = 0$. Moreover, let $\sigma_0^2 = E(\varepsilon_{i0}^2)$.

Clearly, under Assumptions B4 and B5 we have that $\delta_0 = 0$, $\delta = 1$ and $\sigma_0^2 = \sigma^2/(1 - \alpha^2)$.

In view of (6.7) and (6.58), this model can be written as

$$y_{it} = \alpha^t \delta_0 + \left[1 - (1 - \delta)\alpha^t\right]\mu_i + \sum_{s=0}^{t-1} \alpha^s v_{i(t-s)} + \alpha^t \varepsilon_{i0} \quad (t = 1, ..., T). \tag{6.59}$$

So this specification gives rise to a mean-covariance structure that has three additional parameters relative to the stationary model of the previous section. Means, variances, and covariances take now period-specific values given by

$$E(y_{it}) = \alpha^t \delta_0 + \left[1 - (1 - \delta)\alpha^t\right]\mu \tag{6.60}$$

and for $s \leq t$:

$$\omega_{ts} = \left[1 - (1 - \delta)\alpha^t\right]\left[1 - (1 - \delta)\alpha^s\right]\sigma_\mu^2 + \alpha^{t-s}\left[\sigma^2\left(\sum_{j=0}^{s-1}\alpha^{2j}\right) + \alpha^{2s}\sigma_0^2\right]. \tag{6.61}$$

The model with unrestricted initial conditions nests various situations of potential interest, some of which were discussed by Anderson and Hsiao (1981). These include:

- y_{i0} follows the stationary unconditional distribution of the process ($\delta_0 = 0$, $\delta = 1$ and $\sigma_0^2 = \sigma^2/(1 - \alpha^2)$).

- y_{i0} random but uncorrelated to μ_i ($\delta = 0$).

- y_{i0} fixed ($\delta = \sigma_0^2 = 0$).

- y_{i0} mean stationary ($\delta_0 = 0$, $\delta = 1$, σ_0^2 unrestricted).

GMM Estimation   As a result of nonstationarity, none of the moment conditions (6.41b)-(6.41d) hold so that GMM or PML estimators based on them will be inconsistent in general. Consistent estimates of the nonstationary model can be obtained by nonlinear GMM from (6.60) and (6.61).

Alternative representations of the moment conditions for models with unrestricted initial conditions were studied by Ahn and Schmidt (1995). Lack of correlation between errors and lagged ys implies that for $s < t$

$$\omega_{st} = \alpha\omega_{s(t-1)} + c_s. \tag{6.62}$$

where $c_s = Cov(y_{is}, \eta_i)$. Moreover, lack of correlation between the individual effects and the errors implies that[14]

---

[14]Under stationary initial conditions $c_0 = \sigma_\eta^2/(1 - \alpha)$, so that c_s is constant for all s.

$$c_s = \alpha c_{s-1} + \sigma_\eta^2. \tag{6.63}$$

First-differencing (6.62) for given c_s gives the standard linear IV moment conditions (6.25). In addition, substituting (6.62) into (6.63) we have

$$\omega_{st} = \alpha \omega_{s(t-1)} + \alpha \omega_{(s-1)t} - \alpha^2 \omega_{(s-1)(t-1)} + \sigma_\eta^2. \tag{6.64}$$

or

$$E\left[(y_{is} - \alpha y_{i(s-1)} - \eta)(y_{it} - \alpha y_{i(t-1)} - \eta)\right] = \sigma_\eta^2, \tag{6.65}$$

which can be first-differenced to obtain quadratic moment conditions that only depend on α.

The validity of (6.62) and (6.63) depends exclusively on Assumption *B1*. It turns out that all the restrictions implied by *B1* on the covariance matrix and mean vector of the data can be represented as

$$E\left[y_i^{t-2}\left(\Delta y_{it} - \alpha \Delta y_{i(t-1)}\right)\right] = 0 \ (t = 2, ..., T) \tag{6.66a}$$

$$E\left[\left(\Delta y_{i(t-1)} - \alpha \Delta y_{i(t-2)}\right)\left(y_{it} - \alpha y_{i(t-1)} - \eta\right)\right] = 0 \ (t = 3, ..., T) \tag{6.66b}$$

$$E\left(y_{it} - \alpha y_{i(t-1)} - \eta\right) = 0 \ (t = 1, ..., T) \tag{6.66c}$$

In addition, time series homoskedasticity (Assumption *B3*) implies

$$E\left[\left(y_{it} - \alpha y_{i(t-1)} - \eta\right)^2 - \sigma_u^2\right] = 0 \ (t = 1, ..., T), \tag{6.67}$$

where $\sigma_u^2 = \sigma_\eta^2 + \sigma^2$.

Finally, the following four unrestricted moments determine the first and second moments of y_{i0}, c_0 and c_1

$$E(y_{i0} - \mu_0) = 0 \tag{6.68a}$$

$$E\left[y_{i0}^2 - \varphi_0^2\right] = 0 \tag{6.68b}$$

$$E\left[y_{i0}(y_{i2} - \alpha y_{i1} - \eta) - c_0\right] = 0 \tag{6.68c}$$

$$E\left[y_{i1}(y_{i2} - \alpha y_{i1} - \eta) - c_1\right] = 0. \tag{6.68d}$$

In this representation of the moment conditions, the coefficients related to initial conditions and the individual effect variance can be ignored since they only appear through unrestricted moments. Thus, optimal GMM estimates of α, σ_u^2, and η can be obtained from the moment conditions (6.66a) to (6.67) alone. This is useful because it facilitates optimal nonlinear GMM inference on a smaller set of parameters and moments when the main interest is in testing the covariance structure or in estimating autoregressive parameters.

Given the coefficients in the previous parameterization, the variance of the effects and the initial condition parameters can be determined from

$$\sigma_\eta^2 = c_1 - \alpha c_0 \tag{6.69a}$$

$$\delta = \frac{(1-\alpha)}{\sigma_\eta^2} c_0 \tag{6.69b}$$

$$\delta_0 = \mu_0 - \delta\mu \tag{6.69c}$$

$$\sigma_0^2 = \varphi_0^2 - \delta^2 \sigma_\mu^2. \tag{6.69d}$$

The IV moments for errors in levels (6.41b), which we used in the stationary case, are not valid in the absence of mean stationarity since they require the constancy of c_s. To see the connection with the current restrictions, note that under mean stationarity $c_0 = c_1$, so that from (6.68c)-(6.68d) $E\left[\Delta y_{i1}\left(y_{i2} - \alpha y_{i1} - \eta\right)\right] = 0$, which together with (6.66a)-(6.66b) imply (6.41b).

Marginal PML with Unrestricted Initial Conditions   We now consider the integrated MLE under (6.22), which specified that $v_{it} \mid y_i^{t-1}, \mu_i$ is distributed as $\mathcal{N}(0, \sigma^2)$, and the assumption that the pair (y_{i0}, μ_i) is jointly normally distributed with unrestricted mean vector and covariance matrix.

Thus, we retain the assumption of normal effects (6.44), but relax the initial condition assumption (6.43) by considering:

$$y_{i0} \mid \mu_i \sim \mathcal{N}\left(\delta_0 + \delta\mu_i, \sigma_0^2\right). \tag{6.70}$$

In order to derive the likelihood function it is convenient to write model (6.1) using the following stacked notation:

$$B y_i = \alpha y_{i0} d_i + u_i \tag{6.71}$$

where B is a $T \times T$ matrix given by

$$B = \begin{pmatrix} 1 & 0 & \dots & 0 & 0 \\ -\alpha & 1 & \dots & 0 & 0 \\ \vdots & \vdots & & \vdots & \vdots \\ 0 & 0 & \dots & -\alpha & 1 \end{pmatrix}$$

and $y_i = (y_{i1}, ..., y_{iT})'$, $d_i = (1, 0, ..., 0)'$, $u_{it} = \eta_i + v_{it}$, and $u_i = (u_{i1}, ..., u_{iT})'$.
The conditional density of y_i given y_{i0} can then be written as

$$f(y_i \mid y_{i0}) = f(u_i \mid y_{i0}) \left|\det(B)\right|, \tag{6.72}$$

but since B is triangular $\det(B) = 1$, so that the densities of $y_i \mid y_{i0}$ and $u_i \mid y_{i0}$ coincide. Moreover,

$$f(u_i \mid y_{i0}) = f(\bar{u}_i, u_i^* \mid y_{i0}) \left|\det(H)\right| \tag{6.73}$$

where H is the transformation matrix (2.58) that yields the average series and the orthogonal deviations: $H u_i = (\bar{u}_i, u_i^{*\prime})'$. The determinant of the transformation satisfies $|\det(H)| = T^{-1/2}$, which is an irrelevant constant for our purposes.

Under the assumptions of the model, Hu_i is normally distributed as:

$$Hu_i \sim N\left[\begin{pmatrix} \eta \\ 0 \end{pmatrix}, \begin{pmatrix} \sigma_\eta^2 + T^{-1}\sigma^2 & 0 \\ 0 & \sigma^2 I_{T-1} \end{pmatrix}\right]. \tag{6.74}$$

Moreover,

$$Hu_i \mid y_{i0} \sim N\left[\begin{pmatrix} \varphi_0 + \varphi_1 y_{i0} \\ 0 \end{pmatrix}, \begin{pmatrix} \omega^2 & 0 \\ 0 & \sigma^2 I_{T-1} \end{pmatrix}\right], \tag{6.75}$$

where φ_0, φ_1, and ω^2 are the linear projection coefficients of $\bar{u}_i$ on y_{i0}.[15] Therefore,

$$\log f(y_i \mid y_{i0}) \propto -\frac{(T-1)}{2}\log \sigma^2 - \frac{1}{2\sigma^2}(y_i^* - \alpha y_{i(-1)}^*)'(y_i^* - \alpha y_{i(-1)}^*)$$
$$-\frac{1}{2}\log\omega^2 - \frac{1}{2\omega^2}(\bar{y}_i - \alpha\bar{y}_{i(-1)} - \varphi_0 - \varphi_1 y_{i0})^2, \tag{6.76}$$

where y_i^* and $y_{i(-1)}^*$ denote orthogonal deviations of y_i and $y_{i(-1)}$, respectively.[16]

Thus, the Gaussian log likelihood given y_{i0} can be decomposed into a within-group and a between-group component. Note that this is an integrated likelihood that is marginal on η_i but conditional on y_{i0}:

$$f(y_i^T \mid y_{i0}) = \int \prod_{t=1}^T f(y_{it} \mid y_i^{t-1}, \eta_i) dG(\eta_i \mid y_{i0}). \tag{6.77}$$

So, the maximizer of $\sum_i \log f(y_i \mid y_{i0})$ can be regarded as the MLE conditional on y_{i0} under the assumption that $G(\eta_i \mid y_{i0})$ is normal with linear conditional mean and constant variance.

The ML estimates of σ^2, φ_0, φ_1, and ω^2 as functions of the MLE of α are

$$\hat{\sigma}^2 = \frac{1}{N(T-1)}\sum_{i=1}^N (y_i^* - \hat\alpha y_{i(-1)}^*)'(y_i^* - \hat\alpha y_{i(-1)}^*), \tag{6.78}$$

[15]Thus, φ_0 and ω^2 are related to η and σ_η^2 by the expressions:

$$\omega^2 = \left[\sigma_\eta^2 - \varphi_1^2 Var(y_{i0})\right] + \frac{\sigma^2}{T}$$

and $\varphi_0 = \eta - \varphi_1 E(y_{i0})$.
[16]Recall that the WG and the orthogonal-deviations residual sum of squares coincide:

$$(y_i^* - \alpha y_{i(-1)}^*)'(y_i^* - \alpha y_{i(-1)}^*) = (y_i - \alpha y_{i(-1)})'Q(y_i - \alpha y_{i(-1)}).$$

$$\widehat{\varphi} = \left(\sum_{i=1}^{N} f_i f_i'\right)^{-1} \sum_{i=1}^{N} f_i(\overline{y}_i - \widehat{\alpha}\overline{y}_{i(-1)}), \tag{6.79}$$

and

$$\widehat{\omega}^2 = \frac{1}{N} \sum_{i=1}^{N} (\overline{y}_i - \widehat{\alpha}\overline{y}_{i(-1)} - \widehat{\varphi}' f_i)^2 \tag{6.80}$$

where $\widehat{\varphi} = (\widehat{\varphi}_0, \widehat{\varphi}_1)'$ and $f_i = (1, y_{i0})'$.

By substituting (6.78)-(6.80) into (6.76), we obtain a concentrated likelihood that only depends on α, so that the MLE $\widehat{\alpha}$ can be shown to solve

$$
\begin{aligned}
\widehat{\alpha} \;=\; & \arg\min_a \; \Big\{ \log\Big[(y^* - ay^*_{(-1)})'(y^* - ay^*_{(-1)})\Big] \\
& + \frac{1}{(T-1)} \log\Big[(\overline{y} - a\overline{y}_{(-1)})'S_0(\overline{y} - a\overline{y}_{(-1)})\Big]\Big\}
\end{aligned}
\tag{6.81}
$$

where $S_0 = I_N - F(F'F)^{-1}F'$, $F = (f_1, ..., f_N)'$, $y^* = (y_1^{*\prime}, ..., y_N^{*\prime})'$, $y^*_{(-1)} = (y_{1(-1)}^{*\prime}, ..., y_{N(-1)}^{*\prime})'$, $\overline{y} = (\overline{y}_1, ..., \overline{y}_N)'$, and $\overline{y}_{(-1)} = (\overline{y}_{1(-1)}, ..., \overline{y}_{N(-1)})'$.

The first term in the (negative) concentrated likelihood (6.81) corresponds to the WG criterion, and the second term, of order $(T-1)$, can be regarded as providing a small T correction for the WG bias. The estimator and criterion (6.81) were considered by Alvarez and Arellano (1998).[17]

Having estimated the parameters in $f(y_i \mid y_{i0})$, these can be combined with the sample mean and variance of y_{i0}, $\overline{y}_0$ and $\widehat{Var}(y_{i0})$, to obtain the ML estimates of σ_η^2 and η from

$$\widehat{\sigma}_\eta^2 = \widehat{\omega}^2 + \widehat{\varphi}_1^2 \widehat{Var}(y_{i0}) - \frac{\widehat{\sigma}^2}{T} \tag{6.82}$$

$$\widehat{\eta} = \widehat{\varphi}_0 + \widehat{\varphi}_1 \overline{y}_0. \tag{6.83}$$

The resulting estimate of σ_η^2 does not impose non-negativity. ML estimates that enforce $\sigma_\eta^2 > 0$ can be obtained by parameterizing the joint likelihood of y_i^T (as opposed to $y_i^T \mid y_{i0}$) in terms of δ_0, δ, σ_0^2, α, σ^2, and σ_η^2.[18]

In the absence of normality, (6.81) is just a PMLE that will remain consistent as long as the restrictions implied by the model on the unconditional covariance matrix of y_i^T hold. Thus, for fixed T and large N, (6.81) is robust to conditional heteroskedasticity but not to time series heteroskedasticity.

---

[17] Arellano (2000) contains a similar result for VAR processes.

[18] A concentrated full likelihood which is only a function of α and $\lambda = \sigma_\eta^2/\sigma^2$ is given by Alvarez and Arellano (1998).

A GLS Estimator   The log likelihood (6.76) has been written in terms of the transformed system

$$
\begin{pmatrix} \overline{y}_i \\ y_i^* \end{pmatrix} = \begin{pmatrix} \overline{y}_{i(-1)} & 1 & y_{i0} \\ y_{i(-1)}^* & 0 & 0 \end{pmatrix} \begin{pmatrix} \alpha \\ \varphi_0 \\ \varphi_1 \end{pmatrix} + \begin{pmatrix} \varepsilon_i \\ v_i^* \end{pmatrix} \equiv W_i \gamma + u_i^\dagger \qquad (6.84)
$$

with

$$
\begin{pmatrix} \varepsilon_i \\ v_i^* \end{pmatrix} \mid y_{i0} \sim N \left[0, \begin{pmatrix} \omega^2 & 0 \\ 0 & \sigma^2 I_{T-1} \end{pmatrix} \right] \equiv N(0, \Sigma). \qquad (6.85)
$$

OLS estimates of γ in (6.84) set to zero the sample moments $\sum_i W_i' u_i^\dagger$ and are therefore inconsistent because

$$
E \left(y_{i(-1)}^{*\prime} v_i^* \right) + E \left(\overline{y}_{i(-1)} \varepsilon_i \right) \neq 0.
$$

However, a GLS or weighted least-squares estimator that sets $\sum_i W_i' \widetilde{\Sigma}^{-1} u_i^\dagger$ to zero is consistent (as long as $\widetilde{\Sigma}$ is consistent for Σ) because it is solving the ML equations for a fixed value $\widetilde{\Sigma}$, whose population counterpart is given by

$$
E \left(y_{i(-1)}^{*\prime} v_i^* \right) = -\frac{\sigma^2}{\omega^2} E \left(\overline{y}_{i(-1)} \varepsilon_i \right) \qquad (6.86)
$$

and

$$
E \left[\begin{pmatrix} 1 \\ y_{i0} \end{pmatrix} \varepsilon_i \right] = 0. \qquad (6.87)
$$

The form of the GLS estimator of α estimated jointly with the coefficients in the linear projection of η_i on y_{i0} is therefore

$$
\widetilde{\delta} = \left(\sum_{i=1}^N W_i' \widetilde{\Sigma}^{-1} W_i \right)^{-1} \sum_{i=1}^N W_i' \widetilde{\Sigma}^{-1} y_i^\dagger, \qquad (6.88)
$$

where $y_i^\dagger = (\overline{y}_i, y_i^{*\prime})'$, and $\widetilde{\Sigma}$ is a diagonal matrix containing consistent estimates $\widetilde{\omega}^2$ and $\widetilde{\sigma}^2$.

This type of GLS estimator was considered by Blundell and Smith (1991) and has been further discussed by Blundell and Bond (1998). The problem with the GLS estimates of α and φ based on preliminary estimates of ω^2 and σ^2 is that they are only consistent if based on consistent estimates of ω^2 and σ^2, and they are only asymptotically equivalent to ML if based on asymptotically efficient estimates of ω^2 and σ^2. Moreover, estimation of ω^2 and σ^2 requires preliminary estimates of α, whose properties will in general affect those of the variance parameters. This problem arises generally in the GLS estimation of triangular systems (e.g. Lahiri and Schmidt, 1978; Arellano, 1989b).

Conditional PML with Unrestricted Initial Conditions The log likelihood for individual i conditional on η_i and y_{i0}, as given in (6.23), takes the form

$$\ell_i(\theta, \eta_i) = \log f(y_i \mid y_{i0}, \eta_i) \propto -\frac{T}{2} \log \sigma^2 - \frac{1}{2\sigma^2} \sum_{t=1}^{T} (y_{it} - \alpha y_{i(t-1)} - \eta_i)^2$$

where $\theta = (\alpha, \sigma^2)'$. In Section 6.2 we saw that the MLE of α jointly estimated with σ^2 and the η_i coincides with the WG estimator and is therefore inconsistent for fixed T.

The same is true of the maximizer of the log likelihood conditioned on the MLE of η_i, since this is also the WG estimator. To see this, note that the MLE of η_i for given α is

$$\widehat{\eta}_i = \bar{y}_i - \alpha \bar{y}_{i(-1)} = \eta_i + \bar{v}_i \tag{6.89}$$

so that $\widehat{\eta}_i \mid y_{i0}, \eta_i$ has a normal distribution with mean η_i and variance σ^2/T. Hence, the log likelihood conditioned on $\widehat{\eta}_i$ is given by

$$\log f(y_i \mid y_{i0}, \eta_i, \widehat{\eta}_i) = \log \frac{f(y_i \mid y_{i0}, \eta_i)}{f(\widehat{\eta}_i \mid y_{i0}, \eta_i)} = \log f(y_i \mid y_{i0}, \widehat{\eta}_i)$$

$$\propto -\frac{(T-1)}{2} \log \sigma^2 - \frac{1}{2\sigma^2} \sum_{t=1}^{T} (v_{it} - \bar{v}_i)^2, \tag{6.90}$$

which does not depend on η_i, and has the same form as the "WG likelihood" (2.54) that we discussed in Chapter 2 for static regression models.

This situation is in contrast with the result we found under stationarity. Namely, that the likelihood conditioned on $\widehat{\mu}_i$ was the same as the likelihood of the data in first-differences (6.54), so that conditional PML estimates of α and σ^2 were consistent for fixed T.

In the stationary case, however, θ and the effects were information orthogonal, whereas they are not so when initial conditions are unrestricted. Now we have[19]

$$E\left(\frac{\partial^2 \ell_i}{\partial \theta \partial \eta_i} \mid y_{i0}, \eta_i \right) = \begin{pmatrix} -\frac{T}{\sigma^2} E\left(\bar{y}_{i(-1)} \mid y_{i0}, \eta_i \right) \\ 0 \end{pmatrix}, \tag{6.91}$$

whose first term is different from zero. In fact it can be shown that[20]

---

[19]The required derivatives are $(\partial \ell_i / \partial \eta_i) = \sigma^{-2} T \bar{v}_i$, $(\partial^2 \ell_i / \partial \eta_i \partial \alpha) = -\sigma^{-2} T \bar{y}_{i(-1)}$, and $(\partial^2 \ell_i / \partial \eta_i \partial \sigma^2) = -\sigma^{-4} T \bar{v}_i$. For later use, note also that $(\partial^2 \ell_i / \partial \eta_i \partial \eta_i) = -\sigma^{-2} T$.

[20]From (6.7) we have that

$$T \bar{y}_{i(-1)} = \sum_{t=0}^{T-1} y_{it} = \left(\sum_{t=0}^{T-1} \sum_{s=0}^{t-1} \alpha^s \right) \eta_i + \left(\sum_{t=0}^{T-1} \alpha^t \right) y_{i0} + \sum_{t=0}^{T-1} \sum_{s=0}^{t-1} \alpha^s v_{i(t-s)}.$$

The result then follows from taking expectations and adding up the series.

$$E\left(\bar{y}_{i(-1)} \mid y_{i0}, \eta_i\right) = h_T(\alpha)\eta_i + \frac{1}{T}\left(\frac{1-\alpha^T}{1-\alpha}\right)y_{i0} \tag{6.92}$$

where $h_T(\alpha)$ is given in (6.14).

So, following Lancaster (2002), we look for an orthogonal transformation of the effects $\eta_i = \eta(\theta, \lambda_i)$, such that the reparameterized log likelihood

$$\ell_i^*(\theta, \lambda_i) = \ell_i\left(\theta, \eta(\theta, \lambda_i)\right) \tag{6.93}$$

satisfies

$$E\left(\frac{\partial^2 \ell_i^*}{\partial\theta\partial\lambda_i} \mid y_{i0}, \eta_i\right) = 0. \tag{6.94}$$

We wish to examine the fixed T properties of estimates of θ that maximize a pseudo likelihood conditioned on the PMLE of the orthogonalized effects λ_i.

Since we have

$$\frac{\partial\ell_i^*}{\partial\theta} = \frac{\partial\ell_i}{\partial\theta} + \frac{\partial\eta_i}{\partial\theta}\frac{\partial\ell_i}{\partial\eta_i} \tag{6.95}$$

and[21]

$$E\left(\frac{\partial^2 \ell_i^*}{\partial\theta\partial\lambda_i} \mid y_{i0}, \eta_i\right) = \frac{\partial\eta_i}{\partial\lambda_i}E\left(\frac{\partial^2 \ell_i}{\partial\theta\partial\eta_i} \mid y_{i0}, \eta_i\right) + \frac{\partial\eta_i}{\partial\lambda_i}\frac{\partial\eta_i}{\partial\theta}E\left(\frac{\partial^2 \ell_i}{\partial\eta_i\partial\eta_i} \mid y_{i0}, \eta_i\right), \tag{6.96}$$

the function $\eta(\theta, \lambda_i)$ must satisfy the partial differential equations

$$\frac{\partial\eta_i}{\partial\theta} = -E\left(\frac{\partial^2 \ell_i}{\partial\theta\partial\eta_i} \mid y_{i0}, \eta_i\right) \Big/ E\left(\frac{\partial^2 \ell_i}{\partial\eta_i\partial\eta_i} \mid y_{i0}, \eta_i\right), \tag{6.97}$$

or equivalently

$$\frac{\partial\eta_i}{\partial\alpha} = -h_T(\alpha)\eta_i - \frac{1}{T}\left(\frac{1-\alpha^T}{1-\alpha}\right)y_{i0} \tag{6.98}$$

$$\frac{\partial\eta_i}{\partial\sigma^2} = 0. \tag{6.99}$$

Therefore, $\eta(\theta, \lambda_i)$ depends on α but not on σ^2.

Note that because of the invariance of ML estimation, the MLE of λ_i satisfies $\widehat{\eta}_i = \eta(\theta, \widehat{\lambda}_i)$. Therefore, the conditional log density given $\widehat{\lambda}_i$ is related to that given $\widehat{\eta}_i$ by

$$\log f(y_i \mid y_{i0}, \eta_i, \widehat{\lambda}_i) = \log f(y_i \mid y_{i0}, \widehat{\eta}_i) - \log\left|\frac{\partial\eta_i}{\partial\lambda_i}\right|, \tag{6.100}$$

so that $f(y_i \mid y_{i0}, \eta_i, \widehat{\lambda}_i)$ is also independent of η_i. Thus, in order to obtain an approximate conditional likelihood we do not need an explicit expression for $\eta(\theta, \lambda_i)$, but only the log of the Jacobian term $|\partial\eta_i/\partial\lambda_i|$.

[21]Note that there is a term that vanishes: $(\partial^2\eta_i/\partial\theta\partial\lambda_i)E\left(\partial\ell_i/\partial\eta_i \mid y_{i0}, \eta_i\right) = 0$.

Moreover, the conditional scores are given by

$$\frac{\partial \log f(y_i \mid y_{i0}, \widehat{\lambda}_i)}{\partial \alpha} = \frac{\partial \log f(y_i \mid y_{i0}, \widehat{\eta}_i)}{\partial \alpha} - \frac{\partial}{\partial \alpha} \log \left| \frac{\partial \eta_i}{\partial \lambda_i} \right| \qquad (6.101)$$

$$\frac{\partial \log f(y_i \mid y_{i0}, \widehat{\lambda}_i)}{\partial \sigma^2} = \frac{\partial \log f(y_i \mid y_{i0}, \widehat{\eta}_i)}{\partial \sigma^2} \qquad (6.102)$$

or, specifically,

$$\frac{\partial \log f(y_i \mid y_{i0}, \widehat{\lambda}_i)}{\partial \alpha} = \frac{1}{\sigma^2} \left[y'_{i(-1)} Q v_i + \sigma^2 h_T(\alpha) \right] \qquad (6.103)$$

$$\frac{\partial \log f(y_i \mid y_{i0}, \widehat{\lambda}_i)}{\partial \sigma^2} = \frac{1}{2\sigma^4} \left[v'_i Q v_i - (T-1)\sigma^2 \right]. \qquad (6.104)$$

This is so because from (6.98) it turns out that[22]

$$\frac{\partial}{\partial \alpha} \log \left| \frac{\partial \eta_i}{\partial \lambda_i} \right| = -h_T(\alpha). \qquad (6.105)$$

Thus, the conditional PML estimates of α and σ^2 coincide with the GMM estimator based on the following moment conditions

$$E\left(y'_{i(-1)} Q v_i \right) = -\sigma^2 h_T(\alpha) \qquad (6.106)$$

$$E\left(v'_i Q v_i \right) = (T-1)\sigma^2. \qquad (6.107)$$

Condition (6.106) corresponds to the expression for the numerator of the WG bias in (6.13), which was derived under Assumptions *B1* and *B3* only. So the resulting estimates will be consistent and asymptotically normal for fixed T and large N as long as these two moments are satisfied.

An explicit expression for the conditional log likelihood given $\widehat{\lambda}_i$ is

$$\log f(y_i \mid y_{i0}, \widehat{\lambda}_i) \propto -\frac{(T-1)}{2} \log \sigma^2 - \frac{1}{2\sigma^2} v'_i Q v_i + b_T(\alpha) \qquad (6.108)$$

where the log Jacobian is given by

$$b_T(\alpha) = \frac{1}{T} \sum_{t=1}^{T-1} \left(\frac{T-t}{t} \right) \alpha^t. \qquad (6.109)$$

---

[22]To see this, note that from (6.98) we have

$$\frac{\partial^2 \eta_i}{\partial \alpha \partial \lambda_i} = -h_T(\alpha) \frac{\partial \eta_i}{\partial \lambda_i}$$

or equivalently,

$$\frac{\partial^2 \eta_i}{\partial \alpha \partial \lambda_i} \bigg/ \frac{\partial \eta_i}{\partial \lambda_i} = \frac{\partial}{\partial \alpha} \log \left| \frac{\partial \eta_i}{\partial \lambda_i} \right| = -h_T(\alpha).$$

This term is obtained by integrating the function $h_T(\alpha)$, as we have

$$\log \left| \frac{\partial \eta_i}{\partial \lambda_i} \right| = \int_{a_0}^{\alpha} -h_T(s)ds = -b_T(\alpha) + const. \qquad (6.110)$$

where a_0 is some value of α.

The discussion of orthogonalization for the AR model with unrestricted initial conditions is due to Lancaster (2002), who also considered Bayesian inference integrating the orthogonalized effects out with respect to a uniform prior.

Comparison between Conditional and Marginal PML   We can compare marginal PML with conditional PML using the factorization

$$\log f(y_i \mid y_{i0}) = \log f(y_i \mid y_{i0}, \widehat{\lambda}_i) + \log \int f(\widehat{\lambda}_i \mid y_{i0}, \eta_i)dG(\eta_i \mid y_{i0})$$

$$\equiv \log f(y_i \mid y_{i0}, \widehat{\lambda}_i) + \log f(\widehat{\lambda}_i \mid y_{i0}) \qquad (6.111)$$

where the first term on the right-hand side corresponds to (6.108) and the second is

$$f(\widehat{\lambda}_i \mid y_{i0}) = f(\widehat{\eta}_i \mid y_{i0}) \left| \frac{\partial \eta_i}{\partial \lambda_i} \right|. \qquad (6.112)$$

If (y_{i0}, η_i) are jointly normally distributed, $\widehat{\eta}_i \mid y_{i0} \sim \mathcal{N}(\varphi_0 + \varphi_1 y_{i0}, \omega^2)$, so that

$$\log f(\widehat{\lambda}_i \mid y_{i0}) \propto -\frac{1}{2} \log \omega^2 - \frac{1}{2\omega^2} \left(\overline{y}_i - \alpha \overline{y}_{i(-1)} - \varphi_0 - \varphi_1 y_{i0} \right)^2 - b_T(\alpha), \qquad (6.113)$$

in which case the resulting expression for $\log f(y_i \mid y_{i0})$ in (6.111) coincides with (6.76).

Marginal PML is equivalent to a GMM estimator that, in addition to (6.106)-(6.107), uses the moments

$$\frac{1}{\omega^2} E \left[\begin{pmatrix} \overline{y}_{i(-1)} \\ 1 \\ y_{i0} \end{pmatrix} \left(\overline{y}_i - \alpha \overline{y}_{i(-1)} - \varphi_0 - \varphi_1 y_{i0} \right) \right] = \begin{pmatrix} h_T(\alpha) \\ 0 \\ 0 \end{pmatrix} \qquad (6.114)$$

$$\frac{1}{\omega^2} E \left(\overline{y}_i - \alpha \overline{y}_{i(-1)} - \varphi_0 - \varphi_1 y_{i0} \right)^2 = 1. \qquad (6.115)$$

Therefore, the situation is similar to the one discussed for the stationary case. If the (η_i, y_{i0}) are independent draws from some bounded variance distribution, there is additional information about α contained in the marginal likelihood. Nevertheless, this additional information will tend to vanish as the variance of the effects (and hence ω^2) becomes large.

Finally, it is of some interest to compare expression (6.81) for marginal PML with the corresponding expression for conditional PML. Concentrating σ^2 out of the (approximate) conditional likelihood (6.108), the conditional PML estimator of α can be expressed as

$$\widehat{\alpha}_{PML} = \arg\min_{a} \left\{ \log\left[(y^* - ay^*_{(-1)})'(y^* - ay^*_{(-1)})\right] - \frac{2}{(T-1)} b_T(a) \right\}. \quad (6.116)$$

Both (6.81) and (6.116) are modified WG criteria with correction terms of order $(T-1)$. However, whereas marginal PML uses a data-based correction that employs the levels of the data, conditional PML relies exclusively on the Jacobian term $b_T(a)$.

6.4.3 Time Series Heteroskedasticity

In the time series context standard estimators of autoregressive models under the assumption of homoskedasticity remain consistent estimators when the homoskedasticity assumption is false. This is not so, however, in short panels. GMM or PML estimators of α in any of the two previous models will be inconsistent for fixed T as N tends to infinity if the unconditional variances of the errors vary over time.

PML estimators of the conditional mean parameters obtained under the assumption of conditional homoskedasticity, however, are robust to conditional heteroskedasticity in short panels, as long as the restrictions implied by the pseudo likelihood on the unconditional covariance matrix of the data are satisfied. The same will, of course, be true of GMM estimates of the corresponding covariance structures.

Therefore, unless one has a substantive interest in the modelling of conditional variances, robust estimates of α can be obtained in conjunction with the unconditional variances of the errors. Conversely, if one is interested in modelling dispersion in the conditional distributions of $y_{it} \mid y_i^{t-1}, \mu_i$, the use of estimators of (possibly time-varying) unconditional error variances σ_t^2 as estimates of the conditional variances may result in mis-specification.

Time series heteroskedasticity may arise as a result of the presence of aggregate effects in the conditional variance of the process. Thus, time-varying σ's may occur in conjunction with a stationary idiosyncratic process, and even with a stationary aggregate effect. In the latter situation, time series heteroskedasticity would just reflect the fact that in a short panel we condition on the values of the aggregate effects that occur in the sample, and these enter the conditional variance (time effects are discussed in Section 5.2 and later on in this section).

So we also consider a model in which the unconditional variances of the errors are allowed to vary over time in an arbitrary way, hence relaxing Assumption *B3*. In combination with unrestricted initial conditions, this gives rise to a covariance structure characterized by the $(T+4) \times 1$ parameter vector $(c_0, c_1, \sigma_0^2, \sigma_1^2, ..., \sigma_T^2, \alpha)$, and so the number of parameters increases with T.

Controlling for time series heteroskedasticity by means of unrestricted coefficients σ_t^2 is particularly desirable when T is short relative to N. For larger values of T, the homoskedastic model with possibly unrestricted initial conditions becomes more appealing, both because it has a fixed number of parameters (so that it can be expected to perform well under a variety of sample configurations), and because as T increases the homoskedastic PML estimator (6.81) tends to become robust to time series heteroskedasticity (Alvarez and Arellano, 1998).

GMM Estimation   In terms of the moment conditions (6.66a) to (6.68d) the only modification is that (6.67) now becomes a set of unrestricted moments

$$E\left[\left(y_{it} - \alpha y_{i(t-1)} - \eta \right)^2 - \sigma_{ut}^2 \right] = 0 \ (t = 1, ..., T), \qquad (6.117)$$

where $\sigma_{ut}^2 = \sigma_\eta^2 + \sigma_t^2$, so that the only restrictions implied by the model are (6.66a)-(6.66c).

An optimal GMM estimator of α based on the orthogonality conditions (6.66a)-(6.66c) will be asymptotically equivalent to the optimal GMM/MD estimator of α jointly estimated with the remaining parameters in the full parameter vector. This setting is specially convenient when α is the parameter of interest since it can be estimated without having to estimate simultaneously the other parameters in the covariance structure.

Relationship to Linear IV Estimation   The moments (6.25) used by the linear IV estimators of Section 6.3 are the only restrictions implied on the data covariance matrix by a conditional moment specification of the form (6.3). As explained in Section 6.1, the difference with Assumption *B1* is that (6.3) does not rule out correlation between the error v_{it} and the individual effect η_i. Therefore, (6.63) is not valid in this case and all the covariances $c_t = Cov(\eta_i, y_{it})$ should be treated as free parameters. The result is a covariance matrix characterized by a $2(T+1) \times 1$ parameter vector $(c_0, c_1, ..., c_{T-1}, \sigma_0^2, \sigma_1^2, ..., \sigma_T^2, \alpha)$.

When $T = 2$ the models based on *B1* and (6.3) are indistinguishable on the basis of the data covariance matrix, but for $T > 2$ the model based on *B1* satisfies the quadratic restrictions (6.66b) while the model based on (6.3) does not.

6.4.4   Time Effects in Autoregressive Models

Suppose y_{it} can be written as the sum of an aggregate component and an individual-specific component as in (5.18):

$$y_{it} = y_t^a + y_{it}^I. \tag{6.118}$$

If y_{it}^I follows an AR(1) process with individual specific intercepts, using the previous notation we would have

$$y_{it} = \delta_t + \alpha y_{i(t-1)} + \eta_i + v_{it}, \tag{6.119}$$

where

$$\delta_t = y_t^a - \alpha y_{t-1}^a. \tag{6.120}$$

In this model one can set $E(\eta_i) = 0$ without lack of generality, since a non-zero mean would be subsumed in δ_t.

The basic moment equations allowing for time effects, unrestricted initial conditions, and time series heteroskedasticity are given by the following straightforward modification of (6.66a)-(6.66c):[23]

$$E\left[y_i^{t-2}\left(\Delta y_{it} - \alpha \Delta y_{i(t-1)} - \Delta \delta_t\right)\right] = 0 \quad (t = 2, ..., T)$$
$$E\left[\left(\Delta y_{i(t-1)} - \alpha \Delta y_{i(t-2)} - \Delta \delta_{t-1}\right)\left(y_{it} - \alpha y_{i(t-1)} - \delta_t\right)\right] = 0 \quad (t = 3, ..., T)$$
$$E\left(y_{it} - \alpha y_{i(t-1)} - \delta_t\right) = 0 \quad (t = 1, ..., T)$$

These moments can be used to obtain GMM estimates of α and $\delta_1, ..., \delta_T$, and for testing the restrictions implied by the model. The remaining parameters are determined from unrestricted moment equations that are similar to (6.68a)-(6.68d) and (6.117), except for the addition of time-varying intercepts.

Time-varying Autoregressive Linear Projections A more general nonstationary specification for autoregressive equations was considered by Holtz-Eakin, Newey, and Rosen (1988). Their framework was originally motivated by the problem of testing for Granger non-causality conditional on an individual effect (Chamberlain, 1984).

Holtz-Eakin et al. considered period-by-period linear projections of a variable on its own lags, lags of other variables, and an individual effect. No restrictions were placed except for the assumption that projections on the entire past were only a function of a fixed number of lags. To test for Granger non-causality one would then test for the joint significance of the lags of other variables. Clearly, the use of nonstationary projections works against the possibility of a spurious finding of failure of Granger non-causality, but at the expense of potential loss of power.

A scalar first-order version of this model is given by

$$y_{it} = \gamma_t + \alpha_t y_{i(t-1)} + \delta_t \eta_i + v_{it}. \tag{6.122}$$

Since the coefficient of η_i is period-specific, this model contains an interaction of time and individual effects similar to the single-factor model (5.30) discussed in Section 5.2.

---

[23] Further discussion on models with time effects is contained in Crepon, Kramarz, and Trognon (1997).

Letting $\pi_t = \delta_t/\delta_{t-1}$, individual effects can be eliminated by taking the following quasi-differences

$$y_{it} - \pi_t y_{i(t-1)} = c_t + \alpha_t y_{i(t-1)} - \pi_t \alpha_{t-1} y_{i(t-2)} + \left(v_{it} - \pi_t v_{i(t-1)}\right) \quad (6.123)$$

where $c_t = \gamma_t - \pi_t \gamma_{t-1}$.

Thus, the model implies the following orthogonality conditions

$$E\left\{ \begin{pmatrix} 1 \\ y_i^{t-2} \end{pmatrix} \left[y_{it} - c_t - (\alpha_t + \pi_t)\, y_{i(t-1)} + \pi_t \alpha_{t-1} y_{i(t-2)} \right] \right\} = 0 \;\; (t = 3, ..., T)$$

$$(6.124)$$

which satisfy the order condition for identification of the parameters $c_3, ..., c_T$, $\alpha_2, ..., \alpha_T$, and $\pi_3, ..., \pi_T$ as long as $T \geq 4$.

6.5 Mean Stationarity

We have seen that assumptions about initial conditions present a trade-off between robustness and efficiency in the context of short panels. The trade-off is particularly acute for autoregressive models with roots close to the unit circle, since in such a case the IV moment conditions (6.25) may be very weak.

Here we discuss a model that enforces mean stationarity but leaves the initial and subsequent variances unrestricted. That is, we assume that Assumptions *B1* and *B4* hold but not necessarily *B2*, *B3*, or *B5*. So that we have

$$E(y_{it} \mid \mu_i) = \mu_i \;\; (t = 0, 1, ..., T)$$

This implies that $\delta_0 = 0$ and $\delta = 1$ in the model with unrestricted initial conditions and time series heteroskedasticity of the previous section.

As an example, suppose there are a variety of workers indexed by μ_i. The life-cycle earnings of each type follow a stable process (around some common trend) with steady state mean earnings given by μ_i. Our mean stationarity assumption does not refer to the (possibly unobservable) start of an individual's process, but to the first observations in the actual sample. Therefore, in a sample of mature workers it could be reasonable to assume stationary initial conditions, regardless of the nature of the distribution of earnings of the workers at the outset of their working lives. However, if there are young workers in the data, the assumption of mean stationarity requires that, on average, workers of a given type do not do systematically better or worse at the beginning of their careers relative to their steady state earnings.

Under mean stationarity the covariance between y_{it} and μ_i does not depend on t, so that $c_0 = c_1 = ... = c_T = (1 - \alpha)\sigma_\mu^2$, and Δy_{it} is uncorrelated with μ_i. In view of the discussion in the previous section, the implication is that for this model both sets of IV conditions (6.41a) and (6.41b) for errors in differences and levels, respectively, are valid. Adding the mean conditions (6.41c), the full list of restrictions implied by mean stationarity on the data first and second moments is:[24]

$$E\left[y_i^{t-2}\left(\Delta y_{it} - \alpha \Delta y_{i(t-1)}\right)\right] = 0 \ (t = 2, ..., T) \qquad (6.125)$$

$$E\left[\Delta y_{i(t-1)}\left(y_{it} - \alpha y_{i(t-1)} - \eta\right)\right] = 0 \ (t = 2, ..., T) \qquad (6.126)$$

$$E\left(y_{it} - \alpha y_{i(t-1)} - \eta\right) = 0 \ (t = 1, ..., T) \qquad (6.127)$$

$$E\left(y_{i0} - \mu\right) = 0. \qquad (6.128)$$

Note that (6.125)-(6.127) require that $\delta = 1$, but still hold if $\delta_0 \neq 0$, in which case (6.128) would become an unrestricted moment. So we may consider a slight generalization that allows for "aggregate nonstationarity in mean":

$$E\left(y_{i0} \mid \mu_i\right) = \delta_0 + \mu_i, \qquad (6.129)$$

while relying on the moments (6.125)-(6.127). Permitting $\delta_0 \neq 0$ could be useful in a case where the discrepancy between the distribution of initial observations and the steady state distribution is due to a major event that influenced all units in a similar way.

So full covariance-information linear estimation of α is possible for this model using a GMM estimator that combines instruments in levels for equations in differences with instruments in differences for equations in levels. This estimator and the corresponding moments were proposed by Arellano and Bover (1995), and have been further discussed by Ahn and Schmidt (1995) and Blundell and Bond (1998).

Levels & Differences GMM Linear Estimators Moments (6.125)-(6.127) can be written in compact form as

$$E\left(\begin{array}{c} Z_i' D u_i \\ Z_{\ell i}' u_i \end{array}\right) \equiv E\left(Z_i^{\dagger\prime} \mathcal{H} u_i\right) = 0 \qquad (6.130)$$

where $u_i = y_i - \alpha y_{i(-1)}$, Z_i is the matrix of instruments given in (6.29) for equations in differences, $Z_{\ell i}$ is the matrix of instruments for equations in levels that takes the form

$$Z_{\ell i} = \begin{pmatrix} 1 & 0 & 0 & 0 & 0 & \cdots & 0 & 0 \\ 0 & 1 & \Delta y_{i1} & 0 & 0 & & 0 & 0 \\ 0 & 0 & 0 & 1 & \Delta y_{i2} & & 0 & 0 \\ \vdots & \vdots & & & & \ddots & & \vdots \\ 0 & 0 & 0 & 0 & 0 & \cdots & 1 & \Delta y_{i(T-1)} \end{pmatrix}, \qquad (6.131)$$

[24]Mean stationarity also implies

$$E\left[\Delta y_{i(t-j)}\left(y_{it} - \alpha y_{i(t-1)}\right)\right] = 0 \ (t = 2, ..., T; j = 2, ..., t-1),$$

but these moments are redundant given (6.125) and (6.126) since they are linear combinations of them.

$\overline{\mathcal{H}}$ is the $(2T-1) \times T$ selection matrix $\overline{\mathcal{H}} = (D', I_T)'$, where D is the $(T-1) \times T$ first-difference matrix operator, and $Z_i^{\dagger}$ is a block diagonal matrix with blocks Z_i and $Z_{\ell i}$. We can think of the model as specifying different instruments for a system of $T-1$ equations in first-differences followed by T equations in levels. Letting $X_i = (y_{i(-1)}, \iota)$, a GMM estimator of α and η will be of the form:

$$\begin{pmatrix} \widehat{\alpha}_S \\ \widehat{\eta}_S \end{pmatrix} = \left[\left(\sum_{i=1}^{N} X_i' \overline{\mathcal{H}}' Z_i^{\dagger} \right) A_N \left(\sum_{i=1}^{N} Z_i^{\dagger\prime} \overline{\mathcal{H}} X_i \right) \right]^{-1}$$
$$\left(\sum_{i=1}^{N} X_i' \overline{\mathcal{H}}' Z_i^{\dagger} \right) A_N \left(\sum_{i=1}^{N} Z_i^{\dagger\prime} \overline{\mathcal{H}} y_i \right). \qquad (6.132)$$

An optimal two-step choice for A_N can be obtained from the inverse of a consistent estimate of the moment covariance matrix $E \left(Z_i^{\dagger\prime} \overline{\mathcal{H}} u_i u_i' \overline{\mathcal{H}}' Z_i^{\dagger} \right)$. However, unlike in the case of the IV estimators in differences (6.28), this matrix depends on unknown parameters even under conditional homoskedasticity (i.e. it is not just a function of data moments up to a multiplicative constant). The intuition is that since some of the instruments for the equations in levels are not valid for those in differences, and conversely, not all the covariance terms between the two sets of moments will be zero. As a result, when combining levels and differences no one-step GMM estimator is available that achieves asymptotic efficiency under "classical" auxiliary assumptions about the errors.[25]

Interpreting Initial Condition Bias in Short Panels   The initial condition bias is the result of assuming that the initial observations follow the steady state unconditional distribution of the process when the assumption is false. Given the simplicity of the moment conditions (6.126) it is convenient to focus on mean stationarity. We examine the asymptotic bias of a simple IV estimator based on (6.126) when $\delta \neq 1$ and $T = 2$. We have

$$Cov\left(\Delta y_{i1}, y_{i2} - \alpha y_{i1}\right) = Cov\left(\Delta y_{i1}, \eta_i + v_{i2}\right) = Cov\left(\Delta y_{i1}, \eta_i\right) = (1 - \delta)\sigma_{\eta}^2. \qquad (6.133)$$

Thus

$$\frac{Cov\left(y_{i2}, \Delta y_{i1}\right)}{Cov\left(y_{i1}, \Delta y_{i1}\right)} = \alpha + (1 - \delta)\frac{\sigma_{\eta}^2}{Cov\left(y_{i1}, \Delta y_{i1}\right)} \equiv \alpha + b. \qquad (6.134)$$

Since (6.125) and (6.127) remain valid under nonstationarity, (6.126) will be the only source of bias. Therefore, the asymptotic bias of an estimator based on all the moments available will be of the same sign as (6.134) but of a

---

[25] An arbitrary but convenient choice of one-step weight matrix is given by the inverse of $N^{-1} \sum_{i=1}^{N} Z_i^{\dagger\prime} \overline{\mathcal{H}} \overline{\mathcal{H}}' Z_i^{\dagger}$.

smaller magnitude. The bias can take either sign, but inspection of the formula suggests that if there is a bias it will tend to be positive when analysing short panels of households or companies.

The expression for the denominator of the bias term is

$$Cov\,(y_{i1}, \Delta y_{i1}) = (1-\delta)\,[1 - \alpha(1-\delta)]\,(1-\alpha)\sigma_\mu^2 + [\sigma_1^2 - (1-\alpha)\alpha\sigma_0^2]. \quad (6.135)$$

Under full stationarity (i.e. $\delta = 1$ and $\sigma_0^2 = \sigma_1^2/(1-\alpha^2)$), $Cov\,(y_{i1}, \Delta y_{i1}) = \sigma_1^2/(1+\alpha)$ so that it is always positive. More generally, it will remain positive provided $0 \leq \delta < 1$ and $\sigma_1^2 - (1-\alpha)\alpha\sigma_0^2 \geq 0$, in which case the bias will also be positive. If $\delta > 1$ the sign of the bias will depend on the relative magnitudes of the variances of the individual effects and the random errors.

If y_{i0} is fixed ($\delta = \sigma_0^2 = 0$) the bias is always positive and given by

$$b = \frac{\sigma_\eta^2}{\sigma_\eta^2 + \sigma_1^2}. \quad (6.136)$$

Finally, if y_{i0} and μ_i are perfectly correlated (i.e. $y_{i0} = \delta_0 + \delta\mu_i$), so that $\sigma_0^2 = 0$ and $\delta = \sigma_{y0}/\sigma_\mu$, where σ_{y0} denotes the standard deviation of y_{i0}, the bias will be positive whenever $\sigma_{y0} \leq \sigma_\mu$. That is, provided there is no more dispersion in initial conditions than in the distribution of steady state levels of the process ("σ-divergence" in the context of the empirical growth literature). The bias may still be positive under σ-convergence, but the sign will depend on the relative magnitudes of the parameters.

Mean Stationarity Conditional on Time Effects If y_{it} consists of an additive aggregate shock y_t^a plus a mean stationary AR(1) idiosyncratic component y_{it}^I, the mean stationarity condition for the observed data becomes

$$E(y_{it}|\eta_i) = \mu_t. \quad (6.137)$$

That is, we assume mean stationarity conditional upon an aggregate effect (which might be stationary or nonstationary).

The orthogonality conditions in (6.125)-(6.127) remain valid in this case with the addition of a time-varying intercept:

$$E\left[y_i^{t-2}\left(\Delta y_{it} - \alpha\Delta y_{i(t-1)} - \Delta\delta_t\right)\right] = 0 \;\; (t = 2, ..., T) \quad (6.138)$$

$$E\left[\Delta y_{i(t-1)}\left(y_{it} - \alpha y_{i(t-1)} - \delta_t\right)\right] = 0 \;\; (t = 2, ..., T) \quad (6.139)$$

$$E\left(y_{it} - \alpha y_{i(t-1)} - \delta_t\right) = 0 \;\; (t = 1, ..., T). \quad (6.140)$$

6.6   Unit Roots

So far we have considered stable models (with autoregressive roots inside the unit circle) or models in which a unit root is a feature of the specification, like the integrated moving average process used by Hall and Mishkin (1982) to model household income (see Section 5.5). In Hall and Mishkin's example the random walk component is the device used to model permanent income shocks. In such a context the empirical interest is in measuring how large the random walk component is relative to the stationary component, rather than testing for its presence.

Sometimes the presence or absence of unit roots is a central feature of the economic model of interest so that unit root testing is not warranted. Unit roots are not properties of the data, but properties of models that may or may not be of interest depending on the objectives of the research. In this section, however, we take for granted an interest in testing the unit root hypothesis, and examine the nature of the problem in short panels with unobserved heterogeneity.

First of all, the null and alternative hypotheses need to be specified. We begin by considering, as the alternative hypothesis, the stable AR model with unrestricted initial conditions and time series heteroskedasticity. As for the specification of the null, we consider a random walk without drift. The model is

$$y_{i0} = \delta_0 + \delta\mu_i + v_{i0} \tag{6.141a}$$

$$y_{it} = \alpha y_{i(t-1)} + (1-\alpha)\mu_i + v_{it}. \tag{6.141b}$$

Thus, when $\alpha = 1$ we have

$$y_{it} = y_{i(t-1)} + v_{it}, \tag{6.142}$$

so that heterogeneity only plays a role in the determination of the starting point of the process. The implication is that when $\alpha = 1$ only the variance of y_{i0} is identified in the covariance matrix of (y_{i0}, μ_i).

An alternative specification of the null would be a random walk with an individual-specific drift

$$y_{it} = y_{i(t-1)} + \eta_i + v_{it}, \tag{6.143}$$

but this is a model with heterogeneous linear growth that would be more suited for comparisons with stationary models including individual trends.

Under the null $H_0 : \alpha = 1$, pooled OLS in levels is a consistent and asymptotically normal estimator of α in (6.142) for fixed T and large N.[26] Therefore, a standard t-ratio statistic can be used to perform a fixed-T-large-N one-sided test of the unit root hypothesis against the alternative of a stable process.[27] Nevertheless, given the upward bias of OLS in levels under the alternative,

---

[26] Harris and Tzavalis (1999) obtained the fixed-T-large-N limiting distributions of pooled OLS, WG, and WG with individual trends, under the null of a unit root and normally distributed errors.

[27] The OLS t-ratio will only have an asymptotic normal distribution as $N \to \infty$ for fixed T. For large T the distribution will be nonstandard. See Phillips and Moon (2000) for a survey and references on unit root asymptotic results for panels with large T and N.

such a test may have little power to reject the null when the variance of μ_i is large. To illustrate the situation, recall that under stationarity the first-order autocorrelation can be written as (equation (5.16))

$$\rho_1 = \alpha + \frac{(1-\alpha)\lambda}{(1+\lambda)} \tag{6.144}$$

where $\lambda = \sigma_\mu^2/\sigma_0^2$. Therefore, for any value of α, ρ_1 can be made arbitrarily close to one for sufficiently large λ, and as a consequence indistinguishable from a unit root in a finite sample.

The IV Estimator with Unit Roots and Highly Persistent Data
When $\alpha = 1$ the rank condition of the IV moments (6.25) for errors in first-differences fails. Basically, the variables in y_i^{t-2} are uncorrelated with $\Delta y_{i(t-1)}$ when $\alpha = 1$ since in that case $\Delta y_{i(t-1)}$ is the innovation in period $(t-1)$. That is, for $j \geq 2$ we have

$$
\begin{aligned}
Cov(y_{i(t-j)}, \Delta y_{i(t-1)}) &= -(1-\alpha)\left[Cov(y_{i(t-j)}, y_{i(t-2)}) - Cov(y_{i(t-j)}, \mu_i)\right] \\
Cov(y_{i(t-j)}, \Delta y_{it}) &= \alpha Cov(y_{i(t-j)}, \Delta y_{i(t-1)}).
\end{aligned}
$$

Hence, when $\alpha = 1$, the IV moments (6.25) are not only satisfied for the true value of α, but also for any other value. The implication is that GMM estimators of α based on (6.25) are inconsistent when $\alpha = 1$.[28]

Given this situation it is of some interest to examine the identification content of the orthogonality conditions (6.25) with highly persistent data. This can be done by calculating the asymptotic variance of the optimal GMM estimator based on these moment conditions. Here we reproduce the calculations reported by Arellano and Honoré (2001) under stationarity. The idea is to see how the information about α in (6.25) changes as T and α change for values of ρ_1 close to one.

The lower bound on the asymptotic variance of a GMM estimator of α based on (6.25) when the process generating the data is the fully stationary model is given by

$$\sigma_T^2 = \frac{\sigma^2}{E\left(\Delta y_{i(-1)}' Z_i\right)\left[E(Z_i' DD' Z_i)\right]^{-1} E\left(Z_i' \Delta y_{i(-1)}\right)}. \tag{6.145}$$

According to (6.144), for any $0 \leq \alpha \leq \rho_1$ there is a value of λ—or equivalently of $\phi = \sigma_\eta/\sigma$—such that ρ_1 equals a pre-specified value.[29] Thus, Table 6.2 contains the values of σ_T for various values of T and for different pairs (α, ϕ) such that $\rho_1 = 0.99$. Also, the bottom row shows the time series asymptotic standard deviation, evaluated at $T = 14$, for comparisons.

[28]Tests of underidentification in autoregressive models with individual effects are discussed by Arellano, Hansen, and Sentana (1999).

[29]Under stationarity the relation between the two ratios is $\phi^2 = \lambda(1-\alpha)/(1+\alpha)$.

Table 6.2
Asymptotic Standard Deviation Bound for α (σ_T)
$\rho_1 = 0.99$

α	0	0.2	0.5	0.8	0.9	0.99
ϕ	9.9	7.2	4.0	1.4	0.7	0
$T = 2$	14.14	15.50	17.32	18.97	19.49	19.95
$T = 3$	1.97	2.66	4.45	8.14	9.50	10.00
$T = 4$	1.21	1.55	2.43	4.71	5.88	6.34
$T = 9$	0.50	0.57	0.71	1.18	1.61	1.85
$T = 14$	0.35	0.38	0.44	0.61	0.82	0.96
$\left(\frac{1-\alpha^2}{14}\right)^{1/2}$	0.27	0.26	0.23	0.17	0.11	0.04

Table 6.2 shows that with $\rho_1 = 0.99$ there is a very large difference in information between $T = 2$ and $T > 2$. So $T = 2$ seems to be a very special case. Moreover, for given T there is less information on α the closer α is to ρ_1. Often, there will be little information on α with $T = 2$ and the usual values of N. Additional information may be acquired from using some of the additional restrictions discussed above. Particularly large gains can be obtained from employing mean stationarity assumptions, as suggested from the Monte Carlo simulations reported by Arellano and Bover (1995) and Blundell and Bond (1998), and the information bound calculations by Hahn (1999).

Mean Stationarity and Unit Roots   Let us now consider a model that specifies mean stationarity when $|\alpha| < 1$ and a random walk without drift when $\alpha = 1$. This is model (6.141a)-(6.141b) with the restriction $\delta = 1$, which gives rise to

$$y_{it} = \mu_i + v_{it} + \alpha v_{i(t-1)} + \ldots + \alpha^{t-1} v_{i1} + \alpha^t v_{i0}. \qquad (6.146)$$

In this model σ_μ^2 and σ_0^2 are not separately identified when $\alpha = 1$, but the rank condition from moments (6.125)-(6.126) is satisfied. As noted by Arellano and Bover (1995), the reason is that when $\alpha = 1$ we have

$$Cov\left(\Delta y_{i(t-1)}, y_{i(t-1)}\right) = \sigma_t^2 \qquad (6.147)$$

which will be non-zero as long as $\sigma_t^2 > 0$. So the IV moments for the errors in levels (6.126) ensure the determination of α when α equals one. The implication is that GMM estimators of the mean stationary model remain consistent when $\alpha = 1$, and can be used to perform a test of the unit root hypothesis against the mean stationary alternative.

6.7   Estimating and Testing VARs for Firm Employment and Wages

In this section we discuss various aspects of inference with autoregressive models in the context of an empirical illustration. We consider autoregressive employment and wage equations estimated from the panel of firms used by Alonso-Borrego and Arellano (1999). This is a balanced panel of 738 Spanish manufacturing companies, for which there are available annual observations for the period 1983–1990. We consider various specializations of a bivariate VAR(2) model for the logs of employment and wages, denoted n_{it} and w_{it} respectively. Individual and time effects are included in both equations. The form of the model is

$$n_{it} = \delta_{1t} + \alpha_1 n_{i(t-1)} + \alpha_2 n_{i(t-2)} + \beta_1 w_{i(t-1)} + \beta_2 w_{i(t-2)} + \eta_{1i} + v_{1it} \quad (6.148)$$

$$w_{it} = \delta_{2t} + \gamma_1 w_{i(t-1)} + \gamma_2 w_{i(t-2)} + \lambda_1 n_{i(t-1)} + \lambda_2 n_{i(t-2)} + \eta_{2i} + v_{2it}. \quad (6.149)$$

Univariate AR Estimates for Employment   We begin by obtaining alternative estimates of a univariate AR(1) model for employment (setting $\alpha_2 = \beta_1 = \beta_2 = 0$).[30]   Table 6.3 compares OLS estimates in levels, first-differences, and within-groups with those obtained by GMM using as instruments for the equation in first-differences all lags of employment up to $t-2$. The results are broadly consistent with what would be expected for an AR data generation process with unobserved heterogeneity, in light of our previous discussion of biases. Taking GMM estimates as a benchmark, OLS in levels is biased upwards, and WG and OLS in differences are biased downwards, with a much larger bias in the latter.

The one- and two-step GMM estimates in the 4-th and 5-th columns, respectively, are based on the sample moments $b_N(\beta) = (b'_{3N}, ..., b'_{8N})'$, where β is the 7×1 parameter vector $\beta = (\alpha, \Delta\delta_3, ..., \Delta\delta_8)'$ and

$$b_{tN} = \frac{1}{738} \sum_{i=1}^{738} \begin{pmatrix} 1 \\ n_i^{t-2} \end{pmatrix} (\Delta n_{it} - \Delta\delta_t - \alpha\Delta n_{i(t-1)}) \quad (t = 3, ..., 8). \quad (6.150)$$

$b_N(\beta)$ contains 27 orthogonality conditions in total, so that there are 20 over identifying restrictions. These are tested with the Sargan statistic. There is a contrast between the value of the one-step Sargan statistic (35.1), which is too high for a chi-square with 20 degrees of freedom, and the robust two-step statistic which is much smaller (15.5). This should not be taken as evidence against the overidentifying restrictions, but as an indication of the presence of conditional heteroskedasticity (the one-step Sargan statistic would not be distributed as a χ^2 in large samples when the errors are conditionally heteroskedastic even if the overidentifying restrictions hold).

Column 6 in Table 6.3 reports two-step GMM estimates of an AR(2) model. Since one cross-section is spent in constructing the second lag, the two orthogonality conditions in b_{3N} are lost, so we are left with 25 moments. There

---

[30] All the estimates reported in this section were calculated using DPD (Arellano and Bond, 1988).

is a second autoregressive coefficient but $\Delta\delta_3$ is lost, so the total number of parameters is unchanged.

Finally, the last column in Table 6.3 presents continuously updated GMM estimates of the AR(2) model (cf. Hansen, Heaton, and Yaron, 1996). They use the same moments as GMM2, but the weight matrix is continuously updated (as opposed to GMM2 which evaluates it once for all at one-step estimates).[31] The two estimators are asymptotically equivalent, but in finite samples CU-GMM has been found to have less bias and a higher probability of outliers than GMM2. Indeed Alonso-Borrego and Arellano (1999) simulated data as close as possible to the AR(2) employment equation and found evidence that GMM2 was somewhat downward biased in this setting (with a true value of $\alpha_1 = .813$ the median of GMM2 estimates over 1000 replications was .72).

Table 6.3
Univariate AR Estimates for Employment

	OLS-levels	OLS-dif.	WG	GMM1	GMM2	GMM2	CU GMM2
$n_{i(t-1)}$	0.992	0.054	0.69	0.86	0.89	0.75	0.83
	(0.001)	(0.026)	(0.025)	(0.07)	(0.06)	(0.09)	(0.09)
$n_{i(t-2)}$						0.04	0.03
						(0.02)	(0.02)
Sargan	—	—	—	35.1	15.5	14.4	13.0
(d.f.)				(20)	(20)	(18)	(18)
m_1	2.3	−0.6	−9.0	−8.0	−7.6	−6.0	
m_2	2.2	2.3	0.6	0.5	0.5	0.3	

$N = 738$, $T = 8$, $1983 - 1990$. Heteroskedasticity robust standard errors in parentheses. Time dummies included in all equations.

From the orthogonality conditions above only first-differences of time effects are directly estimated. The initial time effect can be estimated as

$$\widehat{\delta}_3 = \frac{1}{738} \sum_{i=1}^{738} (y_{i3} - \widehat{\alpha}_1 y_{i2} - \widehat{\alpha}_2 y_{i1}) \qquad (6.151)$$

[31]Thus, whereas GMM2 solves

$$\widehat{\beta}_{GMM2} = \arg\min_{\beta} b_N(\beta)' \left[V(\widehat{\beta}_{GMM1}) \right]^{-1} b_N(\beta),$$

for continuously updated GMM we have

$$\widehat{\beta}_{CU-GMM} = \arg\min_{\beta} b_N(\beta)' [V(\beta)]^{-1} b_N(\beta).$$

Note that, unlike GMM2, CU-GMM solves a nonlinear optimization problem even if the moment conditions $b_N(\beta)$ are linear in β.

and, given estimates of their changes, the rest can be estimated recursively from $\widehat{\delta}_t = \widehat{\Delta\delta}_t + \widehat{\delta}_{t-1}$ ($t = 4, ..., 8$). Given the large cross-sectional sample size, the realizations of the time effects in the data can be accurately estimated, but with only 6 time series observations we do not have enough information to consider a stochastic model for δ_t. On the other hand, individual effects can be estimated as

$$\widehat{\eta}_i = \frac{1}{T-2} \sum_{s=3}^{T} \widehat{u}_{is} \tag{6.152}$$

where $\widehat{u}_{is} = y_{is} - \widehat{\delta}_s - \widehat{\alpha}_1 y_{i(s-1)} - \widehat{\alpha}_2 y_{i(s-2)}$. Here the situation is the reverse. Since the $\widehat{\eta}_i$ are averages of just $T - 2 = 6$ observations, they will typically be very noisy estimates of realizations of the effects for particular firms. However, the variance of η_i can still be consistently estimated for large N. Optimal estimation of σ_η^2 and the σ_t^2 requires consideration of the data covariance structure, but noting that the errors in levels $u_{it} \equiv \eta_i + v_{it}$ satisfy $Var(u_{it}) = \sigma_\eta^2 + \sigma_t^2$ and $Cov(u_{it}, u_{is}) = \sigma_\eta^2$, simple consistent estimates can be obtained as:

$$\widehat{\sigma}_\eta^2 = \frac{2}{T(T-1)} \sum_{t=2}^{T} \sum_{s=1}^{t-1} \widehat{Cov}\left(\widehat{u}_{it}, \widehat{u}_{is}\right) \tag{6.153}$$

$$\widehat{\sigma}_t^2 = \widehat{Var}(\widehat{u}_{it}) - \widehat{\sigma}_\eta^2, \tag{6.154}$$

where $\widehat{Var}$ and $\widehat{Cov}$ denote cross-sectional sample variances and covariances. For the AR(2) employment equation Alonso-Borrego and Arellano reported $\widehat{\sigma}_\eta^2 = .038$ and $T^{-1} \sum_{t=1}^{T} \widehat{\sigma}_t^2 = .01$. Thus, variation in firm-specific intercepts was approximately 4 times larger than the average random error variance.

In this example time dummies are important for the model to be accepted by the data. Without time dummies, GMM2 estimates of the AR(2) employment equation in first-differences yielded a Sargan statistic of 59.0 ($d.f. = 18$) without constant, and of 62.7 ($d.f. = 18$) with constant (i.e. a linear trend in levels).[32] Thus, implying a sound rejection of the overidentifying restrictions. For the firms in our data set, average growth of employment during the seven-year period 1984–90 is 1 per cent, but this is the result of almost no growth in the first two years, 1 per cent growth in 1986, 2 per cent in 1987–89 and zero or negative growth in 1990. Given such a pattern, it is not surprising that we reject the restrictions imposed by the cross-sectional orthogonality conditions with a common intercept or a linear trend.

Bivariate VAR Estimates for Employment and Wages For the rest of the section we focus on the bivariate model (6.148)-(6.149) since it allows us to illustrate a richer class of problems. Table 6.4 presents OLS in levels and

---

[32]The corresponding parameter estimates were $\widehat{\alpha}_1 = .82$ (.07) and $\widehat{\alpha}_2 = .05$ (.07) in the model without constant, and $\widehat{\alpha}_1 = .53$ (.09) and $\widehat{\alpha}_2 = .06$ (.02) in the model with constant.

GMM2 in differences for employment (columns 1 and 2), and wages (columns 4 and 5). The table also contains GMM estimates that combine levels and differences, but these will be discussed below in conjunction with testing for mean stationarity.

Table 6.4
VAR Estimates

	Employment			Wages		
	OLS-levels	GMM2 dif.	GMM2 lev.&dif.	OLS-levels	GMM2 dif.	GMM2 lev.&dif.
$n_{i(t-1)}$	1.11	0.84	1.17	0.08	−0.04	0.08
	(0.03)	(0.09)	(0.03)	(0.03)	(0.10)	(0.03)
$n_{i(t-2)}$	−0.12	−0.003	−0.13	−0.07	0.05	−0.06
	(0.03)	(0.03)	(0.02)	(0.03)	(0.03)	(0.02)
$w_{i(t-1)}$	0.14	0.08	0.13	0.78	0.26	0.78
	(0.03)	(0.08)	(0.02)	(0.03)	(0.11)	(0.02)
$w_{i(t-2)}$	−0.11	−0.05	−0.11	0.18	0.02	0.08
	(0.03)	(0.02)	(0.02)	(0.03)	(0.02)	(0.02)
$\chi^2_{ce}(2)$	41.7	7.2	43.7	26.1	3.3	10.4
p-value	0.00	0.03	0.00	0.00	0.19	0.006
Sargan	–	36.9	61.2	–	21.4	64.2
(d.f.)		(36)	(48)		(36)	(48)
p-value		0.43	0.096		0.97	0.06
m_1	−0.6	−6.8	−8.0	0.05	−5.7	−9.5
m_2	1.6	0.2	1.3	−2.7	0.5	−0.6

$N = 738$, $T = 8$, 1983–1990. Heteroskedasticity robust standard errors in parentheses. Time dummies included in all equations.
$\chi^2_{ce}(2)$ is a Wald test statistic of the joint significance of cross-effects.

In line with the univariate results for employment, the OLS estimates in levels for both equations are markedly different to GMM2 in differences, and imply a substantially higher degree of persistence, which is consistent with the presence of heterogeneous intercepts (a test of unobserved heterogeneity is discussed below). The GMM estimates use as instruments for the equations in first-differences all the available lags of employment and wages up to $t-2$. With $T = 8$, a second-order VAR and time dummies, there are 36 overidentifying restrictions for each equation. As can be seen in Table 6.4, neither of the Sargan test statistics provide evidence against these restrictions.

Although not pursued here, it may be possible to improve the efficiency by jointly estimating the two equations. Optimal joint GMM estimates would use a weight matrix that takes into account the correlation between the moment conditions of the employment and wage equations.

Testing for Residual Serial Correlation If the errors in levels are serially independent, those in first-differences will exhibit first- but not second-order serial correlation. Moreover, the first-order serial correlation coefficient should be equal to -0.5. In this regard, an informal but often useful diagnostic is provided by the inspection of the autocorrelation matrix for the errors in first-differences. Serial correlation matrices for employment and wages based on GMM residuals in first-differences are shown in Table 6.5, broadly conforming to the expected pattern.

Table 6.5

(a) GMM1 (dif.) Residual Serial Correlation Matrix for Employment

$$
\begin{pmatrix}
1. & & & & \\
-.53 & 1. & & & \\
.10 & -.49 & 1. & & \\
-.04 & -.015 & -.46 & 1. & \\
-.015 & .04 & -.08 & -.44 & 1.
\end{pmatrix}
$$

(b) GMM1 (dif.) Residual Serial Correlation Matrix for Wages

$$
\begin{pmatrix}
1. & & & & \\
-.51 & 1. & & & \\
.03 & -.33 & 1. & & \\
.004 & -.035 & -.42 & 1. & \\
.009 & .00 & -.03 & -.39 & 1.
\end{pmatrix}
$$

Formal tests of serial correlation are provided by the m_1 and m_2 statistics reported in Table 6.4 for the VAR model (and also in Table 6.3 for the univariate results). They are asymptotically distributed as $\mathcal{N}(0,1)$ under the null of no autocorrelation, and have been calculated from residuals in first-differences (except for OLS in levels). So if the errors in levels were uncorrelated, we would expect $m1$ to be significant, but not $m2$, as is the case for the GMM2-dif. estimates for both the employment and wage equations.

The m_j statistics were proposed by Arellano and Bond (1991) and they are moment tests of significance of the average j-th order autocovariance r_j:

$$
r_j = \frac{1}{T-3-j} \sum_{t=4+j}^{T} r_{tj} \tag{6.155}
$$

where $r_{tj} = E\left(\Delta v_{it}\Delta v_{i(t-j)}\right)$. Their null is therefore $H_0 : r_j = 0$ and they are given by

$$
m_j = \frac{\widehat{r}_j}{SE(\widehat{r}_j)} \tag{6.156}
$$

where $\widehat{r}_j$ is the sample counterpart of r_j based on first-difference residuals $\widehat{\Delta v}_{it}$ and $\widehat{r}_{tj} = N^{-1} \sum_{i=1}^{N} \widehat{\Delta v}_{it} \widehat{\Delta v}_{i(t-j)}$.[33]

To obtain an explicit expression for the standard error $SE(\widehat{r}_j)$ used in Table 6.4, we need to introduce some notation. Let us write down the relation between residuals and true errors as $\widehat{\Delta v}_{it} = \Delta v_{it} - \Delta x'_{it}(\widehat{\beta} - \beta)$, where Δx_{it} and $\widehat{\beta} - \beta$ denote the vectors of right-hand-side variables and parameter estimation errors, respectively. Moreover, the latter can be written as $\widehat{\beta} - \beta = P'_N N^{-1} \sum_{i=1}^{N} Z'_i \Delta v_i$. Using this notation the estimated residual autocovariance can be written as:[34]

$$\sqrt{N}\widehat{r}_j = \begin{pmatrix} 1 & -g'_N P'_N \end{pmatrix} \frac{1}{N^{1/2}} \sum_{i=1}^{N} \begin{pmatrix} \varsigma_{ji} \\ Z'_i \Delta v_i \end{pmatrix} + o_p(1) \tag{6.157}$$

where

$$\varsigma_{ji} = \frac{1}{(T-3-j)} \sum_{t=4+j}^{T} \Delta v_{it} \Delta v_{i(t-j)}$$

and

$$g'_N = \frac{1}{N(T-3-j)} \sum_{i=1}^{N} \sum_{t=4+j}^{T} \left(\Delta v_{it} \Delta x'_{i(t-j)} + \Delta v_{i(t-j)} \Delta x'_{it} \right).$$

Thus, under $r_j = 0$, from a standard large-N central limit theorem we may conclude that $\widehat{Var}(\widehat{r}_j)^{-1/2}\sqrt{N}\widehat{r}_j$ has a $\mathcal{N}(0,1)$ distribution with

$$\widehat{Var}(\widehat{r}_j) = \begin{pmatrix} 1 & -g'_N P'_N \end{pmatrix} \frac{1}{N} \sum_{i=1}^{N} \begin{pmatrix} \widehat{\varsigma}_{ji}^2 & \widehat{\varsigma}_{ji}\widehat{\Delta v}'_i Z_i \\ Z'_i \widehat{\Delta v}_i \widehat{\varsigma}_{ji} & Z'_i \widehat{\Delta v}_i \widehat{\Delta v}'_i Z_i \end{pmatrix} \begin{pmatrix} 1 \\ -P_N g_N \end{pmatrix}, \tag{6.158}$$

and hence also $m_j \sim \mathcal{N}(0,1)$ asymptotically, with

$$SE(\widehat{r}_j) = \left[\widehat{Var}(\widehat{r}_j)/N \right]^{1/2}.$$

The estimates in Table 6.4 are based on the assumption that given individual and time effects n_{it} and w_{it} only depend on the past two observations. Provided

[33] Alternatively, we could consider a $(T-3-j)$ degrees of freedom test of the joint hypothesis

$$H_0 : r_{(j+4)j} = r_{(j+5)j} = ... = r_{Tj}.$$

[34] The $o_p(1)$ remainder in the expression for $\sqrt{N}\widehat{r}_j$ is given by

$$\sqrt{N} \left(\widehat{\delta} - \delta \right)' \frac{1}{N} \sum_{i=1}^{N} \left(\frac{1}{T-3-j} \sum_{t=4+j}^{T} \Delta x_{it} \Delta x'_{i(t-j)} \right) \left(\widehat{\delta} - \delta \right).$$

T is sufficiently large, the m_j statistics can be used to test assumptions on lag length.[35]

Testing for Stationarity in Mean of Initial Observations We turn to consider GMM estimates that combine levels and differences, as shown in columns 3 (employment) and 6 (wages) of Table 6.4. For the employment equation, estimates are based on the following 40 moments for errors in differences:

$$b_{tN}^d = \sum_{i=1}^{738} \binom{n_i^{t-2}}{w_i^{t-2}} (\Delta n_{it} - \Delta \delta_{1t} - \alpha_1 \Delta n_{i(t-1)} - \alpha_2 \Delta n_{i(t-2)}$$

$$-\beta_1 \Delta w_{i(t-1)} - \beta_2 \Delta w_{i(t-2)}) \quad (6.159)$$

$$(t = 4, ..., 8),$$

together with 6 moments for the period-specific constants:

$$b_{tN}^c = \sum_{i=1}^{738} (n_{it} - \delta_{1t} - \alpha_1 n_{i(t-1)} - \alpha_2 n_{i(t-2)} - \beta_1 w_{i(t-1)} - \beta_2 w_{i(t-2)}) \quad (6.160)$$

$$(t = 3, ..., 8),$$

and 12 additional moments for errors in levels:

$$b_{tN}^\ell = \sum_{i=1}^{738} \binom{\Delta n_{i(t-1)}}{\Delta w_{i(t-1)}} (n_{it} - \delta_{1t} - \alpha_1 n_{i(t-1)} - \alpha_2 n_{i(t-2)}$$

$$-\beta_1 w_{i(t-1)} - \beta_2 w_{i(t-2)}) \quad (6.161)$$

$$(t = 3, ..., 8).$$

The moments are functions of the 10×1 parameter vector

$$\beta = (\delta_3, ..., \delta_8, \alpha_1, \alpha_2, \beta_1, \beta_2),$$

so that there are 48 overidentifying restrictions. The estimates for the wage equation were obtained in exactly the same manner.[36] We report two-step

---

[35]Holtz-Eakin, Newey, and Rosen (1988) paid particular attention to the specification of lag lengths, and Pakes and Griliches (1984) considered similar issues in the context of distributed lag models with exogenous variables.

[36]Employment and wage changes lagged two periods or more are not used as instruments for the equations in levels because they are redundant given those already included. To see this note that, for example, we have

$$E\left(\Delta z_{i(t-2)} u_{it}\right) = E\left(\Delta z_{i(t-2)} \Delta u_{it}\right) + E\left(\Delta z_{i(t-2)} u_{i(t-1)}\right),$$

where $z_{it} = (n_{it}, w_{it})'$ and

$$u_{it} = n_{it} - \delta_{1t} - \alpha_1 n_{i(t-1)} - \alpha_2 n_{i(t-2)} - \beta_1 w_{i(t-1)} - \beta_2 w_{i(t-2)}.$$

robust estimates whose weight matrix is based on the kind of one-step residuals described above.

Note that, contrary to what we would expect under mean stationarity, the combined levels & differences GMM estimates in both equations are closer to the OLS-levels estimates than to GMM in differences. A test of the moment restrictions (6.161) is a test of whether, given an aggregate time effect, the mean of the distribution of initial observations and the mean of the steady state distribution coincide. This can be done by computing incremental Sargan test statistics.[37] Specifically, under the null of mean stationarity, the difference between the *lev.&dif.* and the *dif.* Sargan statistics would be asymptotically distributed as a χ^2 with 12 degrees of freedom. Since we obtain $\Delta S_n = 24.3$ (*p*-val. 0.0185) for employment, and $\Delta S_w = 42.8$ (*p*-val. 0.00) for wages, the null is rejected for the two equations, although somewhat more marginally so in the case of employment.

Testing for the Presence of Unobserved Heterogeneity In the absence of unobserved heterogeneity OLS in levels are consistent estimates, but more generally estimation (e.g. of the employment equation) could be based on the following 60 sample moments

$$b_{tN}^* = \sum_{i=1}^{738} \begin{pmatrix} 1 \\ n_i^{t-1} \\ w_i^{t-1} \end{pmatrix} \left(n_{it} - \delta_{1t} - \alpha_1 n_{i(t-1)} - \alpha_2 n_{i(t-2)} \right.$$
$$\left. - \beta_1 w_{i(t-1)} - \beta_2 w_{i(t-2)} \right) \tag{6.162}$$
$$(t = 3, ..., 8).$$

Given the 46 moments in (6.159) and (6.160), (6.162) adds the following 14 moments:

$$b_{3N}^h = \sum_{i=1}^{738} \begin{pmatrix} n_{i1} \\ n_{i2} \\ w_{i1} \\ w_{i2} \end{pmatrix} \left(n_{i3} - \delta_{13} - \alpha_1 n_2 - \alpha_2 n_{i1} - \beta_1 w_{i2} - \beta_2 w_{i1} \right) \tag{6.163}$$

$$b_{tN}^h = \sum_{i=1}^{738} \begin{pmatrix} n_{i(t-1)} \\ w_{i(t-1)} \end{pmatrix} \left(n_{it} - \delta_{1t} - \alpha_1 n_{i(t-1)} - \alpha_2 n_{i(t-2)} \right.$$
$$\left. - \beta_1 w_{i(t-1)} - \beta_2 w_{i(t-2)} \right) \tag{6.164}$$
$$(t = 4, ..., 8).$$

Thus a test for the validity of the moments (6.163) and (6.164) can be regarded as testing for the presence of unobserved heterogeneity. This can

[37]See Section A.8 in the Appendix.

be done by calculating combined GMM estimates based on (6.159), (6.160), (6.163), and (6.164)—or equivalently levels-GMM estimates based on (6.162)— and obtaining the corresponding incremental Sargan tests relative to GMM in differences. Testing procedures along these lines were suggested by Holtz-Eakin (1988) and Arellano (1993).

The resulting estimates for employment and wages are very close to OLS, and both incremental tests reject the absence of unobserved heterogeneity. The incremental Sargan statistics ($d.f. = 14$) take the values $\Delta S_n^h = 36.0$ (p-val. 0.001) for employment, and $\Delta S_w^h = 47.2$ (p-val. 0.00) for wages.

Testing for Granger Non-causality with and without Heterogeneity The hypothesis that employment does not Granger-cause wages conditional on individual and time effects imposes the restrictions $\lambda_1 = \lambda_2 = 0$. Conversely, to test whether wages Granger-cause employment we would examine the validity of the restrictions $\beta_1 = \beta_2 = 0$ (cf. Granger, 1969).[38] The testing of these restrictions is of some interest in our example because a version of model (6.148)-(6.149) in which the wage equation only includes its own lags can be regarded as the reduced form of an intertemporal labour demand model under rational expectations (as in Sargent, 1978).

Wald test statistics of the joint significance of cross-effects are reported in Table 6.4 for the two equations. For the GMM2 estimates in first-differences we find that (at the 5 per cent level) wages Granger-cause employment, but employment does not Granger-cause wages.

An interesting point is that conditioning on individual effects is crucial for this result. As shown in Table 6.4, if the tests were based upon the OLS estimates in levels, the hypothesis that employment does not Granger-cause wages would be clearly rejected. This illustrates how lack of control of individual heterogeneity could result in a spurious rejection of non-causality.

Another aspect of some interest is that Granger non-causality would also be rejected using the estimates that impose mean stationarity of the initial observations. Thus, in short panels assumptions about initial conditions also matter for the assessment of non-causality.

---

[38] As explained in Section 6.4, Chamberlain (1984) and Holtz-Eakin, Newey, and Rosen (1988) considered non-causality tests in a more general setting that allowed for time-varying coefficients in the projections on lagged dependent variables and individual effects.

Part III

Dynamics and Predeterminedness

7

Models with both Strictly Exogenous and Lagged Dependent Variables

7.1   The Nature of the Model

In Chapters 1 and 2 we considered regression models with strictly exogenous regressors and individual effects. In this chapter we extend these models to include lags of the dependent variable as additional explanatory variables allowing for serial correlation of unknown form. The prototypical equation takes the form

$$y_{it} = \alpha y_{i(t-1)} + x'_{it}\beta + \eta_i + v_{it}, \tag{7.1}$$

together with the assumption

$$E\left(v_{it} \mid x_{i1}, ..., x_{iT}, \eta_i\right) = 0 \ \ (t = 1, ..., T). \tag{7.2}$$

An equation of this type might also contain lags of x and/or additional lags of y, but (7.1) captures the essential feature of the model that we wish to discuss in this section. Namely, a dynamic effect of x on y for which the speed of adjustment is governed by the coefficient of lagged y.

Assumption (7.2) implies that x is uncorrelated to past, present, and future values of v, and hence it is a strictly exogenous variable. It does not rule out correlation between x and the individual effect η. Lagged y will be correlated by construction with the effects η and with lagged v, but it may also be correlated with contemporaneous v if v is serially correlated, which is not ruled out by (7.2). Thus, lagged y is effectively an endogenous explanatory variable in equation (7.1) with respect to both η and v.

Examples include partial adjustment models of firm investment or labour demand, and household consumption or labour supply models with habits (e.g.

Bover, 1991, or Becker, Grossman, and Murphy, 1994). In these applications the coefficient α captures the magnitude of adjustment costs or the extent of habits. It therefore has a structural significance. Moreover, there are often reasons to expect serial correlation in the transitory errors v of the economic model. In those cases lagged y must be treated as an endogenous explanatory variable. That is, one would not regard equation (7.1) as a linear projection of y on lagged y, x, and η. The reason is that even if $\alpha = 0$ in (7.1) the coefficient of lagged y in the projection will in general be different from zero if v is serially correlated.

Assumption (7.2) implies that for all t and s

$$E\left[x_{is}\left(\Delta y_{it} - \alpha \Delta y_{i(t-1)} - \Delta x'_{it}\beta\right)\right] = 0. \tag{7.3}$$

Thus, the model generates internal moment conditions that, subject to a rank condition, will ensure identification in spite of serial correlation of unspecified form and the endogeneity of lagged y. Essentially, we are exploiting the strict exogeneity of x in order to use lags and leads of x that do not have a direct effect on Δy_{it} as instruments for $\Delta y_{i(t-1)}$.

For example, if the model contains the contemporaneous and first lag of a scalar variable x and $T = 3$, we have three instruments x_1, x_2, and x_3 for the single equation in first-differences

$$y_3 - y_2 = \alpha\left(y_2 - y_1\right) + \beta_0\left(x_3 - x_2\right) + \beta_1\left(x_2 - x_1\right) + \left(v_3 - v_2\right), \tag{7.4}$$

so that the coefficients α, β_0, β_1 are potentially just identifiable from the moment conditions $E\left(x_{is}\Delta v_{i3}\right) = 0$, $(s = 1, 2, 3)$.

The models in this chapter should not be regarded as an extension of the autoregressive models of Chapter 6 with the addition of strictly exogenous variables. The purpose of the AR models was to capture time series dependence, so that it was natural to start with serially uncorrelated errors. Here, however, lagged y appears in a structural role, and we consider models where its effect is identified regardless of the form of serial correlation. We shall also consider inference imposing restrictions on the error autocovariances, but retaining the assumption of identification with unrestricted autocorrelation.

7.2 An Example: Cigarette Addiction

As an illustration, we consider Becker, Grossman, and Murphy's analysis of cigarette consumption for US state panel data (1994), extending a similar discussion by Arellano and Honoré (2001). The empirical model is

$$c_{it} = \theta c_{i(t-1)} + \beta\theta c_{i(t+1)} + \gamma p_{it} + \eta_i + \delta_t + v_{it} \tag{7.5}$$

where:

c_{it} = Annual per capita cigarette consumption in packs by state.

p_{it} = Average cigarette price per pack.

θ = A measure of the extent of addiction (for $\theta > 0$).

β = Discount factor.

Becker et al. are interested in testing whether smoking is addictive by considering the response of cigarette consumption to tax-induced exogenous changes in cigarette prices.

Equation (7.5) can be obtained as an approximation to the first-order conditions of utility maximization in a life-cycle model with certainty and habits, in which utility in period t depends on cigarette consumption in t and $t-1$. The degree of addiction is measured by θ, which will be positive if smoking is addictive. Furthermore, the price coefficient γ should be negative due to concavity of the utility . With certainty, the marginal utility of wealth is constant over time but not cross-sectionally. The state specific intercept η_i is intended to capture such variation, although according to the theory γ would also be a function of the marginal utility of wealth. Finally, the δ_ts represent aggregate shocks, possibly correlated with prices, which are treated as period specific parameters.

Equation (7.5) captures the fact that addictive behaviour implies that past consumption increases current consumption, holding the current price and the marginal utility of wealth fixed. Moreover, a rational addict will decrease current consumption in response to an anticipated decrease in future consumption.

The errors v_{it} represent unobserved life-cycle utility shifters, which are likely to be autocorrelated. Therefore, even in the absence of addiction ($\theta = 0$) and serial correlation in prices, we would expect to find dependence over time in c_{it}. As spelled out below, current consumption depends on prices in all periods through the effects of past and future consumption, but it is independent of past and future prices when $c_{i(t-1)}$ and $c_{i(t+1)}$ are held fixed. Exploiting this fact, the strategy of Becker et al. is to identify θ, β, and γ from the assumption that prices are strictly exogenous relative to the unobserved utility shift variables, which enables them to use lagged and future prices as instrumental variables. The required exogenous variation in prices comes from changes in cigarette tax rates. A crucial ingredient of this identification arrangement is the assumption that agents are able to anticipate future prices without error.

Becker, Grossman, and Murphy use annual US state data over the period 1955–1985 ($N = 50$, $T = 31$). Price variation arising from differences in excise taxes on cigarettes across states and time is an essential source of exogenous variation in this exercise. In addition, thanks to the panel nature of the data, the aggregate component of the errors can be held fixed through the use of time dummies. For these reasons a similar exercise with aggregate time series data, although technically possible, would lack the empirical justification for using prices as instruments that the state-level analysis has. On the other hand, individual-level panel data, while potentially useful in characterizing heterogeneity in the degree of addiction, would not add identifying content to the model if the only source of exogenous price variation remained state-level differences in fiscal policies.

Relation to the Joint Process of Consumption and Prices   Finally, it is instructive to consider the statistical nature of model (7.5) and its relation to the bivariate autoregressive representation of the joint process of c_{it} and p_{it}. Letting u_{it} be the composite error term in (7.5), and L and L^{-1} denote the lag and forward operators, respectively, the equation can be written as

$$\left(1 - \theta L - \beta \theta L^{-1}\right) c_{it} = \gamma p_{it} + u_{it} \tag{7.6}$$

or

$$\frac{\theta}{\lambda} \left(1 - \lambda L\right) \left(1 - \beta \lambda L^{-1}\right) c_{it} = \gamma p_{it} + u_{it} \tag{7.7}$$

where λ is the stable root of the equation $\beta \theta \lambda^2 - \lambda + \theta = 0$. Thus, we can express current consumption as a function of past and future prices of the form

$$c_{it} = \gamma \sum_{j=-\infty}^{\infty} \psi_j p_{i(t+j)} + \sum_{j=-\infty}^{\infty} \psi_j u_{i(t+j)} \tag{7.8}$$

where the coefficients ψ_j are functions of θ and β.

Equation (7.8) is a regression of c_{it} on past and future prices of the type considered by Sims (1972). Becker et al.'s model is effectively placing a set of restrictions on the coefficients of this regression. Aside from stationarity, the error process is left unrestricted, and so is the price process. In conjunction with univariate processes for u and p one can obtain the autoregressive or moving average representations of the joint process of c_{it} and p_{it}.

It is interesting to note that while p is a strictly exogenous variable relative to v in equation (7.5), it is nevertheless Granger-caused by c. What is meant by this is that, regardless of the form of the univariate process of p, as long as $\psi_j \neq 0$ for some $j > 0$ the projection of p on lagged p and lagged c will have non-zero coefficients on some lagged c (Sims, 1972). Therefore, p would not be described as "strictly exogenous" according to Sims's statistical definition, even if it is strictly exogenous relative to v in model (7.5).[1] Granger non-causality and statistical strict exogeneity will only occur if $\beta = 0$, in which case $\psi_j = 0$ for all $j > 0$, which corresponds to the model with "myopic habits" also considered by Becker et al.

---

[1] Another example of this situation is provided by Arellano and Honoré (2001, pp. 3240-3241).

7.3   GMM Estimation

7.3.1   2SLS Estimation from a Large T Perspective

Becker et al. treated the individual effects in (7.5) as parameters to be jointly estimated with the remaining coefficients. They employed 2SLS estimators using $p_{i(t-1)}$, p_{it}, $p_{i(t+1)}$, and state and time dummies as instrumental variables. This is a natural perspective given the sample size of the state panel they used where $N = 50$ and $T = 31$. It is nevertheless useful to relate this type of estimator to estimators in deviations in order to exhibit some equivalences and the connection with the perspective adopted in small T large N environments.

Let the stacked form of a generic model that includes (7.1) and (7.5) as special cases be

$$y = W\delta + C\eta + v \qquad (7.9)$$

where η is an $N \times 1$ vector of individual effects and $C = I_N \otimes \iota_T$ is an $NT \times N$ matrix of individual dummies. The NT-row matrix of explanatory variables W will contain observations of $y_{i(t-1)}$ and x_{it} in model (7.1), and of $c_{i(t-1)}$, $c_{i(t+1)}$, p_{it}, and time dummies in model (7.5). Moreover, let Z be an NT-row matrix of instruments with at least as many columns as W. In a version of Becker et al.'s example Z contains $p_{i(t-1)}$, p_{it}, $p_{i(t+1)}$, and time dummies, whereas in model (7.1) it may contain observations of x_{it}, $x_{i(t-1)}$, ..., $x_{i(t-j)}$ for some given j, and the actual value of T will be adjusted accordingly.

A 2SLS estimator of (δ, η) in (7.9) using Z and the individual dummies as instruments, $Z^\dagger = (Z, C)$ say, is given by

$$\begin{pmatrix} \tilde{\delta} \\ \tilde{\eta} \end{pmatrix} = \left[W^{\dagger\prime} Z^\dagger \left(Z^{\dagger\prime} Z^\dagger \right)^{-1} Z^{\dagger\prime} W^\dagger \right]^{-1} W^{\dagger\prime} Z^\dagger \left(Z^{\dagger\prime} Z^\dagger \right)^{-1} Z^{\dagger\prime} y$$

$$\equiv \left(\widehat{W}^{\dagger\prime} \widehat{W}^\dagger \right)^{-1} \widehat{W}^{\dagger\prime} y \qquad (7.10)$$

where $W^\dagger = (W, C)$ and $\widehat{W}^\dagger = \left(\widehat{W}, C \right)$ denotes the fitted value of $W^\dagger$ in a regression on (Z, C).

The estimator $\tilde{\delta}$ is numerically the same as the *within-group 2SLS estimator* based on all variables y, W, and Z in deviations from time means:

$$\tilde{\delta} = \left[W'\overline{Q}Z \left(Z'\overline{Q}Z \right)^{-1} Z'\overline{Q}W \right]^{-1} W'\overline{Q}Z \left(Z'\overline{Q}Z \right)^{-1} Z'\overline{Q}y \qquad (7.11)$$

where $\overline{Q} = I_N \otimes Q$ and Q is the within-group operator introduced in (2.18).

We can see this by taking into account that $\overline{Q} = I_{NT} - C \left(C'C \right)^{-1} C'$ and using the result from partitioned regression:

$$\tilde{\delta} = \left(\widehat{W}' \overline{Q} \widehat{W} \right)^{-1} \widehat{W}' \overline{Q} y. \qquad (7.12)$$

Since $\widehat{W}$ is the fitted value in a regression of W on Z and C, it turns out that $\overline{Q}\widehat{W}$ is the fitted value in a regression of $\overline{Q}W$ on $\overline{Q}Z$, which is given by $\overline{QW} = \overline{Q}Z \left(Z'\overline{Q}Z\right)^{-1} Z'\overline{Q}W$. Substituting this expression in (7.12), the equivalence with (7.11) follows.

The estimator $\tilde{\delta}$ will be consistent as $T \to \infty$ as long as $E\left(z_{it}v_{it}\right) = 0$, so that it will retain time series consistency even if z_{it} is only predetermined. Consistency as $N \to \infty$ for fixed T, however, requires that

$$E\left[\left(z_{it} - \overline{z}_i\right)\left(v_{it} - \overline{v}_i\right)\right] = 0. \tag{7.13}$$

Such condition will be satisfied if z_{it} is strictly exogenous for v_{it} as it is the case in both models (7.1) and (7.5). In what follows we consider the estimation of model (7.1) from a small T, large N perspective. This will let us provide further discussion of the link with the within-group 2SLS estimator (7.11).

7.3.2 Optimal IV Estimation in a Small T, Large N Context

Let us rewrite model (7.1)-(7.2) with an explicit intercept as

$$y_{it} = \gamma_0 + w'_{it}\gamma_1 + u_{it} = (1, w'_{it})\gamma + u_{it} \tag{7.14}$$
$$u_{it} = \eta_i + v_{it} \tag{7.15}$$

$$E\left(v_{it} \mid x_i, \eta_i\right) = 0 \quad (t = 1, ..., T), \tag{7.16}$$

where $w_{it} = \left(y_{i(t-1)}, x'_{it}\right)'$, $\gamma_1 = \left(\alpha, \beta'\right)'$, and γ_0 denotes a constant term, so that the individual effect η_i has been redefined to have zero mean. Also $\gamma = (\gamma_0, \gamma'_1)'$ and $x_i = (x'_{i0}, ..., x'_{iT})'$. Moreover, for notational convenience we assume that y_{i0} and x_{i0} are observed. Thus, we start with a panel with $T + 1$ time series observations, but we only have T observations of the vector w_{it} for individual i.

Without further restrictions, this model is a special case of the linear structural equation discussed in Section 2.5.2 in which $y_{i(t-1)}$ is the endogenous explanatory variable and x_i is the vector of instruments. Namely, letting $v_i = (v_{i1}, ..., v_{iT})'$, $y_i = (y_{i1}, ..., y_{iT})'$, and $W_i = (w_{i1}, ..., w_{iT})'$, the unfeasible optimal instrumental-variable estimator of γ_1 based on the conditional moment restriction for the errors in orthogonal deviations $E\left(v_i^* \mid x_i\right) = 0$ is

$$\widehat{\gamma}_{1UIV} = \left[\sum_{i=1}^{N} E\left(W_i^{*'} \mid x_i\right)\Omega^{-1}\left(x_i\right)W_i^*\right]^{-1} \sum_{i=1}^{N} E\left(W_i^{*'} \mid x_i\right)\Omega^{-1}\left(x_i\right)y_i^* \tag{7.17}$$

where $\Omega\left(x_i\right) = Var\left(v_i^* \mid x_i\right)$, $v_i^* = Av_i$, $y_i^* = Ay_i$, $W_i^* = AW_i$ and A denotes the $(T-1) \times T$ orthogonal deviations transformation matrix introduced in Section 2.2.2. A feasible counterpart requires estimates of $E\left(W_i^* \mid x_i\right)$ and $\Omega\left(x_i\right)$.

The within-group 2SLS estimator corresponding to (7.11) can be written as

$$\tilde{\gamma}_1 = \left(\sum_{i=1}^{N} \widetilde{W}_i^{*\prime} W_i^* \right)^{-1} \sum_{i=1}^{N} \widetilde{W}_i^{*\prime} y_i^* \tag{7.18}$$

where

$$\widetilde{W}_i^* = Z_i^* \widehat{\Pi} \equiv Z_i^* \left(\sum_{i=1}^{N} Z_i^{*\prime} Z_i^* \right)^{-1} \left(\sum_{i=1}^{N} Z_i^{*\prime} W_i^* \right) \tag{7.19}$$

and Z_i^* is a matrix of instruments in orthogonal deviations.[2] Thus, $\tilde{\gamma}_1$ is an estimator of the form of (7.17) with $\widetilde{W}_i^*$ and an identity matrix in place of $E\left(W_i^{*\prime} \mid x_i \right)$ and $\Omega\left(x_i \right)$, respectively.

For example, if Z_i^* contains x_{it}^* and $x_{i(t-1)}^*$, the instruments used by $\tilde{\gamma}_1$ consist of the sample counterparts of the linear projections

$$E^* \left(w_{it}^* \mid x_{it}^*, x_{i(t-1)}^* \right) = \pi_0' x_{it}^* + \pi_1' x_{i(t-1)}^* \tag{7.20}$$

with the same coefficients for all t. However, in a panel with large N and small T we may consider estimators based on less restrictive projections of the form

$$E^* \left(w_{it}^* \mid x_{i0}, ..., x_{iT} \right) = \pi_{t0}' x_{i0} + ... + \pi_{tT}' x_{iT} \tag{7.21}$$

with unrestricted coefficients for each t. In contrast with (7.20), the projection (7.21) not only depends on all lags and leads of x, but also the coefficients are period-specific. Naturally, in a large T, fixed N environment it would not be possible to obtain consistent estimates of the coefficients of (7.21) without restrictions. Next we turn to consider estimators of this kind.

7.3.3 GMM with the Number of Moments Increasing with T

Let us consider GMM estimators based on the moment conditions $E\left(v_i^* \otimes x_i \right) = 0$. This runs in parallel to a similar discussion for static models in Section 2.3.3. Letting $Z_i = I_{(T-1)} \otimes x_i'$, these estimators take the form

$$\hat{\gamma}_{1GMM} = \left[\left(\sum_i W_i^{*\prime} Z_i \right) A_N \left(\sum_i Z_i' W_i^* \right) \right]^{-1} \left(\sum_i W_i^{*\prime} Z_i \right) A_N \left(\sum_i Z_i' y_i^* \right), \tag{7.22}$$

where A_N is a weight matrix that needs to be chosen.

The model can be regarded as an incomplete system of $(T-1)$ simultaneous equations with T endogenous variables $y_{i0}^*, ..., y_{i(T-1)}^*$, a vector of instruments

---

[2]To go from deviations-from-time-means to orthogonal deviations note that, as explained in Section 2.2.2, $Q = A'A$.

given by x_i, and cross-equation restrictions (since the same coefficients occur in the equations for different periods). From this perspective, a 2SLS estimator of the system uses

$$A_N = \left(\sum_i Z_i' Z_i \right)^{-1} = I_T \otimes \left(\sum_i x_i x_i' \right)^{-1} \tag{7.23}$$

The difference between this 2SLS estimator and (7.18) is that the latter uses (7.20) to form predictions of w_{it}^*, whereas the former uses period-specific projections on all lags and leads as in (7.21).

Similarly, a three-stage least-squares estimator (3SLS) is based on

$$A_N = \left(\sum_i Z_i' \widetilde{\Omega} Z_i \right)^{-1} = \widetilde{\Omega}^{-1} \otimes \left(\sum_i x_i x_i' \right)^{-1} \tag{7.24}$$

where $\widetilde{\Omega} = N^{-1} \sum_i \widetilde{v}_i^* \widetilde{v}_i^{*\prime}$ and the $\widetilde{v}_i^*$ are 2SLS residuals. Finally, a weight matrix that is robust to both heteroskedasticity and serial correlation is

$$A_N = \left(\sum_i Z_i' \widetilde{v}_i^* \widetilde{v}_i^{*\prime} Z_i \right)^{-1} \tag{7.25}$$

The latter gives rise to Chamberlain's (1984) robust generalization of 3SLS for model (7.1).

Estimating the intercept Having estimated γ_1, a consistent estimate of γ_0 can be obtained as

$$\widehat{\gamma}_0 = \frac{1}{NT} \sum_{i=1}^{N} \sum_{t=1}^{T} (y_{it} - w_{it}' \widehat{\gamma}_{1GMM}). \tag{7.26}$$

Alternatively, we may consider the joint estimation of γ_0 and γ_1 by GMM from the moment conditions

$$E\left(y_i - \iota_T \gamma_0 - W_i \gamma_1\right) = 0 \tag{7.27}$$
$$E\left[Z_i'\left(y_i^* - W_i^* \gamma_1\right)\right] = 0, \tag{7.28}$$

or equivalently

$$E\left[\begin{pmatrix} I_T & 0 \\ 0 & Z_i \end{pmatrix}' \begin{pmatrix} u_i \\ u_i^* \end{pmatrix} \right] = E\left(Z_i^{\circ\prime} u_i^{\circ}\right) = 0, \tag{7.29}$$

where $u_i^{\circ} = H^{\circ} u_i$ and $H^{\circ} = (I_T, A')'$. This leads to estimators of the form

$$\begin{pmatrix} \widehat{\gamma}_0 \\ \widehat{\gamma}_1 \end{pmatrix} = \left[\left(\sum_i W_i^{\circ\prime} Z_i^{\circ} \right) A_N^{\circ} \left(\sum_i Z_i^{\circ\prime} W_i^{\circ} \right) \right]^{-1} \left(\sum_i W_i^{\circ\prime} Z_i^{\circ} \right) A_N^{\circ} \left(\sum_i Z_i^{\circ\prime} y_i^{\circ} \right) \tag{7.30}$$

where $y_i^{\circ} = H^{\circ} y_i$ and $W_i^{\circ} = H^{\circ} (\iota_T, W_i)$.

Expression (7.30) is similar to the "levels & differences" or "system" estimator for AR models discussed in Section 6.5, in the sense that both combine moment conditions for errors in levels and deviations. The same argument can be used to estimate coefficients on time-invariant explanatory variables that are assumed to be uncorrelated with the effects.

7.3.4 Explanatory Variables Uncorrelated with the Effects

The previous setting also suggests a generalization to a case where a subset of the xs are uncorrelated with the effects. Suppose that a subset $x_{1i} = (x'_{1i1}, ..., x'_{1iT})'$ of x_i are uncorrelated with the effects whereas the remaining x_{2i} are correlated, as in the static Hausman and Taylor models of Section 3.4. In such case we obtain a GMM estimator of the same form as (7.30), but using an augmented matrix of instruments given by

$$Z_i^\circ = \begin{pmatrix} I_T \otimes (1, x'_{1i}) & 0 \\ 0 & I_{(T-1)} \otimes x'_{2i} \end{pmatrix}. \tag{7.31}$$

If all xs are uncorrelated with the effects, the second block of moments in orthogonal deviations drops out and we are just left with the moments in levels

$$E(u_i \otimes x_{\ell i}) = E(Z'_{\ell i} u_i) = E[Z'_{\ell i}(y_i - W_{\ell i}\gamma)] = 0 \tag{7.32}$$

where $Z_{\ell i} = (I_T \otimes x'_{\ell i})$, $x_{\ell i} = (1, x'_i)'$ and $W_{\ell i} = (\iota_T, W_i)$.

7.3.5 Enforcing Restrictions in the Covariance Matrix

Let the marginal covariance matrix of u_i be $E(u_i u'_i) = \Omega$. The general form of Ω is

$$\Omega = \sigma_\eta^2 \iota_T \iota'_T + E(v_i v'_i), \tag{7.33}$$

which is not restrictive if $E(v_i v'_i)$ is unrestricted. However, we may consider restricting Ω by restricting the time series properties of v_i. For example, by considering the standard error components structure

$$\Omega = \sigma_\eta^2 \iota_T \iota'_T + \sigma^2 I_T, \tag{7.34}$$

or some other ARMA process for v_i, so that Ω can be expressed as a function of a smaller set of coefficients $\Omega(\theta)$.

We may consider estimating γ imposing the constraints in Ω. Even if Ω does not depend directly on γ, enforcing the covariance restrictions in Ω will in general lead to more efficient but less robust estimates of γ. This is so because the model is a simultaneous system as opposed to a multivariate regression (Rothenberg, 1973).[3] It may also help identification in a way that we shall pursue in the next section.

---

[3]See also section B.6 in the Appendix.

The set of moments is now

$$E\left(Z_i^{\circ\prime} u_i^{\circ}\right) = 0 \tag{7.35}$$

$$E\left\{vech\left[u_i u_i^\prime - \Omega\left(\theta\right)\right]\right\} = 0 \tag{7.36}$$

and this can be used as the basis for covariance restricted GMM estimators for models with all, part, or none of the xs correlated with the effects, something which will be reflected in the choice of Z_i° as explained above.

The covariance structures to be considered in the present context are of the type we discussed in Chapter 5, so that the discussion in that chapter is relevant here, both in terms of possible models and characterization of restrictions.

It is possible that some of the covariance restrictions may be expressed as simple instrumental variable restrictions. For example, if v_{it} is serially uncorrelated then the error in orthogonal deviations in period t v_{it}^* is not only orthogonal to x_i but also to $y_{i0}, ..., y_{i(t-1)}$, which suggests the use of GMM estimators with an increasing number of instruments of the type discussed in Section 5.4.2 and Chapter 6.

7.4   Maximum Likelihood

7.4.1   Estimation with Unrestricted Covariance Matrix

Bhargava and Sargan (1983) considered Gaussian ML estimators of model (7.1) under the assumption of lack of correlation between x's and the effects. They completed the model with a linear reduced form equation for y_{i0}:

$$y_{i0} = x_{\ell i}^\prime \mu + u_{i0} \tag{7.37}$$

and the conditional normality assumption for $u_i^\dagger = (u_{i0}, u_i^\prime)^\prime$:

$$u_i^\dagger \mid x_{\ell i} \sim \mathcal{N}\left(0, \Omega^\dagger\right). \tag{7.38}$$

The full system can be expressed as

$$B y_i - \Gamma x_{\ell i} = u_i^\dagger \tag{7.39}$$

where $\Gamma = (\mu, \Gamma_1^\prime)^\prime$, $\Gamma_1 = (\gamma_0 \iota_T, 0, I_T \otimes \gamma_1^\prime)$, and $B = \{b_{jk}\}$ is a lower triangular matrix such that $b_{jj} = 1$, $b_{j(j-1)} = -\alpha$, and $b_{jk} = 0$ for all other j and k. The log likelihood, apart from a constant term, is given by

$$L = -\frac{N}{2} \log \det \Omega^\dagger - \frac{1}{2} \sum_i u_i^{\dagger\prime} \Omega^{\dagger-1} u_i^\dagger + N \log |\det B| \tag{7.40}$$

$$= -\frac{N}{2}\log\det\Omega - \frac{1}{2}\sum_i u_i'\Omega^{-1}u_i + \frac{N}{2}\log\omega^{00} - \frac{\omega^{00}}{2}\sum_i (u_{i0} - u_i'f_{10})^2$$

where $f_{10} = -\omega^{10}/\omega^{00}$ and

$$\Omega^{\dagger -1} = \begin{pmatrix} \omega_{00} & \omega_{01} \\ \omega_{10} & \Omega \end{pmatrix}^{-1} = \begin{pmatrix} \omega^{00} & \omega^{01} \\ \omega^{10} & \Omega^{11} \end{pmatrix}. \tag{7.41}$$

Moreover, since B is triangular and all its diagonal elements are equal to one, $\log\det B = 0$, and therefore the Jacobian term will not occur here.[4]

The ML estimator of μ is given by

$$\widehat{\mu} = (X'X)^{-1}X'(y_0 - Uf_{10}) \tag{7.42}$$

where X is a matrix with N rows whose i-th row is given by $x'_{\ell i} = (1, x'_i)$, $y_0 = (y_{10}, ..., y_{N0})'$, and $U = (u_1, ..., u_N)'$.

Letting $M = I_N - X(X'X)^{-1}X'$ and concentrating the likelihood with respect to μ, we obtain the following expression that will be used below:

$$\begin{aligned} L^{\dagger} &= -\frac{N}{2}\log\det\Omega - \frac{1}{2}tr\left(\Omega^{-1}U'U\right) \\ &+ \frac{N}{2}\log\omega^{00} - \frac{\omega^{00}}{2}(y_0 - Uf_{10})' M(y_0 - Uf_{10}). \end{aligned} \tag{7.43}$$

Further concentrating the likelihood with respect to f_{10}, ω^{00}, and Ω, aside from constant terms, we obtain[5]

$$L_C = -\frac{N}{2}\log\det\left(\frac{U'U}{N}\right) + \frac{N}{2}\log\det\left(\frac{U'MU}{N}\right). \tag{7.44}$$

The maximum likelihood estimator of γ is therefore given by

$$\widehat{\gamma}_{ML} = \arg\max L_C.$$

[4]We have made use of the following formulae for the determinant and the inverse of a partitioned matrix: $\det\Omega^{\dagger} = (\det\Omega)/\omega^{00}$ and $\Omega^{11} = \Omega^{-1} + \omega^{00}f_{10}f_{01}$.

[5]To see this note that substituting the MLE $\widehat{f}_{10} = (U'MU)^{-1}U'My_0$ we get

$$N/\widehat{\omega}^{00} = \left(y_0 - U\widehat{f}_{10}\right)' M\left(y_0 - U\widehat{f}_{10}\right) = y_0'My_0 - y_0'MU\left(U'MU\right)^{-1}U'My_0.$$

Furthermore, using the formulae for the determinant of a partitioned inverse, this equals

$$\frac{\det\begin{pmatrix} u_0'Mu_0 & u_0'MU \\ U'Mu_0 & U'MU \end{pmatrix}}{\det(U'MU)} = \frac{\det\left(U^{\dagger\prime}MU^{\dagger}\right)}{\det(U'MU)} = \frac{(\det B)\det(Y'MY)(\det B')}{\det(U'MU)} = \frac{\det(Y'MY)}{\det(U'MU)}.$$

Since $\det(Y'MY)$ is constant, the result follows.

Asymptotic Equivalence to 3SLS   Regardless of normality, $\widehat{\gamma}_{ML}$ can be shown to be asymptotically equivalent to the 3SLS estimator based on the moments (7.32).[6] The 3SLS estimator in this case minimizes

$$b_N' V_N b_N = tr\left[\left(\frac{\widehat{U}'\widehat{U}}{N}\right)^{-1} U'X\left(X'X\right)^{-1} X'U\right] \tag{7.45}$$

with $b_N = \sum_i \left(u_i \otimes x_{\ell i}\right) = vec\left(U'X\right)$ and $V_N = \left(\widehat{U}'\widehat{U}/N\right) \otimes \left(X'X\right)$, where $\widehat{U}$ denote 2SLS residuals.

It is of some interest to compare the first-order conditions of ML with those of 3SLS. The former are

$$-tr\left[\left(\frac{U'U}{N}\right)^{-1} U'\left(dU\right)\right] + tr\left[\left(\frac{U'MU}{N}\right)^{-1} U'M\left(dU\right)\right] = 0 \tag{7.46}$$

or

$$tr\left[\left(\frac{U'MU}{N}\right)^{-1} U'X\left(X'X\right)^{-1} X'\left(dU\right)\right]$$
$$= tr\left\{\left[\left(\frac{U'U}{N}\right)^{-1} - \left(\frac{U'MU}{N}\right)^{-1}\right] U'\left(dU\right)\right\}, \tag{7.47}$$

whereas the 3SLS estimator solves

$$tr\left[\left(\frac{\widehat{U}'\widehat{U}}{N}\right)^{-1} U'X\left(X'X\right)^{-1} X'\left(dU\right)\right] = 0. \tag{7.48}$$

The *rhs* of (7.47) is asymptotically negligible and the *lhs* is similar to (7.48), except that the estimated covariance matrix is not fixed but continuously updated.

7.4.2   MLE with Covariance Restrictions

If the partial adjustment model started in the distant past, it implies

$$y_{i0} = \sum_{k=0}^{\infty} \alpha^k \beta' x_{i(-k)} + \frac{\eta_i}{1-\alpha} + \sum_{k=0}^{\infty} \alpha^k v_{i(-k)}, \tag{7.49}$$

so that the error term in Bhargava and Sargan's equation for y_{i0} (7.37) takes the form

[6]This is generally true for any linear-in-variables simultaneous system without covariance restrictions (Sargan, 1964).

$$u_{i0} = \varepsilon_i + \frac{\eta_i}{1-\alpha} + \sum_{k=0}^{\infty} \alpha^k v_{i(-k)} \tag{7.50}$$

where ε_i is the error in the prediction of $\sum_{k=0}^{\infty} \alpha^k \beta' x_{i(-k)}$ based on x_i:

$$\varepsilon_i = \sum_{k=0}^{\infty} \alpha^k \beta' x_{i(-k)} - \sum_{k=0}^{\infty} \alpha^k \beta' E\left(x_{i(-k)} \mid x_i\right). \tag{7.51}$$

Thus, the variance of u_{i0} is unrestricted since so is the variance of ε_i, but the covariances between u_{i0} and subsequent u_{it} are given by

$$E\left(u_{i0} u_{it}\right) = \frac{\sigma_\eta^2}{1-\alpha} + \sum_{k=0}^{\infty} \alpha^k E\left(v_{i(-k)} v_{it}\right). \tag{7.52}$$

If the autocovariances of the v_{it} process are unrestricted, the terms $E\left(u_{i0} u_{it}\right)$ will be unrestricted as well. However, restrictions in $E\left(v_{i(-k)} v_{it}\right)$ may imply restrictions in $E\left(u_{i0} u_{it}\right)$. In particular, if v_{it} is white noise then for $t = 1, ..., T$:

$$E\left(u_{i0} u_{it}\right) = \frac{\sigma_\eta^2}{1-\alpha}. \tag{7.53}$$

Bhargava and Sargan considered estimation by ML subject to (7.53) and the error components structure (7.34). To do so, they maximized the concentrated likelihood (7.43) as a function of γ, σ_η^2/σ^2, σ^2, and the variance of ε_i.

Under normality the covariance-restricted ML estimator of Bhargava–Sargan is asymptotically equivalent to the optimal GMM estimator based on the moments

$$E\left(Z_{\ell i}' u_i\right) = 0 \tag{7.54}$$

$$E\left[\text{vech}\left(u_i u_i' - \sigma_\eta^2 \iota_T \iota_T' - \sigma^2 I_T\right)\right] = 0 \tag{7.55}$$

$$E\left(u_{i0} u_i - \frac{\sigma_\eta^2}{1-\alpha} \iota_T\right) = 0. \tag{7.56}$$

However, under non-normality the MLE will be suboptimal relative to the optimal GMM estimator for the reasons explained in the context of the estimation of covariance structures in Chapter 5. Minimum distance estimators and specification tests for this type of model under non-normality were considered in Arellano (1989a,b, 1990).

7.4.3   MLE with Correlated xs

In the likelihood model (7.37)-(7.39) the effects are independent of the xs. This can be relaxed by assuming

$$u_i \mid x_{\ell i} \sim \mathcal{N}\left[E\left(\eta_i \mid x_{\ell i}\right) \iota_T, \Omega\right] \tag{7.57}$$

with

$$E\left(\eta_i \mid x_{\ell i}\right) = x'_{\ell i}\lambda. \tag{7.58}$$

The previous development can then be repeated after redefining $u_i^\dagger$ as

$$u_i^\dagger = \begin{pmatrix} u_{i0} \\ u_i - (x'_{\ell i}\lambda)\,\iota_T \end{pmatrix}, \tag{7.59}$$

which leads to a correlated random effects likelihood that can be maximized with or without imposing covariance restrictions in the error process

To see the form of the concentrated likelihood without covariance restrictions that only depends on γ_1, it is useful to write the full system of $T+1$ equation as follows:

$$y_{i0} = x'_{\ell i}\mu + u_{i0} \tag{7.60}$$

$$y_{i1} = x'_{\ell i}\mu_1 + v_{i1} \tag{7.61}$$

$$y_{it}^* = w_{it}^{*\prime}\gamma_1 + u_{it}^* \quad (t = 1, ..., T-1). \tag{7.62}$$

That is, we have changed the parameterization from λ (including an intercept) to the coefficients μ_1 of the reduced form equation for y_{i1}, and transformed the remaining $T-1$ equations in orthogonal deviations.

Using similar arguments as before, the concentrated likelihood as a function of γ_1 alone is therefore

$$L_C^* = -\frac{N}{2}\log\det\left(\frac{U^{*\prime}U^*}{N}\right) + \frac{N}{2}\log\det\left(\frac{U^{*\prime}MU^*}{N}\right), \tag{7.63}$$

where $U^* = (u_1^*, ..., u_N^*)'$ is an $N \times (T-1)$ matrix of errors in orthogonal deviations. Moreover, the maximizier of L_C^* is asymptotically equivalent to the correlated effects 3SLS estimator (7.22)-(7.24).

8

Predetermined Variables

In Chapter 2 we considered regression models with regressors that could be correlated with a time-invariant unobserved heterogeneity component, but that were strictly exogenous in the sense of being uncorrelated to past, present, and future time-varying errors.

In Section 2.5.2 we considered the extension to structural equations by relying on external instruments. The situation there was that endogenous regressors could be correlated with time-varying errors at all lags and leads, and the instruments were strictly exogenous. Both instruments and endogenous explanatory variables were allowed to be correlated with the effects. Chapter 7 was devoted to a prominent special model of this kind. Namely, a dynamic model containing both lags of the dependent variable and strictly exogenous explanatory variables. The lagged dependent variable was treated as an endogenous variable since we allowed for unrestricted serial correlation, and the strict exogeneity assumption was key to identification.

These "all-or-nothing" settings may be too restrictive in a time series environment, since it is possible to imagine situations in which explanatory variables may be correlated with errors at certain periods but not at others, and such patterns may provide essential information for the identification of parameters of interest.

We have already encountered examples of this type of situation. One is the measurement error model of Chapter 4 in which mismeasured regressors were correlated with contemporaneous errors but not with lagged or future errors, as long as measurement errors were not serially correlated. Another example is the autoregressive model of Chapter 6 in which the lagged dependent variable can be regarded as a regressor that is correlated to past errors but not to current or future errors. In the two examples, regressors were correlated with the effects.

In this chapter we consider models in which the time-varying errors are uncorrelated with current and lagged values of certain conditioning variables but not with their future values, so that they are *predetermined* with respect to the time varying errors. Some of these variables may be explanatory variables included in the equation or lags of them, but others may be external predetermined instruments. Moreover, the equation may contain explanatory endogenous variables whose lags may or may not be part of the conditioning set.

Autoregressive models and dynamic regressions ("partial adjustment with feedback") in which lagged dependent variables and other regressors are treated as predetermined are specific examples. The main emphasis in this chapter, however, is in an incomplete model that specifies orthogonality conditions between a structural error and predetermined instruments. In our context, predeterminedness is defined relative to a specific structural error. By "predetermined variables" we just refer to variables that are potentially correlated to lagged values of the structural error but are uncorrelated to present and future values.

An alternative approach to models with predetermined and/or endogenous regressors is to consider complete systems. For example, by considering VAR versions of the models discussed in Chapter 6, or structural transformations of those VAR models. In this chapter, however, we have in mind situations in which a researcher is interested in modelling certain equations but not others. Thus, we focus on incomplete models with unspecified feedback processes, and restrictions specifying that errors are mean independent to certain variables in a sequential way.

8.1   Introduction and Examples

The previous chapter considered econometric models with lagged dependent variables whose errors were mean independent of past and future values of certain variables z_{it}

$$E\left(v_{it} \mid z_{i1}, ..., z_{iT}\right) = 0, \tag{8.1}$$

and referred to these variables as strictly exogenous with respect to v_{it}. We now consider models whose errors satisfy *sequential moment conditions* of the form

$$E\left(v_{it} \mid z_{i1}, ..., z_{it}\right) = 0. \tag{8.2}$$

Autoregressive Processes   An example of (8.2) is the AR model with individual effects that we discussed in Chapter 6. In this case

$$v_{it} = y_{it} - \alpha y_{i(t-1)} - \eta_i$$

and $E\left(v_{it} \mid y_{i0}, ..., y_{i(t-1)}, \eta_i\right) = 0$, so that (8.2) is satisfied with $z_{it} = y_{i(t-1)}$.

In what follows we present several other instances that illustrate the scope of sequential moment assumptions.

8.1.1   Partial Adjustment with Feedback

Another example is a sequential version of the partial adjustment model. The equation is the same as (7.1):

$$y_{it} = \alpha y_{i(t-1)} + x'_{it}\beta + \eta_i + v_{it} \tag{8.3}$$

but in this instance the errors are assumed to satisfy

$$E\left(v_{it} \mid y_i^{t-1}, x_i^t, \eta_i\right) = 0, \tag{8.4}$$

so that equation (8.3) is regarded as a parameterization of the regression function $E\left(y_{it} \mid y_i^{t-1}, x_i^t, \eta_i\right)$.

There are two main differences between the behaviour of the vs and xs that is assumed in this model and that of (7.1)-(7.2). Firstly, (8.4) implies lack of autocorrelation in v_{it} since lagged vs are linear combinations of the variables in the conditioning set, whereas (7.2) by itself does not restrict the serial dependence of the errors. Secondly, in contrast with (8.4), Assumption (7.2) implies that y does not Granger-cause x, in the sense that forecasts of x_{it} given x_i^{t-1}, y_i^{t-1}, and additive effects are not affected by y_i^{t-1}. Thus, (7.2) rules out the possibility of feedback from lagged y to current xs, whereas feedback is allowed in (8.4).

Without further restrictions the two models are not nested. This situation can be illustrated using the example with $T = 3$ given in (7.4) (cf. Arellano and Honoré, 2001, p. 3237):

$$\Delta y_{i3} = \alpha \Delta y_{i2} + \beta_0 \Delta x_{i3} + \beta_1 \Delta x_{i2} + \Delta v_{i3}.$$

Under Assumption (7.2) the coefficients α, β_0, β_1 are potentially just identifiable from the moment conditions

$$E\left[\begin{pmatrix} x_{i1} \\ x_{i2} \\ x_{i3} \end{pmatrix} \Delta v_{i3}\right] = 0. \tag{8.5}$$

Under Assumption (8.4) the three parameters are also potentially just identifiable from

$$E\left[\begin{pmatrix} y_{i1} \\ x_{i1} \\ x_{i2} \end{pmatrix} \Delta v_{i3}\right] = 0, \tag{8.6}$$

but the two models only have two moment restrictions in common, which in this example are not enough to identify the three parameters.

8.1.2   Euler Equation for Household Consumption

The next example is an intertemporal consumption model with uncertainty of the type developed by Zeldes (1989), who used individual after-tax returns and food consumption from the PSID (as Hall and Mishkin, 1982, did).[1] Suppose each period t a family i chooses consumption c_{it} and portfolio shares to maximize the expected value of a time-separable life-cycle utility function. In the absence of liquidity constraints, optimal consumption must satisfy the following Euler equation

$$E_{t-1}\left[\left(\frac{1+r_{it}}{1+\delta_i}\right)U'_{it}\left(c_{it}\right)\right] = U'_{i(t-1)}\left(c_{i(t-1)}\right) \tag{8.7}$$

where $U'_{it}(.)$ denotes the marginal utility of consumption, $E_{t-1}(.)$ is a conditional expectation given information available at time $t-1$, δ_i is a household-specific rate of time preference, and r_{it} is the rate of return of a riskless asset. Equivalently, we can write

$$\frac{(1+r_{it})\,U'_{it}\left(c_{it}\right)}{(1+\delta_i)\,U'_{i(t-1)}\left(c_{i(t-1)}\right)} = 1+\varepsilon_{it} \tag{8.8}$$

where ε_{it} is an expectational error that satisfies $E_{t-1}\left(\varepsilon_{it}\right) = 0$ and is therefore uncorrelated with information known to the consumer at time $t-1$.

Suppose the utility of consumption has constant relative risk aversion coefficient α

$$U_{it}\left(c_{it}\right) = \frac{c_{it}^{1-\alpha}}{1-\alpha}e^{\theta_{it}} \tag{8.9}$$

and θ_{it} captures differences in preferences across families and time, which are specified as

$$\theta_{it} = \beta' x_{it} + \phi_t + \zeta_i + \xi_{it}. \tag{8.10}$$

In Zeldes's model, the vector x_{it} contains age and family size variables, and ζ_i, ϕ_t, and ε_{it} are, respectively, family, time, and residual effects. With this specification the log of (8.8) is given by

$$\log\left(1+r_{it}\right) - \alpha\Delta\log c_{it} - \beta'\Delta x_{it} - \delta_t - \eta_i = v_{it} + \log\left(1+\varepsilon_{it}\right) \tag{8.11}$$

where $\eta_i = \log\left(1+\delta_i\right)$, $\delta_t = \Delta\phi_t$ and $v_{it} = \Delta\xi_{it}$. Moreover, using a second-order Taylor approximation $\log\left(1+\varepsilon_{it}\right) \simeq \varepsilon_{it} - \varepsilon_{it}^2/2$, we can write

$$\log\left(1+\varepsilon_{it}\right) = E_{t-1}\log\left(1+\varepsilon_{it}\right) + e_{it} \simeq -\frac{1}{2}Var_{t-1}\left(\varepsilon_{it}\right) + e_{it} \tag{8.12}$$

where by construction $E_{t-1}\left(e_{it}\right) = 0$. The conditional variance $Var_{t-1}\left(\varepsilon_{it}\right)$ may contain additive individual and time effects that would be subsumed into

---

[1] Zeldes used this framework to derive and test implications for consumption in the presence of borrowing constraints, which we ignore. See also Runkle (1991) and Keane and Runkle (1992).

δ_t and η_i, but otherwise it is assumed not to change with time $t - 1$ variables. Hence, the basic empirical equation becomes

$$\log (1 + r_{it}) = \alpha \Delta \log c_{it} + \beta' \Delta x_{it} + \delta_t + \eta_i + u_{it} \tag{8.13}$$

where

$$u_{it} = v_{it} + e_{it}. \tag{8.14}$$

Thus, the equation's error term u_{it}, net of individual and time effects, is made of two components: the unobservable change in tastes v_{it} and the expectational error e_{it}.[2]

In this model both returns and consumption growth at time t can be correlated with e_{it}, and are therefore treated as endogenous variables. Zeldes's identifying assumption is of the form of (8.2) with the instrument vector z_{it} containing Δx_{it}, lagged income, and marginal tax rates.

Lagged es should be uncorrelated to current es as long as they are in the agents' information sets, but vs may be serially correlated (unless ξ is a random walk). So serial correlation in u cannot be ruled out. Moreover, lagged consumption may be correlated to v even if it is not correlated to e. Thus, the presence of the taste shifter v rules out lagged consumption variables as instruments. Lack of orthogonality between lagged c and u in this model does not necessarily imply a violation of the Euler condition.

Finally, note that the model's martingale property $E_{t-1}e_{it} = 0$ implies that for a variable z_{it} in the information set a time average of the form

$$\frac{1}{T} \sum_{t=1}^{T} z_{it} e_{it} \to 0$$

as $T \to \infty$. However, the cross-sectional average $N^{-1} \sum_{i=1}^{N} z_{it} e_{it}$ need not converge to zero as $N \to \infty$ if e_{it} contains aggregate shocks (cf. Chamberlain, 1984, p. 1311, Zeldes, 1989, p. 318, and our discussion of Hall and Mishkin's model in Section 5.5). The cross-sectional limit will only vanish if the es are independent idiosyncratic shocks, that in model (8.13) requires us to assume that aggregate shocks affect all households in the same way and can be captured by time dummies.

Related examples that feature similar expectational errors are Euler-equation models for labour supply (MaCurdy, 1985), firm employment (Arellano and Bond, 1991, Schiantarelli and Sembenelli, 1993), and investment (Bond and Meghir, 1994). In the investment literature, company panel relationships between investment and q have also been identified through sequential moment restrictions by Hayashi and Inoue (1991), and Blundell, Bond, Devereux, and Schiantarelli (1992).

---

[2]Without the approximation, the model is nonlinear in variables and it has multiplicative individual effects.

8.1.3   Cross-Country Growth and Convergence

Our last example is a cross-country panel equation of the determinants of growth of the type considered by Caselli, Esquivel, and Lefort (1996). These authors estimated five 5-year period growth equations for 97 countries of the form

$$y_{it} - y_{i(t-5)} = \beta y_{i(t-5)} + s'_{i(t-5)}\gamma + \overline{f}'_{i(t-5)}\delta + \xi_t + \eta_i + v_{it} \qquad (8.15)$$

$$(t = 1965, 1970, 1975, 1980, 1985)$$

where y_{it} denotes log per-capita GDP in country i in year t, $s_{i(t-5)}$ is a vector of stock variables measured in year $t-5$ (including human capital indicators such as the log- secondary school enrolment rate), $\overline{f}_{i(t-5)}$ is a vector of flow variables measured as averages from $t-5$ to $t-1$: $\overline{f}_{i(t-5)} = \left(f_{i(t-5)} + ... + f_{i(t-1)}\right)/5$ (such as the rates of investment, population growth, and government expenditure), ξ_t captures global shocks, and η_i is a country effect that may represent differences in technology.

Caselli, Esquivel, and Lefort completed the specification with the following identifying assumptions:

$$E\left(v_{i1965} \mid y_{i1960}, s_{i1960}\right) = 0 \qquad (8.16)$$

$$E\left(v_{it} \mid y_{i1960}, s_{i1960}, ..., y_{i(t-5)}, s_{i(t-5)}, \overline{f}_{i1960}, ..., \overline{f}_{i(t-10)}\right) = 0 \qquad (8.17)$$

$$(t = 1970, ..., 1985).$$

That is, the country-specific time-varying shock in year t, v_{it}, is uncorrelated to the stock variables dated $t-5$ or earlier, including the output variable $y_{i(t-5)}$, and to the average flow variables dated $t-10$ or earlier. Thus, the stock variables dated $t-5$ are treated as predetermined for v_{it}, whereas the flow variables dated $t-5$ are predetermined for $v_{i(t+5)}$, and the assumptions restrict the dependence over time of v_{it}. Moreover, all explanatory variables are allowed to be correlated with the country effects η_i.

Islam (1995) considered an equation similar to (8.15) and allowed for correlation between the country effects and the determinants of growth in s and f, but treated them as strictly exogenous for v. Islam's identifying assumptions did not restrict the form of serial correlation in v. However, as argued by Caselli et al., except for indicators of a country's geography and climate, strict exogeneity assumptions do not seem very useful in the growth context. Variables like the investment rate or the population growth rate are potentially both effects and causes of economic growth.

The models of Caselli et al. (1996) and Islam (1995) illustrate our earlier discussion of the contrast between the partial adjustment equations with and without strictly exogenous variables in (7.1)-(7.2) and (8.3)-(8.4).

If β is negative, equation (8.15) can be regarded as a description of the convergence of output from an initial level to a steady state level, and it is broadly consistent with a variety of neoclassical growth models (see Barro and Sala-i-Martin, 1995). The variables s, f and η are therefore interpreted as determinants of a country's steady state level of income. The smaller the value of β the faster the (conditional) convergence to the steady state. If on the contrary $\beta = 0$ then there is no convergence, and s, f, and η measure differences in steady-state growth rates.

Panel data analyses of growth and convergence were preceded by cross-sectional analyses in which growth over the 25-year interval 1960–1985 was related to 1960 income and other determinants (as in Mankiw, Romer, and Weil, 1992). These studies typically found a negative but small effect of initial income, that implied a convergence rate in the range of 2–3 per cent.

Caselli et al. and others (e.g. Benhabib and Spiegel, 2000; Forbes, 2000; and Levine, Loayza, and Beck, 2000) considered panel analyses over 5- or 10-year subperiods as a way of controlling for unobserved constant differences in steady state growth, and lack of exogeneity of the observed determinants. Growth over long time spans of at least 5 years is chosen as a way to abstract from business cycle effects.

The GMM panel estimates of β reported by Caselli, Esquivel, and Lefort are also negative but of a larger magnitude than the cross-sectional estimates, implying a 10 per cent convergence rate.[3] Nevertheless, an open question is the extent to which these estimates are affected by finite sample biases in the GMM estimates (e.g. Bond, Hoeffler, and Temple, 2001).

From a substantive point of view, however, explaining the uncovered heterogeneity in steady state income levels seems at least as crucial as finding good estimates of the convergence coefficient.

8.2   Large T Within-Group Estimation

Let us consider a generic linear model that includes the previous examples as special cases:

$$y_{it} = w_{it}'\delta + \eta_i + v_{it}, \tag{8.18}$$

so that the errors satisfy condition (8.2), which for covenience we rewrite as

$$E\left(v_{it} \mid z_i^t\right) = 0 \tag{8.19}$$

for some vector z_{it} and $z_i^t = (z_{i1}, ..., z_{it})$.

If T is large, the sample realizations of the effects η_i may be treated as parameters that are jointly estimated with the common parameter vector δ. Thus, if all the variables in w_{it} are predetermined (i.e. if the w_{it} are functions

---

[3]The coefficient β can be regarded as approximating $-\left(1 - e^{-\lambda\tau}\right)$, where λ is the convergence rate and $\tau = 5$, so that $\lambda \simeq -(1/\tau)\ln(1 + \beta)$.

of the variables in the conditioning set z_i^t), the within-group OLS estimator of δ is consistent as $T \to \infty$:

$$\widehat{\delta}_{WG} = \left(\sum_{i=1}^{N} \sum_{t=1}^{T-1} w_{it}^* w_{it}^{*\prime} \right)^{-1} \sum_{i=1}^{N} \sum_{t=1}^{T-1} w_{it}^* y_{it}^* \qquad (8.20)$$

where as usual starred variables denote forward orthogonal deviations. An example in which all w_{it} are predetermined is the partial adjustment regression model (8.3)-(8.4).

Large T consistency of $\widehat{\delta}_{WG}$ hinges on the condition $E\left(w_{it}v_{it}\right) = 0$. This estimator, however, is not unbiased for fixed T since $E\left(w_{it}^* v_{it}^*\right) \neq 0$. Moreover, the bias does not tend to zero as N increases. Intuitively, as $N \to \infty$ the cross-sectional sample average

$$\frac{1}{N} \sum_{i=1}^{N} w_{it}^* v_{it}^*$$

approaches $E\left(w_{it}^* v_{it}^*\right)$, but it does not get closer to zero for a given value of T. Therefore, $\widehat{\delta}_{WG}$ is inconsistent in a fixed T, large N setting (detailed expressions for the bias in the case of a pure autoregressive model are given in Section 6.2, and illustrative calculations provided in Table 6.1).

If some of the w_{it} are endogenous explanatory variables (that is, if they are not functions of z_i^t), subject to identification, a within-group 2SLS estimator of the type described in (7.11) or (7.18) is consistent for large T:

$$\widehat{\delta}_{WG,2SLS} = \left(\sum_{i=1}^{N} \sum_{t=1}^{T-1} \widehat{w}_{it}^* w_{it}^{*\prime} \right)^{-1} \sum_{i=1}^{N} \sum_{t=1}^{T-1} \widehat{w}_{it}^* y_{it}^*. \qquad (8.21)$$

The vector $\widehat{w}_{it}^*$ denotes the estimated linear projection of w_{it}^* on $z_{it}^*, ..., z_{i(t-J)}^*$ for some pre-specified maximum lag value J:

$$\widehat{w}_{it}^* = \widehat{\pi}_0' z_{it}^* + ... + \widehat{\pi}_j' z_{i(t-J)}^* \quad (t = 1, ..., T-1) . \qquad (8.22)$$

Examples with both endogenous and predetermined explanatory variables are the consumption Euler equation and cross-country growth models.

In parallel with the previous case, large T consistency of $\widehat{\delta}_{WG,2SLS}$ requires that $E\left(z_{i(t-j)}v_{it}\right) = 0$ for $j = 1, ..., J$, a condition that is satisfied under the model's assumptions. But fixed T large N consistency would require $E\left(z_{i(t-j)}^* v_{it}^*\right) = 0$, which does not hold because z_{it} is only a predetermined variable relative to v_{it}.

8.3 Small T GMM Estimation

8.3.1 Moments and Weight Matrices

GMM estimators of δ in (8.18) based on the moments for the errors in first-differences

$$E\left[z_i^t\left(v_{i(t+1)} - v_{it}\right)\right] = 0 \ (t = 1, ..., T-1) \tag{8.23}$$

or in orthogonal deviations

$$E\left(z_i^t v_{it}^*\right) = 0 \ (t = 1, ..., T-1) \tag{8.24}$$

are consistent for large N and fixed T. The orthogonality between v_{it}^* and z_i^t is due to the fact that v_{it}^* is a forward deviation that only depends on current and future values of the errors.[4] Backward deviations or standard deviations from time means could not be used to express moment conditions of this type.

A generic compact expression that encompasses (8.23) and (8.24) is

$$E\left(Z_i'Ku_i\right) \equiv E\left[Z_i'K\left(y_i - W_i\delta\right)\right] = 0 \tag{8.25}$$

where Z_i is a block-diagonal matrix whose t-th block is given by $z_i^{t'}$, $y_i = (y_{i1}, ..., y_{iT})'$, $W_i = (w_{i1}', ..., w_{iT}')'$, $u_i = (u_{i1}, ..., u_{iT})'$, and $u_{it} = \eta_i + v_{it}$. Moreover, K represents any $(T-1) \times T$ upper-triangular transformation matrix of rank $(T-1)$, such that $K\iota = 0$, where ι is a $T \times 1$ vector of ones.

Orthogonality between K and ι ensures that the transformation eliminates any fixed effects, whereas by being upper triangular the transformed vector of errors Ku_i may depend on present and future errors but not on lagged ones. Note that both the first-difference matrix operator and the forward orthogonal deviations operator satisfy these requirements.

The form of a GMM estimator of δ based on (8.25) is

$$\widehat{\delta} = \left[\left(\sum_{i=1}^{N} W_i'K'Z_i\right) A_N \left(\sum_{i=1}^{N} Z_i'KW_i\right)\right]^{-1} \left(\sum_{i=1}^{N} W_i'K'Z_i\right) A_N \left(\sum_{i=1}^{N} Z_i'Ky_i\right). \tag{8.26}$$

Given identification, $\widehat{\delta}$ is consistent and asymptotically normal as $N \to \infty$ for fixed T (Hansen, 1982). An optimal choice of the weight matrix A_N is a consistent estimate of the inverse of $E\left(Z_i'Ku_iu_i'K'Z_i\right)$ up to scale.

We consider three alternative estimators depending on the choice of A_N. Firstly, a one-step weight matrix given by

$$A_N = \left(\sum_{i=1}^{N} Z_i'KK'Z_i\right)^{-1} \tag{8.27}$$

---

[4]This type of moment conditions was introduced by Arellano and Bover (1995). A closely related transformation was used by Hayashi and Sims (1983) for time series models.

This choice is optimal under conditional homoskedasticity $E(v_{it}^2|z_i^t) = \sigma^2$ and lack of autocorrelation $E(v_{it}v_{i(t+j)}|z_i^{t+j}) = 0$ for $j > 0$, since in this case we have

$$E\left(Z_i'Kv_iv_i'K'Z_i\right) = \sigma^2 E\left(Z_i'KK'Z_i\right). \tag{8.28}$$

A second, more general, two-step choice of A_N is given by

$$A_N = \left(\sum_{i=1}^{N} Z_i'K\widetilde{\Omega}K'Z_i\right)^{-1}, \tag{8.29}$$

where $\widetilde{\Omega} = N^{-1}\sum_{i=1}^{N} \widetilde{u}_i\widetilde{u}_i'$, and $\widetilde{u}_i$ is a vector of one-step residuals.[5] This choice is optimal if conditional variances and autocovariances are constant:

$$E(v_{it}^2|z_i^t) = E(v_{it}^2) \tag{8.30}$$

$$E\left(v_{it}v_{i(t+j)}|z_i^{t+j}\right) = E\left(v_{it}v_{i(t+j)}\right). \tag{8.31}$$

Thirdly, the standard two-step robust choice is

$$A_N = \left(\sum_{i=1}^{N} Z_i'K\widetilde{u}_i\widetilde{u}_i'K'Z_i\right)^{-1}, \tag{8.32}$$

which is an optimal weight matrix even if the conditional variances and auto-covariances of the errors are not constant. In contrast, the two-step estimator based on (8.29) does not depend on the data fourth-order moments but it is asymptotically less efficient than the estimator that uses (8.32) unless (8.30) and (8.31) are satisfied, in which case they are asymptotically equivalent (Arellano and Bond, 1991, p. 279).

The GMM estimators for autoregressive models that we discussed in Section 6.3 can be regarded as a special case of those presented here.

It is also useful to compare the estimator in (7.22) for dynamic models with strictly exogenous variables with that in (8.26). In both cases we have a system of transformed equations for different periods, but while in (7.22) the same instruments are valid for all equations (as in a standard simultaneous equations model), in (8.26) different instruments are valid for different equations, and we have an increasing set of instruments available as time progresses. Clearly, it is possible to combine features of the two settings (e.g. a model containing both predetermined and strictly exogenous variables).

8.3.2   The Irrelevance of Filtering

Arellano and Bover (1995) showed that a GMM estimator of the form given in (8.26) is invariant to the choice of K, provided K satisfies the required

---

[5]Note that $\widetilde{\Omega}$ is a consistent estimate of $\Omega = E\left(u_iu_i'\right)$, but not of $E\left(v_iv_i'\right)$. However, $K\widetilde{\Omega}K'$ is a consistent estimate of $KE\left(v_iv_i'\right)K'$.

conditions, and A_N depends on K as in (8.27), (8.29), or (8.32). Another requirement of the invariance result is that all the available instruments are used each period, so that Z_i is a block-diagonal matrix with an increasing number of instruments per block as indicated above.

To see this, first note the invariance of a GMM criterion function to linear transformations of the moments and the weight matrix. We have

$$\left(\sum_i \xi_i(\delta)\right)' V_N^{-1} \left(\sum_i \xi_i(\delta)\right) = \left(\sum_i \xi_i^*(\delta)\right)' V_N^{*-1} \left(\sum_i \xi_i^*(\delta)\right), \quad (8.33)$$

for $\xi_i^*(\delta) = F\xi_i(\delta)$ and $V_N^* = FV_N F'$, where F is a fixed non-singular transformation matrix. Thus, the GMM estimator that minimizes the left-hand side of (8.33) is numerically the same as the one that minimizes the right-hand side.

Next, let us rearrange the moments in $Z_i' K u_i$ as follows:

$$
\begin{aligned}
\xi_i(\delta) &= \begin{pmatrix} Ku_i \otimes z_{i1} \\ K_1 u_i \otimes z_{i2} \\ \vdots \\ K_{T-2} u_i \otimes z_{i(T-1)} \end{pmatrix} \quad (8.34) \\
&= \begin{pmatrix} K \otimes I_{r_1} & 0 & \cdots & 0 \\ 0 & K_1 \otimes I_{r_2} & & 0 \\ \vdots & & \ddots & \vdots \\ 0 & 0 & \cdots & K_{T-2} \otimes I_{r_{T-1}} \end{pmatrix} \begin{pmatrix} u_i \otimes z_{i1} \\ u_i \otimes z_{i2} \\ \vdots \\ u_i \otimes z_{i(T-1)} \end{pmatrix} \\
&= K^\dagger C \left(z_i^{T-1} \otimes u_i\right)
\end{aligned}
$$

where K_s is the $(T-s-1) \times T$ submatrix that results when the first s rows of K are eliminated, I_{r_s} is an identity matrix of the same order as the vector z_{is}, and C is a selection matrix such that

$$\begin{pmatrix} u_i \otimes z_{i1} \\ \vdots \\ u_i \otimes z_{i(T-1)} \end{pmatrix} = C \begin{pmatrix} z_{i1} \otimes u_i \\ \vdots \\ z_{i(T-1)} \otimes u_i \end{pmatrix}. \quad (8.35)$$

With this notation the estimator (8.26) can be regarded as the minimizer of the *rhs* of (8.33) with

$$V_N = K^\dagger C \sum_{i=1}^{N} \left(z_i^{T-1} z_i^{T-1\prime} \otimes \Psi_i\right) C' K^{\dagger\prime}. \quad (8.36)$$

The one-step estimator with weight matrix (8.27) corresponds to (8.36) with $\Psi_i = I_T$, whereas the two-step weight matrices (8.29) and (8.32) correspond to $\Psi_i = \tilde{\Omega}$ and $\Psi_i = \tilde{u}_i \tilde{u}_i'$, respectively.

Now, any other valid transformation K^* can be written as $K^* = \Phi K$ with $\Phi = K^* K' (KK')^{-1}$. Similarly, the submatrix K_s^* can be written as $K_s^* = \Phi_s K_s$ with $\Phi_s = K_s^* K_s' (K_s K_s')^{-1}$. Therefore, the resulting $\xi_i^*(\delta)$ and V_N^* will be of the form $F\xi_i(\delta)$ and $FV_N F'$ with F given by

$$
F = \begin{pmatrix}
\Phi \otimes I_{r_1} & 0 & \cdots & 0 \\
0 & \Phi_1 \otimes I_{r_2} & & 0 \\
\vdots & & \ddots & \vdots \\
0 & 0 & \cdots & \Phi_{T-2} \otimes I_{r_{T-1}}
\end{pmatrix},
\tag{8.37}
$$

which proves that all the estimators of the form (8.26) are identical regardless of the choice of K.

Some Convenient Filters Despite the irrelevance of filtering, specific choices of K may be computationally advantageous. Recall that we obtained the forward orthogonal deviations operator as

$$
A = (DD')^{-1/2} D
$$

where D is the first-difference operator, so that $AA' = I_{(T-1)}$ (see Section 2.2.2). Therefore, for $K = A$, the one-step weight matrix (8.27) simply becomes $\left(\sum_{i=1}^N Z_i' Z_i \right)^{-1}$. Hence, the one-step GMM estimator can be obtained as a matrix-weighted average of cross-sectional IV estimators:

$$
\widehat{\delta} = \left(\sum_{t=1}^{T-1} W_t^{*\prime} Z_t (Z_t' Z_t)^{-1} Z_t' W_t^* \right)^{-1} \sum_{t=1}^{T-1} W_t^{*\prime} Z_t (Z_t' Z_t)^{-1} Z_t' y_t^*,
\tag{8.38}
$$

where $W_t^* = (w_{1t}^{*\prime}, ..., w_{Nt}^{*\prime})'$, $y_t^* = (y_{1t}^*, ..., y_{Nt}^*)'$, and $Z_t = (z_1^{t\prime}, ..., z_N^{t\prime})'$. This is a useful computational feature of orthogonal deviations when T is not a very small number.

Similarly, for K given by

$$
K = \left(D \widetilde{\Omega} D' \right)^{-1/2} D
\tag{8.39}
$$

where $\left(D \widetilde{\Omega} D' \right)^{-1/2}$ denotes the upper-triangular Cholesky decomposition of $\left(D \widetilde{\Omega} D' \right)^{-1}$, the two-step weight matrix (8.29) also becomes $\left(\sum_{i=1}^N Z_i' Z_i \right)^{-1}$. Thus, the corresponding two-step GMM estimator can also be written in the form of (8.38) after replacing orthogonal deviations by observations transformed according to (8.39). This type of GLS transformation was suggested by Keane and Runkle (1992) and it removes serial correlation from the first differenced errors when the errors in levels have estimated covariance matrix $\widetilde{\Omega}$.

8.4 Optimal Instruments

Let us consider the form of the information bound and the optimal instruments for model (8.18)-(8.19) in a small T context. Since $E(\eta_i|z_i^T)$ is unrestricted, all the information about δ is contained in $E(v_{it} - v_{i(t+1)}|z_i^t) = 0$ for $t = 1, ..., T-1$.

For a single period the information bound is

$$J_{0t} = E\left(\frac{d_{it}d_{it}'}{w_{it}}\right)$$

where $d_{it} = E(w_{it} - w_{i(t+1)}|z_i^t)$ and $w_{it} = E[(v_{it} - v_{i(t+1)})^2|z_i^t]$ (cf. Chamberlain, 1987, and Appendix B). Thus, for a single period the optimal instrument is $m_{it} = d_{it}/w_{it}$, in the sense that under suitable regularity conditions the unfeasible IV estimator

$$\widetilde{\delta}_{(t)} = \left(\sum_{i=1}^N m_{it}\Delta w_{i(t+1)}'\right)^{-1}\left(\sum_{i=1}^N m_{it}\Delta y_{i(t+1)}\right) \tag{8.40}$$

satisfies $\sqrt{N}\left(\widetilde{\delta}_{(t)} - \delta\right) \overset{d}{\to} \mathcal{N}\left(0, J_{0t}^{-1}\right)$.

If the transformed errors were conditionally serially uncorrelated, the total information would be the sum of the information bounds for each period. In Section 2.2.2 we obtained forward orthogonal deviations as a filter applied to the differenced data that removed the moving average serial correlation induced by differencing when v_{it} is *iid*. Generalizing this idea we can obtain a forward filter that removes conditional serial correlation to arbitrary first-differenced errors that satisfy sequential moment restrictions. This is achieved by the following recursive transformation proposed by Chamberlain (1992b):

$$\widetilde{v}_{i(T-1)} = v_{i(T-1)} - v_{iT}$$

$$\widetilde{v}_{it} = (v_{it} - v_{i(t+1)}) - \tau_{t1i}\widetilde{v}_{i(t+1)} - \tau_{t2i}\widetilde{v}_{i(t+2)} - ... - \tau_{t(T-t-1)i}\widetilde{v}_{i(T-1)} \tag{8.41}$$

for $t = T - 2, ..., 1$, where

$$\tau_{tji} \equiv \tau_{tj}\left(z_i^{t+j}\right) = \frac{E[(v_{it} - v_{i(t+1)})\widetilde{v}_{i(t+j)}|z_i^{t+j}]}{E(\widetilde{v}_{i(t+j)}^2|z_i^{t+j})} \quad (j = 1, ..., T-t-1). \tag{8.42}$$

The interest in this transformation is that it satisfies the same conditional moment restrictions as the original errors in first-differences, namely

$$E(\widetilde{v}_{it}|z_i^t) = 0, \tag{8.43}$$

but additionally it satisfies by construction the lack of dependence requirement:[6]

---

[6]To see that this is the kind of conditional lack of serial correlation that is required, notice that $E\left(\widetilde{v}_{it} \mid z_i^t\right) = 0$ and $E\left(\widetilde{v}_{i(t+j)} \mid z_i^{t+j}\right) = 0$ imply, respectively, that

$$E(\widetilde{v}_{it}\widetilde{v}_{i(t+j)}|z_i^{t+j}) = 0 \text{ for } j = 1, ..., T - t - 1. \tag{8.44}$$

Therefore, in terms of the transformed errors the information bound can be written as

$$J_0 = \sum_{t=1}^{T-1} E\left(\frac{\widetilde{d}_{it}\widetilde{d}_{it}'}{\widetilde{\omega}_{it}}\right) \tag{8.45}$$

where $\widetilde{d}_{it} = E\left(\widetilde{w}_{it}|z_i^t\right)$ and $\widetilde{\omega}_{it} = E\left(\widetilde{v}_{it}^2|z_i^t\right)$. The variables $\widetilde{w}_{it}$ and $\widetilde{y}_{it}$ denote the corresponding transformations to the first-differences of w_{it} and y_{it} such that $\widetilde{v}_{it} = \widetilde{y}_{it} - \widetilde{w}_{it}'\delta$.

Thus, the optimal instruments for all periods are $\widetilde{m}_{it} = \widetilde{d}_{it}/\widetilde{\omega}_{it}$, in the sense that under suitable regularity conditions the unfeasible IV estimator

$$\widetilde{\delta} = \left(\sum_{i=1}^{N}\sum_{t=1}^{T-1} \widetilde{m}_{it}\widetilde{w}_{it}'\right)^{-1}\left(\sum_{i=1}^{N}\sum_{t=1}^{T-1} \widetilde{m}_{it}\widetilde{y}_{it}\right) \tag{8.46}$$

satisfies $\sqrt{N}\left(\widetilde{\delta} - \delta\right) \xrightarrow{d} \mathcal{N}\left(0, J_0^{-1}\right)$.[7]

The optimal IV estimator (8.46) is unfeasible on two accounts. Firstly, it uses a data dependent filter whose weights are unknown functions of the conditioning variables. Secondly, the optimal instruments $\widetilde{m}_{it}$ depend on unknown conditional expectations of the filtered data.

A feasible estimator that achieves the bound could be potentially constructed by replacing the unknown functions with nonparametric regression estimators. Alternatively, one could use a GMM estimator based on an expanding set of instruments as N tends to infinity. Hahn (1997) showed that a GMM estimator that uses an increasing number of instruments attains the efficiency bound in a model with sequential moment restrictions. Moreover, he discussed the rate of growth of the number of instruments that is required for semi-parametric efficiency when using Fourier and polynomial series.

Lack of Serial Correlation   Suppose that the original errors are conditionally serially uncorrelated so that

$$E\left(v_{it}v_{i(t+j)} \mid z_i^{t+j}\right) = 0.$$

$E\left[h_t\left(z_i^t\right)\widetilde{v}_{it}\right] = 0$ and $E\left[h_{t+j}\left(z_i^{t+j}\right)\widetilde{v}_{i(t+j)}\right] = 0$ for any functions $h_t\left(.\right)$ and $h_{t+j}\left(.\right)$. If $E\left(\widetilde{v}_{it}\widetilde{v}_{i(t+j)} \mid z_i^{t+j}\right) = 0$ then

$$E\left[\widetilde{v}_{it}\widetilde{v}_{i(t+j)}h_t\left(z_i^t\right)h_{t+j}\left(z_i^{t+j}\right)\right] = 0,$$

so that the information bound for any $h_t\left(.\right)$ and $h_{t+j}\left(.\right)$ is the sum of the information bounds for each period.

[7]The optimality result can be extended in a straightforward way to multi-equation and nonlinear contexts as long as the effects and the time-varying errors enter additively. The general formulation is in Chamberlain (1992b).

This is, for example, a property of the partial adjustment regression model (8.3)-(8.4), but not necessarily of Zeldes's Euler equation (8.13) since unobserved taste changes may be serially correlated.

In this case the weights (8.42) are equal to zero for $j > 1$ and the optimal filter becomes

$$\tilde{v}_{i(T-1)} = v_{i(T-1)} - v_{iT}$$

$$\tilde{v}_{it} = \left(v_{it} - v_{i(t+1)}\right) + \frac{\sigma_{i(t+1)}^2}{\tilde{\sigma}_{i(t+1)}^2}\tilde{v}_{i(t+1)} \quad (t = T-2, ..., 1) \tag{8.47}$$

where $\sigma_{it}^2 = E\left(v_{it}^2 \mid z_i^t\right)$ and $\tilde{\sigma}_{it}^2 = E\left(\tilde{v}_{it}^2 \mid z_i^t\right)$.

If the conditional variances are constant but there is unconditional time series heteroskedasticity, so that $E(v_{it}^2|z_i^t) = \sigma_t^2$ and $E\left(\tilde{v}_{it}^2 \mid z_i^t\right) = \tilde{\sigma}_t^2$, we have

$$\tilde{v}_{it} = v_{it} - \frac{1}{\left(\sigma_{(t+1)}^{-2} + ... + \sigma_T^{-2}\right)}\left(\sigma_{(t+1)}^{-2}v_{i(t+1)} + ... + \sigma_T^{-2}v_{iT}\right) \quad (t = T-1, ..., 1)$$

$$\tag{8.48}$$

and

$$\tilde{\sigma}_t^2 = \sigma_t^2 + \frac{1}{\left(\sigma_{(t+1)}^{-2} + ... + \sigma_T^{-2}\right)}. \tag{8.49}$$

Other Special Cases If the v_{it}s are conditionally homoskedastic and serially uncorrelated, so that $E(v_{it}^2|z_i^t) = \sigma^2$ and $E(v_{it}v_{i(t+j)}|z_i^{t+j}) = 0$ for $j > 0$, the $\tilde{v}_{it}$s boil down to ordinary forward orthogonal deviations:

$$\tilde{v}_{it} = v_{it} - \frac{1}{(T-t)}(v_{i(t+1)} + ... + v_{iT}) \equiv \frac{1}{c_t}v_{it}^* \text{ for } t = T-1, ..., 1.$$

where $c_t^2 = (T-t)/(T-t+1)$. In such a case the optimal instrument is $\tilde{m}_{it} = c_t\sigma^{-2}E(w_{it}^*|z_i^t)$ so that

$$\hat{\delta} = \left[\sum_{i=1}^N \sum_{t=1}^{T-1} E\left(w_{it}^*|z_i^t\right) w_{it}^{*\prime}\right]^{-1} \sum_{i=1}^N \sum_{t=1}^{T-1} E\left(w_{it}^*|z_i^t\right) y_{it}^* \tag{8.50}$$

$$= \left[\sum_{i=1}^N \mathcal{E}_T\left(W_i^{*\prime}\right) W_i^*\right]^{-1} \sum_{i=1}^N \mathcal{E}_T\left(W_i^{*\prime}\right) y_i^* \tag{8.51}$$

and

$$J_0 = \frac{1}{\sigma^2}\sum_{t=1}^{T-1} E[E(w_{it}^*|z_i^t)E(w_{it}^{*\prime}|z_i^t)] = \frac{1}{\sigma^2}E\left[\mathcal{E}_T\left(W_i^{*\prime}\right)\mathcal{E}_T\left(W_i^*\right)\right], \tag{8.52}$$

where we have introduced the notation

$$\mathcal{E}_T \left(W_i^{*\prime} \right) = \left[E \left(w_{i1}^* | z_i^1 \right), ..., E \left(w_{i(T-1)}^* | z_i^{T-1} \right) \right]. \qquad (8.53)$$

If we further assume that the conditional expectations $E(w_{it}^* | z_i^t)$ are linear:

$$E(w_{it}^* | z_i^t) = \Pi_t z_i^t \qquad (8.54)$$

with

$$\Pi_t = E(w_{it}^* z_i^{t\prime}) [E(z_i^t z_i^{t\prime})]^{-1}, \qquad (8.55)$$

then

$$J_0 = \frac{1}{\sigma^2} \sum_{t=1}^{T-1} E(w_{it}^* z_i^{t\prime}) [E(z_i^t z_i^{t\prime})]^{-1} E(z_i^t w_{it}^{*\prime}) \qquad (8.56)$$

which coincides with the inverse of the asymptotic covariance matrix of the standard GMM estimator (8.26) under the stated assumptions.

Note that the one-step GMM estimator is of the form of (8.50) with the unrestricted sample linear projection $\widehat{\Pi}_t z_i^t$ in place of $E(w_{it}^* | z_i^t)$. On the other hand, the within-group OLS and 2SLS estimators (8.20) and (8.21) are also of the form of (8.50), but in place of $E(w_{it}^* | z_i^t)$ they use w_{it}^* or $\widehat{w}_{it}^*$, neither of which are in the admissible set of instruments for fixed T, large N consistency.

If we assume that the conditional variances and autocovariances are constant, but we allow for constant autocorrelation and unconditional time series heteroskedasticity, as in (8.30) and (8.31), the $\widetilde{v}_{it}$ are equivalent to the population counterpart of the Keane and Runkle filter (8.39). Note that this filter can also be expressed as a GLS transformation of the errors in orthogonal deviations (instead of first-differences):

$$K = (A\Omega A')^{-1/2} A. \qquad (8.57)$$

Thus, in this case

$$\widetilde{\delta} = \left[\sum_{i=1}^N \mathcal{E}_T \left(W_i^{*\prime} \right) \Omega^{*-1} W_i^* \right]^{-1} \sum_{i=1}^N \mathcal{E}_T \left(W_i^{*\prime} \right) \Omega^{*-1} y_i^* \qquad (8.58)$$

and

$$J_0 = E \left[\mathcal{E}_T \left(W_i^{*\prime} \right) \Omega^{*-1} \mathcal{E}_T \left(W_i^* \right) \right] \qquad (8.59)$$

where $\Omega^* = E \left(u_i^* u_i^{*\prime} \right) = A\Omega A'$.

Note that we do not consider the question of the impact on the bound for δ of assuming conditional homoskedasticity, lack of serial correlation, and linearity of $E(w_{it}^* | z_i^t)$. Here, we have merely particularized the bound for δ based on $E(v_{it} | z_i^t) = 0$ to cases where the additional restrictions happen to occur in the population but are not used in the calculation of the bound.

A Comparable Expression for the General Case The transformation that was presented in (8.41) as a forward filter applied to the first-differences can also be expressed in terms of orthogonal deviations.

A matrix formulation that goes in parallel to the special cases discussed above is as follows. Let us consider the notation

$$
\mathcal{V}_T\left(v_i^*\right) = \begin{pmatrix}
E(v_{i1}^{*2}|z_i^1) & E(v_{i1}^*v_{i2}^*|z_i^2) & \cdots & E(v_{i1}^*v_{i(T-1)}^*|z_i^{T-1}) \\
E(v_{i1}^*v_{i2}^*|z_i^2) & E(v_{i2}^{*2}|z_i^2) & \cdots & E(v_{i2}^*v_{i(T-1)}^*|z_i^{T-1}) \\
\vdots & & \ddots & \vdots \\
E(v_{i1}^*v_{i(T-1)}^*|z_i^{T-1}) & & \cdots & E(v_{i(T-1)}^{*2}|z_i^{T-1})
\end{pmatrix},
$$

(8.60)

and let $\mathcal{H}_i$ be the upper-triangular matrix such that

$$
\mathcal{V}_T\left(\mathcal{H}_i^{-1}v_i^*\right) = \mathcal{V}_T\left(\tilde{v}_i\right) = \begin{pmatrix}
E(\tilde{v}_{i1}^2|z_i^1) & & 0 \\
& \ddots & \\
0 & & E(\tilde{v}_{i(T-1)}^2|z_i^{T-1})
\end{pmatrix} \equiv \Lambda_i.
$$

By conditional Cholesky factorization, $\mathcal{H}_i$ is given by

$$
\mathcal{H}_i = \begin{pmatrix}
1 & h_{11}\left(z_i^2\right) & h_{12}\left(z_i^3\right) & \cdots & h_{1(T-2)}\left(z_i^{T-1}\right) \\
0 & 1 & h_{21}\left(z_i^3\right) & & h_{2(T-3)}\left(z_i^{T-1}\right) \\
\vdots & & & & \vdots \\
0 & 0 & 0 & \ddots & h_{(T-2)1}\left(z_i^{T-1}\right) \\
0 & 0 & 0 & \cdots & 1
\end{pmatrix}
$$

(8.61)

where $h_{tj}\left(z_i^{t+j}\right) = E\left(v_{it}^*\tilde{v}_{i(t+j)} \mid z_i^{t+j}\right)/E\left(\tilde{v}_{i(t+j)}^2 \mid z_i^{t+j}\right)$, which are just orthogonal-deviation counterparts of (8.42).

Thus, the optimal estimator in the general case (8.46) can be written as

$$
\tilde{\delta} = \left\{ \sum_{i=1}^N \mathcal{E}_T\left(W_i^{*\prime}\mathcal{H}_i^{-1\prime}\right) \Lambda_i^{-1}\mathcal{H}_i^{-1}W_i^* \right\}^{-1} \sum_{i=1}^N \mathcal{E}_T\left(W_i^{*\prime}\mathcal{H}_i^{-1\prime}\right) \Lambda_i^{-1}\mathcal{H}_i^{-1}y_i^*,
$$

(8.62)

and the information bound is

$$
J_0 = E\left[\mathcal{E}_T\left(W_i^{*\prime}\mathcal{H}_i^{-1\prime}\right) \Lambda_i^{-1}\mathcal{E}_T\left(\mathcal{H}_i^{-1}W_i^*\right)\right].
$$

(8.63)

8.5 Instruments Uncorrelated with the Effects

8.5.1 System Estimators

We have already discussed system estimators that combined moment restrictions in levels and deviations (or differences) in various contexts. We considered models that contained a subset of strictly exogenous variables that were un-correlated with the effects in both static (Section 3.4) and dynamic settings (Section 7.3.4). Moreover, we also considered mean-stationary autoregressive models in which lagged dependent variables in first-differences were valid in-struments for the equation errors in levels (Section 6.5). The use of moment restrictions in levels may afford large information gains—but also biases if the restrictions are violated—and this has been shown in several instances.[8]

We now consider instrumental variables that are uncorrelated with the ef-fects in the context of sequential moment conditions. Let us suppose as before that

$$y_{it} = \delta' w_{it} + \eta_i + v_{it}$$

$$E(v_{it}|z_i^t) = 0,$$

but in addition a subset z_{1it} of the predetermined instruments in z_{it} are assumed to be uncorrelated with the effects:

$$E\left[z_{1it}\left(\eta_i - \eta\right)\right] = 0 \tag{8.64}$$

where $\eta = E\left(\eta_i\right)$. The implication is that for $s \leq t$:

$$E\left[z_{1is}\left(\eta_i - \eta + v_{it}\right)\right] = 0. \tag{8.65}$$

Given the basic moment restrictions for the errors in first-differences con-sidered earlier

$$E\left[z_i^{t-1}\left(\Delta y_{it} - \delta' \Delta w_{it}\right)\right] = 0 \tag{8.66}$$

and the moments involving the levels' intercept η

$$E\left(y_{it} - \eta - \delta' w_{it}\right) = 0, \tag{8.67}$$

Assumption (8.64) adds the following restrictions in levels[9]

$$E\left[z_{1it}\left(y_{it} - \eta - \delta' w_{it}\right)\right] = 0. \tag{8.68}$$

These two sets of moments can be combined using the Arellano and Bover (1995) GMM estimator. A generic compact expression for the full set of mo-ments is

[8]See Arellano and Bover, 1995; Blundell and Bond, 1998; and Hahn, 1999.

[9]Note, for example, that $E\left[z_{1i(t-1)}\left(y_{it} - \eta - \delta' w_{it}\right)\right] = 0$ is not an extra restriction since it follows from two existing restrictions:

$$\begin{aligned} E\left[z_{1i(t-1)}\left(y_{it} - \eta - \delta' w_{it}\right)\right] &= E\left[z_{1i(t-1)}\left(\Delta y_{it} - \delta' \Delta w_{it}\right)\right] \\ &\quad + E\left[z_{1i(t-1)}\left(y_{i(t-1)} - \eta - \delta' w_{i(t-1)}\right)\right]. \end{aligned}$$

$$E\left[\left(\begin{array}{cc} Z_{\ell i} & 0 \\ 0 & Z_i \end{array}\right)' \left(\begin{array}{c} u_i \\ K u_i \end{array}\right)\right] = E\left(Z_i^{\dagger'} u_i^{\dagger}\right) = E\left[Z_i^{\dagger'}\left(y_i^{\dagger} - W_i^{\dagger}\delta^{\dagger}\right)\right] = 0$$

(8.69)

where u_i, K, and Z_i are as in (8.25), $Z_{\ell i}$ is the following block-diagonal matrix

$$Z_{\ell i} = \left(\begin{array}{ccc} (1, z_{1i1}') & \cdots & 0 \\ & \ddots & \\ 0 & & (1, z_{1iT}') \end{array}\right),$$

(8.70)

and $\delta^{\dagger} = (\delta', \eta)'$. With these changes, the form of the GMM estimator is similar to that of (8.26):

$$\hat{\delta}^{\dagger} = \left[\left(\sum_{i=1}^{N} W_i^{\dagger'} Z_i^{\dagger}\right) A_N \left(\sum_{i=1}^{N} Z_i^{\dagger'} W_i^{\dagger}\right)\right]^{-1} \left(\sum_{i=1}^{N} W_i^{\dagger'} Z_i^{\dagger}\right) A_N \left(\sum_{i=1}^{N} Z_i^{\dagger'} y_i^{\dagger}\right).$$

(8.71)

The standard robust choice of A_N is the inverse of an unrestricted estimate of the variance matrix of the moments $N^{-1} \sum_{i=1}^{N} Z_i^{\dagger'} \tilde{u}_i^{\dagger} \tilde{u}_i^{\dagger'} Z_i^{\dagger}$ for some preliminary consistent residuals $\tilde{u}_i^{\dagger}$. The difference in this case is that, contrary to GMM estimators based exclusively in moments for the errors in differences, an efficient one-step estimator under restrictive assumptions does not exist. Since $E\left(Z_i^{\dagger'} \tilde{u}_i^{\dagger} \tilde{u}_i^{\dagger'} Z_i^{\dagger}\right)$ depends on the errors in levels, at the very least it will be a function of the ratio of variances of η_i and v_{it}. Moreover, as explained in Section 6.5, since some of the instruments for the equations in levels are not valid for those in differences, and conversely, not all the covariance terms between the two sets of moments will be zero.

8.5.2 Stationarity Restrictions

A leading case of uncorrelated predetermined instruments are first-differences of predetermined instruments that exhibit constant correlation with the effects (Arellano and Bover, 1995). Suppose that we can partition

$$z_{it} = \left(\begin{array}{c} z_{Ait} \\ z_{Bit} \end{array}\right)$$

such that the variables in z_{Ait} have constant correlation with the effects over time, in which case

$$E\left(\eta_i \Delta z_{Ait}\right) = 0.$$

(8.72)

Constant correlation over time will be expected when z_{Ait} is conditionally stationary in mean (Blundell and Bond, 1998). That is, when

$$E\left(\Delta z_{Ait} \mid \eta_i\right) = 0. \tag{8.73}$$

This situation leads to a list of orthogonality conditions of the form (8.69) with $z_{1it} = \Delta z_{Ait}$, $z_{2i1} = z_{i1}$, and $z_{2it} = z_{Bit}$ for $t > 1$.

Blundell and Bond (2000) employed moment restrictions of this type in their empirical analysis of Cobb-Douglas production functions using firm panel data. They found that moment conditions for the production function in first-differences of the form (8.66) were not very informative, due to the fact that firm output, capital, and employment were highly persistent. In contrast, the first-difference instruments for production function errors in levels turned out to be informative and empirically valid.

8.5.3   Illustration: A Dynamic Evaluation of Job Training

We next consider as an illustration of the use of stationarity restrictions, an evaluation of training example discussed by Chamberlain (1993) and Arellano and Honoré (2001).

Suppose that y_{it}^* denotes latent earnings of worker i in period t in the absence of training, and that there is a common effect of training for all workers. Actual earnings y_{it} are observed for $t = 1, ..., s-1, s+1, ..., T$. Training occurs in period s $(1 < s < T)$, so that y_{it}^* is observed for all workers in the pre-training period:

$$y_{it} = y_{it}^* \text{ for } t = 1, ..., s-1,$$

and y_{is}^* is unobservable while training takes place[10].

We wish to measure the effect of training on earnings in subsequent periods, denoted by $\delta_{s+1}, ..., \delta_T$:

$$y_{it} = y_{it}^* + \delta_t w_i \ (t = s+1, ..., T), \tag{8.74}$$

where w_i is a dummy variable that equals 1 in the event of training.

We assume that y_{it}^* follows a stable AR(1) process with a stationary individual-specific mean:

$$y_{it}^* = \alpha y_{i(t-1)}^* + \eta_i + v_{it} \tag{8.75}$$

so that $E(v_{it}|y_i^{*(t-1)}) = 0$ and $Cov(\Delta y_{it}^*, \eta_i) = 0$.

We also assume that w_i depends on lagged earnings $y_{i1}, ..., y_{i(s-1)}$ and η_i, but conditionally on these variables it is randomly assigned. That is, we assume that w_i is independent of after-training earnings shocks $v_{is}, v_{i(s+1)}, ..., v_{iT}$.

Then we have:

$$y_{i(s+1)} = \alpha^2 y_{i(s-1)} + \delta_{s+1} w_i + (1+\alpha)\eta_i + (v_{i(s+1)} + \alpha v_{is}) \tag{8.76}$$

$$y_{it} = \alpha y_{i(t-1)} + (\delta_t - \alpha\delta_{t-1})w_i + \eta_i + v_{it} \ (t = s+2, ..., T) \tag{8.77}$$

Let us now consider the orthogonality conditions implied by the model in the absence of the stationarity restriction. Firstly, as long as we observe

---

[10]Actually, y_{is}^* is a censored variable that may be available for workers that do not experience training, but we ignore this possibility.

at least three pre-training periods ($s \geq 4$), the autoregressive parameter of the earnings process can be determined from the pre-training data using the standard moment conditions for the errors in first-differences:

$$E\left[y_i^{t-2}\left(\Delta y_{it} - \alpha \Delta y_{i(t-1)}\right)\right] = 0 \ (t = 3, ..., s-1). \tag{8.78}$$

Secondly, upon substitution of $\eta_i = y_{i(s-1)} - \alpha y_{i(s-2)} - v_{i(s-1)}$ in (8.76) we obtain the following moments that are informative about the short-run effect of training δ_{s+1}:

$$E\left\{y_i^{s-2}\left[y_{i(s+1)} - \left(1 + \alpha + \alpha^2\right)y_{i(s-1)} + \alpha\left(1+\alpha\right)y_{i(s-2)} - \delta_{s+1}w_i\right]\right\} = 0. \tag{8.79}$$

The construction of these moments requires one post-training period and at least two pre-training periods. Nevertheless, unless we have at least three pre-training periods, α and δ_{s+1} cannot be separately identified from (8.78) and (8.79).

Next, dividing (8.76) by $(1+\alpha)$ and subtracting the result from equation (8.77) at $t = s+2$, we obtain a transformed residual that gives rise to the moments

$$E\left\{y_i^{s-1}\left[y_{i(s+2)} - \frac{(1+\alpha+\alpha^2)}{(1+\alpha)}y_{i(s+1)} + \frac{\alpha^2}{(1+\alpha)}y_{i(s-1)}\right.\right.$$

$$\left.\left. - \left(\delta_{(s+2)} - \frac{(1+\alpha+\alpha^2)}{(1+\alpha)}\delta_{(s+1)}\right)w_i\right]\right\} = 0. \tag{8.80}$$

Given α and δ_{s+1}, these moments are informative about the effect of training after two periods $\delta_{(s+2)}$.

Finally, the effects of training for the remaining periods $\delta_{(s+3)}, ..., \delta_T$ are identified from the moments:

$$E\left[y_i^{t-2}\left(\Delta y_{it} - \alpha \Delta y_{i(t-1)} + \Delta(\delta_t - \alpha\delta_{t-1})w_i\right)\right] = 0 \ (t = s+3, ..., T). \tag{8.81}$$

The additional orthogonality conditions implied by mean stationarity are:

$$E\left[\Delta y_{i(t-1)}\left(y_{it} - \alpha y_{i(t-1)}\right)\right] = 0 \ (t = 3, ..., s-1) \tag{8.82}$$

$$E\left[\Delta y_{i(s-1)}\left(y_{i(s+1)} - \alpha^2 y_{i(s-1)} - \delta_{s+1}w_i\right)\right] = 0 \tag{8.83}$$

$$E\left[\Delta y_{i(s-1)}\left(y_{it} - \alpha y_{i(t-1)} + (\delta_t - \alpha\delta_{t-1})w_i\right)\right] = 0 \ (t = s+2, ..., T). \tag{8.84}$$

We would expect $E\left(\Delta y_{i(s-1)}w_i\right) < 0$, since there is evidence of a dip in the pre-training earnings of participants (Ashenfelter and Card, 1985). Thus, (8.83) can be expected to be more informative about δ_{s+1} than (8.79). Moreover, the stationarity restrictions make it possible to identify both α and δ_{s+1} from data containing just two pre-training periods and one post-training period combining the moments (8.79) and (8.83).

8.5.4 Time-Invariant Explanatory Variables

Sometimes the effect of a vector of time-invariant explanatory variables is of interest, a parameter vector γ, say, in a model of the form

$$y_{it} = \delta' w_{it} + \gamma' \zeta_i + \eta_i + v_{it} \tag{8.85}$$

$$E\left(v_{it} \mid z_i^t\right) = 0$$

where for convenience we assume that ζ_i contains an intercept and therefore $E(\eta_i) = 0$ without lack of generality. If ζ_i is orthogonal to $(\eta_i + v_{it})$ then δ and γ can be jointly estimated using a system GMM estimator that combines the moments (8.66) with

$$E\left[\zeta_i \left(y_{it} - \delta' w_{it} - \gamma' \zeta_i\right)\right] = 0. \tag{8.86}$$

However, if the components of ζ_i (other than the intercept) are not orthogonal to $(\eta_i + v_{it})$, the corresponding elements of γ cannot be identified from the basic moments because the time-invariant explanatory variables are absorbed into the individual effect.

In principle, the availability of predetermined instruments that are uncorrelated with the effects might help to identify such parameters. Indeed, this was the motivation Hausman and Taylor (1981) had for considering uncorrelated strictly exogenous variables (see Section 3.4). However, moments in levels that are derived from stationarity restrictions, as in (8.72), are unlikely to serve that purpose. The problem is that if $E(\eta_i \Delta z_{Ait}) = 0$ holds we may expect that $E(\zeta_i \Delta z_{Ait}) = 0$ will also hold, in which case changes in z_{Ait} would not help the identification of γ.

8.5.5 Levels Moments Implied by Lack of Serial Correlation

The basic model with sequential moment conditions that we consider in this chapter, as shown in (8.18)-(8.19), may or may not restrict the serial correlation properties of the errors depending on the nature of the variables in the conditioning set. Moreover, restriction (8.19) does not rule out the correlation between the errors v_{it} and the effects η_i. Sometimes, a natural starting point for an empirical analysis will be the stronger assumption

$$E\left(v_{it} \mid z_i^t, \eta_i\right) = 0 \tag{8.87}$$

which implies (8.19) and also lack of correlation between v_{it} and η_i. If z_{it} includes $y_{i(t-1)}$ and $w_{i(t-1)}$ then (8.87) implies that the v_{it} are not autocorrelated. Examples of this situation are the autoregressive models of Chapter 6 and the partial adjustment model in (8.3)-(8.4).

The point we wish to make here is that if the v_{it} are serially uncorrelated and have constant (or lack of) correlation with the effects, then $\Delta v_{i(t-1)}$ can be used as an instrument for the errors in levels:

$$E\left(\Delta v_{i(t-1)} u_{it}\right) = 0. \tag{8.88}$$

In effect, we have

$$E\left(\Delta v_{i(t-1)} u_{it}\right) = E\left(\Delta v_{i(t-1)} \eta_i\right) + E\left(\Delta v_{i(t-1)} v_{it}\right) = 0$$

as long as the vs are not autocorrelated and $E\left(v_{it}\eta_i\right)$ does not vary with t.[11]

Condition (8.88) is the type of quadratic moment restriction considered by Ahn and Schmidt (1995) for autoregressive models (see Section 6.4.2). In principle, their use makes the estimation problem nonlinear, although an alternative is to evaluate $\Delta v_{i(t-1)}$ using a preliminary consistent estimator of δ, and use the resulting residual as an instrument for the levels equation as part of a system estimator of the type described earlier.

Note that if $y_{i(t-1)}$ and $w_{i(t-1)}$ belong to z_{it} and they are mean stationary in such a way that

$$E\left[\left(\begin{array}{c} \Delta y_{i(t-1)} \\ \Delta w_{i(t-1)} \end{array}\right) u_{it}\right] = 0, \tag{8.89}$$

then the moment condition (8.88) becomes redundant given (8.89). The reason is that since $\Delta v_{i(t-1)} = \Delta y_{i(t-1)} - \delta'\Delta w_{i(t-1)}$, (8.88) is a linear combination of (8.89).

8.6 Estimating the Effect of Fertility on Female Labour Participation

In this section we illustrate various aspects of inference from sequential moment restrictions in the context of an empirical illustration. We consider the relationship between female labour force participation and fertility, discussing several variations on the estimates reported by Carrasco (2001) for a linear probability model. Our discussion extends a similar illustration in Arellano and Honoré (2001).

The data come from the PSID for the years 1986–89. The sample consists of 1442 women aged between 18 and 55 in 1986, that are married or cohabiting. The dependent variable is a binary indicator of participation in year t (defined as positive annual hours of work). Fertility is also a dummy variable, which takes the value one if the age of the youngest child in $t+1$ is 1. The equation also includes an indicator of whether the woman has a child aged between 2 and 6, and individual effects.

---

[11]If the vs are uncorrelated with the effects it is also true that $E\left(v_{i(t-1)} u_{it}\right) = 0$, but $v_{i(t-1)}$ cannot be used as an instrument since it depends on the unobservable individual effects.

Individual effects capture tastes for work, and the permanent components of market wage and household income. The time-varying errors include idiosyncratic labour market shocks to participation (like a job promotion or a dismissal). Since these shocks are also likely to affect fertility decisions, the fertility indicator is treated as an endogenous explanatory variable, in the sense of being correlated not only with the effects but also with the contemporaneous time-varying errors. The presence of a child aged 2–6 is the result of past fertility decisions, and so it should be treated as a predetermined variable that is correlated with the effects.

An indicator of whether a woman has two children of the same sex is used as an external instrument for fertility. The choice of this instrument is motivated by the fact that, in the PSID sample, women with two children of the same sex have a significantly higher probability of having a third child (Angrist and Evans, 1998). Note that we would expect the "same sex" instrumental variable to be correlated with the fixed effect. The reason is that it will be a predictor of preferences for children, given that the sample includes women with less than two children. Moreover, it may be affected by past labour shocks through past fertility decisions, and so it may be treated as a predetermined but not strictly exogenous instrument. Therefore, provided we use a linear specification, the relationship of interest fits in the framework of sequential moment conditions introduced in the earlier sections of this chapter.[12]

Table 8.1 reports the results for two versions of the model with and without lagged participation as an additional explanatory variable, using DPD (Arellano and Bond, 1988). If there are fixed costs of work, we would expect lagged participation to affect current participation other things being equal.

The last three columns present GMM estimates in orthogonal deviations that treat fertility as endogenous, and the "kids 2–6" and "same sex" indicators as predetermined variables. Column 5 contains the estimates based on the basic set of moments, whereas columns 6 and 7 use additional predetermined instruments for the errors in levels. Columns 1–4 report the results from other methods of estimation for comparisons. The estimated equations without individual effects also include a constant, age, race, and education dummies (not reported).

There is a noticeable difference between the OLS and 2SLS estimated effects of fertility, both of which neglect unobserved heterogeneity. Since we expect the fertility, "kids 2–6", and "same sex" variables to be all correlated with the effects, the relative magnitudes of the OLS and 2SLS biases are unclear a priori. Notice also the evidence from the serial correlation statistics $m1$ and $m2$ of persistent positive autocorrelation in the residuals in levels, which is consistent with the presence of fixed effects (these test statistics are asymptotically dis-

---

[12]See Carrasco (2001) for further discussion and additional estimates of linear and nonlinear models.

tributed as a $\mathcal{N}(0,1)$ under the null of no autocorrelation, and they are similar to those discussed in the context of autoregressive models in Section 6.7).

Table 8.1
Female Labour Force Participation
Linear Probability Models (N=1442, 1986-1989)

Variable	OLS	2SLS[1]	WG	GMM St.Ex[2]	GMM Pred[3]	GMM ℓAB[4]	GMM ℓAS[5]
Fertility	−0.15	−1.01	−0.06	−0.08	−0.13	−0.14	−0.16
	(8.2)	(2.1)	(3.8)	(2.8)	(2.2)	(2.4)	(2.8)
Kids 2–6	−0.08	−0.24	0.001	−0.005	−0.09	−0.08	−0.08
	(5.2)	(2.6)	(0.04)	(0.4)	(2.7)	(3.1)	(2.9)
Sargan				48.	18.	26.	73.
(d.f.)				(22)	(10)	(19)	(15)
$m1$	19.	5.7	−10.	−10.	−10.	−9.6	−10.
$m2$	16.	12.	−1.7	−1.7	−1.6	−1.5	−1.5
Models including lagged participation							
Fertility	−0.09	−0.33	−0.06	−0.09	−0.14	−0.18	−0.15
	(5.2)	(1.3)	(3.7)	(3.1)	(2.2)	(3.0)	(2.4)
Kids 2–6	−0.02	−0.07	−0.000	−0.02	−0.10	−0.07	−0.06
	(2.1)	(1.3)	(0.00)	(1.1)	(3.5)	(3.1)	(2.6)
Partic (−1)	0.63	0.61	0.03	0.36	0.29	0.42	0.37
	(42.)	(30.)	(1.7)	(8.3)	(6.3)	(14.)	(11.)
Sargan				51.	25.	43.	30.
(d.f.)				(27)	(15)	(27)	(20)
$m1$	−7.0	−5.4	−13.	−14.	−13.	−16.	−15.
$m2$	3.1	2.8	−1.3	1.5	1.2	2.0	1.8

Heteroskedasticity robust t-ratios shown in parentheses.
[1]External instrument: Previous children of same sex.
[2]IVs: All lags and leads of "kids 2–6" and "same sex" variables.
[3]IVs: Lags of "kids 2–6" and "same sex" up to $t-1$.
GMM IVs in bottom panel also include lags of partic. up to $t-2$.
[4]Add. IVs for levels: First diff. of "kids 2–6" and "same sex".
[5]Add. IV for levels: First diff. of lagged residual.

The within-groups estimator in column 3 controls for unobserved heterogeneity, but in doing so we would expect it to introduce biases due to lack of strict exogeneity of the explanatory variables. Note also the expected contrast between the very small WG estimate of the effect of lagged participation and the very large ones in the first two columns.

The GMM estimates in column 4 deal with the endogeneity of fertility and control for fixed effects, but treat the "kids 2–6" (k_{it}) and "same sex" (s_{it}) variables as strictly exogenous. Specifically, the estimates without lagged participation are based on the 24×1 vector of moments[13]

$$
b_{eN} = \sum_{i=1}^{1442} \begin{pmatrix} z_{i1986} \\ z_{i1987} \\ z_{i1988} \\ z_{i1989} \end{pmatrix} \otimes \begin{pmatrix} \Delta y_{i1987} - \beta_1 \Delta f_{i1987} - \beta_2 \Delta k_{i1987} \\ \Delta y_{i1988} - \beta_1 \Delta f_{i1988} - \beta_2 \Delta k_{i1988} \\ \Delta y_{i1989} - \beta_1 \Delta f_{i1989} - \beta_2 \Delta k_{i1989} \end{pmatrix} \tag{8.90}
$$

where $z_{it} = (k_{it}, s_{it})'$.

The GMM estimates in column 5 treat k_{it} and s_{it} as predetermined. Those in the top half are based on the following subset of 12 moments:

$$
b_{dN} = \sum_{i=1}^{1442} \begin{pmatrix} \begin{pmatrix} z_{i1986} \end{pmatrix} (\Delta y_{i1987} - \beta_1 \Delta f_{i1987} - \beta_2 \Delta k_{i1987}) \\ \begin{pmatrix} z_{i1986} \\ z_{i1987} \end{pmatrix} (\Delta y_{i1988} - \beta_1 \Delta f_{i1988} - \beta_2 \Delta k_{i1988}) \\ \begin{pmatrix} z_{i1986} \\ z_{i1987} \\ z_{i1988} \end{pmatrix} (\Delta y_{i1989} - \beta_1 \Delta f_{i1989} - \beta_2 \Delta k_{i1989}) \end{pmatrix}. \tag{8.91}
$$

The estimates that include lagged participation add one coefficient to the estimation error and use the level of the endogenous variable lagged two periods or more as additional instruments, that adds 6 moments to either (8.90) or (8.91) (since y_{i1985} is observed in our data set).

Treating the instruments as strictly exogenous (column 4) we obtain a smaller effect of fertility on participation (in absolute value) than treating the variables as predetermined (column 5). Moreover, the hypothesis of strict exogeneity of k_{it} and s_{it} is rejected at the 5 per cent level from the difference in the Sargan statistics in both panels. To see this, note that b_{dN} contains a subset of the moments in b_{eN}. If the additional 12 moment restrictions used in b_{eN} are valid we would expect the difference in Sargan tests to be approximately distributed as a chi-square with 12 degrees of freedom. This is a very unlikely event, however, in view of the large values of the incremental Sargan statistics, which are $48. - 18. = 30.$ and $51. - 25. = 26.$ for the top and bottom panels, respectively.[14]

The $m1$ and $m2$ statistics have been calculated from residuals in first-differences for the within-group and GMM estimates. So if the errors in levels were uncorrelated, we would expect $m1$ to be significant, but not $m2$, as is the case here (cf. Arellano and Bond, 1991). Nevertheless, the values of both $m2$ and the Sargan statistics for the GMM estimates that treat instruments as predetermined are somewhat marginal, possibly indicating that the data do not sit well with the linear probability specification.

---

[13]These moments can be written indistinctly in first-differences or orthogonal deviations without altering the form of the estimator.

[14]The GMM estimates in columns 4 and 5 are "one-step", but all test statistics reported are robust to heteroskedasticity.

Using Predetermined Instruments for the Errors in Levels The last two columns of Table 8.1 report two-step GMM estimates that in addition to the moments used in column 5 employ some predetermined instruments for the errors in levels.[15] The "system" GMM estimates in the top half of column 6 are based on b_{dN} and the following moments in levels:

$$
b_{\ell N} = \sum_{i=1}^{1442} \left(\begin{pmatrix} 1 \\ \Delta z_{i87} \end{pmatrix} \begin{pmatrix} (y_{i1986} - \gamma - \beta_1 f_{i1986} - \beta_2 k_{i1986}) \\ (y_{i1987} - \gamma - \beta_1 f_{i1987} - \beta_2 k_{i1987}) \\ (y_{i1988} - \gamma - \beta_1 f_{i1988} - \beta_2 k_{i1988}) \\ (y_{i1989} - \gamma - \beta_1 f_{i1989} - \beta_2 k_{i1989}) \end{pmatrix} \right). \tag{8.92}
$$

The estimates for the model with lagged participation in the bottom half of column 6 include both Δz_{it} and $\Delta y_{i(t-1)}$ as instruments for the errors in levels.

The validity of Δz_{it} as an instrument for the errors in levels depends on whether the correlation between z_{it} and the effects changes over the four-year period covered by the sample or not. The incremental Sargan tests do not reject the additional moment restrictions in the comparisons between columns 5 and 6.

Finally, the estimates in column 7 use moments in levels of the same type as (8.92), but in place of Δz_{it} they use the lagged residual in first-differences (e.g. for the model without lagged participation the instrument is $\Delta \hat{v}_{i(t-1)} = \Delta y_{i(t-1)} + .13\Delta f_{i(t-1)} + .09\Delta k_{i(t-1)}$). The validity of this instrument requires lack of serial correlation and lack of correlation between errors and effects. In the comparison between columns 5 and 7, the incremental Sargan tests clearly reject the restriction for the top half estimates, but not for those that include lagged participation.

Despite the low values of the incremental Sargan statistics—which may be due to lack of power—the validity of the levels restrictions in our example is suspect, since we found that the two-step system estimates differed noticeably from the preliminary ones (not reported) used in calculating the weight matrix.

8.7 Other Estimation Methods

IV Estimation When T/N Tends to a Constant We have discussed OLS and 2SLS within-group estimators of models with predetermined variables that are consistent for large T but not for large N and fixed T. On the other hand, we have also considered GMM estimators that are consistent for fixed

---

[15]The two-step weight matrix depends on one-step system GMM residuals that use $\left(\sum_{i=1}^{N} z_i^{\dagger\prime} z_i^{\dagger} \right)^{-1}$ as weights, in the notation of (8.71). We report two-step estimates in this case because the one-step weights are not optimal even with *iid* errors.

T and large N, and under certain assumptions achieve the information bound. However, we may be concerned with the properties of these estimators when T/N is not negligible. Indeed, we saw in Chapter 6 that GMM estimators of autoregressive models are asymptotically biased when T/N tends to a non-zero constant (Alvarez and Arellano, 1998), and we may expect similar results to extend to other models with predetermined variables.

An instrumental variable estimator of the form

$$\widetilde{\delta} = \left[\sum_{i=1}^{N} \sum_{t=1}^{T-1} \varphi_t \left(z_i^t \right) w_{it}^{*\prime} \right]^{-1} \sum_{i=1}^{N} \sum_{t=1}^{T-1} \varphi_t \left(z_i^t \right) y_{it}^* \qquad (8.93)$$

will be consistent for large N, fixed T as long as $\varphi \left(z_i^t \right)$ is only a function of z_i^t, $E \left(y_{it}^* - \delta' w_{it}^* \mid z_i^t \right) = 0$, and the rank condition is satisfied. Ordinary one-step GMM estimators are like (8.93) with

$$\varphi_t \left(z_i^t \right) = \widehat{\Pi}_t z_i^t \qquad (8.94)$$

and $\widehat{\Pi}_t = \left(\sum_{i=1}^{N} w_{it}^* z_i^{t\prime} \right) \left(\sum_{i=1}^{N} z_i^t z_i^{t\prime} \right)^{-1}$. That is, they use as instruments the cross-section specific unrestricted linear projections of w_{it}^* on z_i^t. Thus, when T is not fixed, the instruments depend on an increasing number of estimated coefficients, which may cause the estimates to be asymptotically biased if T and N increase at the same rate.

Consistency and lack of asymptotic bias for large N, large T or both will be ensured if $\varphi_t \left(z_i^t \right)$ only depends on a fixed number of estimated coefficients. An example is a *"stacked" IV estimator* that uses the first J lags $z_{i(t-1)}, ..., z_{i(t-J)}$ to form a common instrument for all periods:

$$\widehat{\delta}_s = \left(M_{ZW}' M_{ZZ}^{-1} M_{ZW} \right)^{-1} M_{ZW}' M_{ZZ}^{-1} M_{ZY} \qquad (8.95)$$

where $M_{ZW} = \sum_{i=1}^{N} Z_i' \Delta W_i$, $M_{ZY} = \sum_{i=1}^{N} Z_i' \Delta y_i$, $M_{ZZ} = \sum_{i=1}^{N} Z_i' D D' Z_i$, D is the first-difference matrix operator, and

$$\Delta y_i = \begin{pmatrix} \Delta y_{i(J+1)} \\ \vdots \\ \Delta y_{iT} \end{pmatrix}, \Delta W_i = \begin{pmatrix} \Delta w_{i(J+1)}' \\ \vdots \\ \Delta w_{iT}' \end{pmatrix},$$

$$Z_i = \begin{pmatrix} z_{iJ} & \cdots & z_{i1} \\ \vdots & & \vdots \\ z_{i(T-1)} & \cdots & z_{i(T-J)} \end{pmatrix}.$$

Note that in the calculation of this estimator the first J cross-sections are lost.[16]

[16]The Anderson–Hsiao estimators of AR models discussed in Section 6.3 are stacked IV estimators of this type.

Alternatively, we may use an estimator of the form (8.93) that sets

$$\varphi_t \left(z_i^t \right) = \Pi_t \left(\widehat{\theta} \right) z_i^t, \tag{8.96}$$

where $\Pi_t \left(\widehat{\theta} \right)$ is an estimate of the projection matrix Π_t subject to the restrictions derived from a stationary specification of the joint process of w_{it} and z_{it}. In this way, the resulting estimator may still achieve the fixed T information bound under a certain set of assumptions (cf. Arellano, 2000).

LIML Analogue Estimators The conclusion from a sizeable Monte Carlo literature on the finite sample properties of GMM in the dynamic panel data context, is that GMM estimators that use the full set of moments available for errors in first-differences can be severely biased, specially when the instruments are weak and the number of moments is large relative to the cross-sectional sample size (Arellano and Bond, 1991; Kiviet, 1995; Ziliak, 1997; Blundell and Bond, 1998; and Alonso-Borrego and Arellano, 1999, amongst others).

This has prompted consideration of alternative estimation criteria that give rise to estimators that are asymptotically equivalent to GMM as $N \to \infty$ for fixed T, but may have very different finite sample properties.

From the simultaneous equations literature, it is known that the effect of weak instruments on the distributions of 2SLS and "limited information maximum likelihood" (LIML) estimators differs substantially, in spite of the fact that both estimators have the same asymptotic distribution. While LIML is approximately median unbiased, 2SLS is biased towards OLS, and in the case of lack of identification it converges to a random variable with the OLS probability limit as its central value. In contrast, LIML has no moments, and as a result its distribution has thicker tails than that of 2SLS and a higher probability of outliers (cf. Phillips, 1983). Moreover, numerical comparisons of the distributions of the two estimators tended to favour LIML. Thus, it is natural to consider LIML analogues in the panel data context, and compare their finite sample properties with those of GMM estimators.

Following Alonso-Borrego and Arellano (1999), a non-robust LIML analogue $\widehat{\delta}_{LIML1}$ minimizes a criterion of the form

$$\ell_C(\delta) = \frac{(y^* - W^*\delta)'M(y^* - W^*\delta)}{(y^* - W^*\delta)'(y^* - W^*\delta)} \tag{8.97}$$

where starred variables denote orthogonal deviations, $y^* = (y_1^{*\prime}, ..., y_N^{*\prime})'$, $W^* = (W_1^{*\prime}, ..., W_N^{*\prime})'$, $Z = (Z_1', ..., Z_N')'$, and $M = Z(Z'Z)^{-1}Z'$. The resulting estimator is

$$\widehat{\delta}_{LIML1} = (W^{*\prime}MW^* - \widehat{\ell}W^{*\prime}W^*)^{-1}(W^{*\prime}My^* - \widehat{\ell}W^{*\prime}y^*) \tag{8.98}$$

where $\widehat{\ell}$ is the minimum eigenvalue of the matrix $\Psi^{*\prime}M\Psi^*(\Psi^{*\prime}\Psi^*)^{-1}$, and $\Psi^* = (y^*, W^*)$.

Despite its name, this estimator does not correspond to any meaningful maximum likelihood estimator. It is only a LIML analogue estimator in the sense of the minimax instrumental variable interpretation given by Sargan (1958) to the original LIML estimator, and generalized to robust contexts by Hansen, Heaton, and Yaron (1996).[17]

The robust LIML analogue $\widehat{\delta}_{LIML2}$, or "continuously updated GMM" estimator in the terminology of Hansen et al. (1996), minimizes a criterion of the form

$$\ell_R(\delta) = (y^* - W^*\delta)' Z \left(\sum_{i=1}^{N} Z_i' u_i^*(\delta) u_i^*(\delta)' Z_i \right)^{-1} Z' (y^* - W^*\delta) \qquad (8.99)$$

where $u_i^*(\delta) = y_i^* - W_i^*\delta$. Note that LIML2, unlike LIML1, does not solve a standard minimum eigenvalue problem, and requires the use of numerical optimization methods (an illustration for autoregressive models was provided in Section 6.7).

The Monte Carlo results and the empirical illustrations for autoregressive models reported by Alonso-Borrego and Arellano showed that GMM estimates can exhibit large biases when the instruments are poor, while LIML and symmetrically normalized GMM estimators (proposed in the same paper) remained essentially unbiased. However, these estimators always had a larger interquartile range than GMM, although the differences were small except in the almost unidentified cases.

For an autoregressive model, Alvarez and Arellano (1998) showed that under the same conditions used to establish (6.36), as $T/N \to c$

$$\sqrt{NT} \left[\widehat{\alpha}_{LIML1} - \left(\alpha - \frac{1}{(2N - T)}(1 + \alpha) \right) \right] \xrightarrow{d} \mathcal{N}\left(0, 1 - \alpha^2\right). \qquad (8.100)$$

Therefore, as T and N tend to infinity the non-robust LIML estimator has a smaller asymptotic bias than the corresponding GMM estimator.

Empirical Likelihood Estimation   An alternative one-step method that achieves the same (first-order) asymptotic efficiency as robust GMM is provided by maximum empirical likelihood estimation (cf. Qin and Lawless, 1994; and Imbens, 1997).

The maximum empirical likelihood estimator maximizes a multinomial pseudo likelihood function subject to the orthogonality conditions. The procedure works because the multinomial pseudo likelihood (or empirical likelihood) is

---

[17]See Arellano (2002) for a survey of Sargan's work on instrumental variable estimation and its connections with GMM.

not restrictive. Letting p_i be the probability of observation i, the multinomial log likelihood of the data is given by

$$L = \sum_{i=1}^{N} \log p_i. \tag{8.101}$$

The empirical likelihood estimator maximizes this function subject to the restrictions $p_i \geq 0$, $\sum_{i=1}^{N} p_i = 1$, and

$$\sum_{i=1}^{N} p_i Z_i' (y_i^* - W_i^* \delta) = 0. \tag{8.102}$$

The Lagrangian is given by

$$\mathcal{L} = \sum_{i=1}^{N} \log p_i + \lambda \left(1 - \sum_{i=1}^{N} p_i \right) - N\phi' \sum_{i=1}^{N} p_i Z_i' (y_i^* - W_i^* \delta) \tag{8.103}$$

where λ and ϕ are Lagrange multipliers. Taking derivatives of $\mathcal{L}$ with respect to p_i, we obtain the first-order conditions:

$$\frac{1}{p_i} - \lambda - N\phi' Z_i' (y_i^* - W_i^* \delta) = 0.$$

Multiplying by p_i and adding equations we find that $\lambda = N$, so that the constrained probabilities are

$$p_i = \frac{1}{N} \left(\frac{1}{1 + \phi' Z_i' (y_i^* - W_i^* \delta)} \right). \tag{8.104}$$

Therefore, the multipliers of the moment conditions can be determined as implicit functions $\phi(\delta)$ solving the following system of equations subject to $1 + \phi' Z_i' (y_i^* - W_i^* \delta) \geq 1/N$ for a given value of δ:

$$\frac{1}{N} \sum_{i=1}^{N} \left(\frac{1}{1 + \phi' Z_i' (y_i^* - W_i^* \delta)} \right) Z_i' (y_i^* - W_i^* \delta) = 0. \tag{8.105}$$

The concentrated likelihood function for δ is

$$L_c(\delta) = \prod_{i=1}^{N} \frac{1}{N} \left(\frac{1}{1 + \phi(\delta)' Z_i' (y_i^* - W_i^* \delta)} \right), \tag{8.106}$$

so that the estimator is given by

$$\widehat{\delta}_{MEL} = \arg\min \sum_{i=1}^{N} \log \left[1 + \phi(\delta)' Z_i' (y_i^* - W_i^* \delta) \right]. \tag{8.107}$$

A test of overidentifying restrictions is provided by the pseudo likelihood ratio statistic

$$\mathcal{R} = 2 \sum_{i=1}^{N} \log \left[1 + \phi(\widehat{\delta}_{MEL})' Z_i' \left(y_i^* - W_i^* \widehat{\delta}_{MEL} \right) \right] \qquad (8.108)$$

which is asymptotically distributed as χ^2 with as many degrees of freedom as the number of overidentifying restrictions.

Empirical likelihood estimators will also be invariant to normalization due to the invariance property of maximum likelihood estimators. Other one-step estimators with an information-theoretic interpretation can be considered by minimizing alternative concepts of closeness between the estimated distribution and the empirical distribution. An appealing member of this class is the exponential tilting estimator discussed by Imbens (1997) and Imbens, Spady, and Johnson (1998). The higher-order asymptotic biases of empirical likelihood and related estimators have been studied by Newey and Smith (2002).

Imbens (1997) reported GMM and empirical likelihood estimates for an autoregressive covariance structure with random effects and a white noise measurement error, using PSID earnings. Nevertheless, little is known as yet on the relative merits of these estimators in panel data models, concerning computational aspects and their finite sample properties.

Part IV

Appendices

Appendices

A

Generalized Method of Moments Estimation

In the next two appendices we review the basic estimation theory of the generalized method of moments (GMM) and optimal instrumental variables. For the most part, we restrict attention to *iid* observations.

A.1 Method of Moment Estimation Problems

Linear Regression   Economists often use linear regression to quantify a relationship between economic variables. A linear regression between y and x is a relationship of the form

$$y = x'\beta + \varepsilon \tag{A.1}$$

where β and ε are chosen in such a way that ε is uncorrelated with x (which typically includes a constant term). Thus, the parameter vector β satisfies

$$E\left[x\left(y - x'\beta\right)\right] = 0. \tag{A.2}$$

If $E\left(xx'\right)$ has full rank then (A.2) has a unique solution

$$\beta = \left[E\left(xx'\right)\right]^{-1} E\left(xy\right). \tag{A.3}$$

An important property of linear regression is that it is an optimal predictor of y given x in the following sense:

$$\beta = \arg\min_{b} E\left[\left(y - x'b\right)^2\right]. \tag{A.4}$$

That is, it minimizes the expected squared linear prediction error. This is why $x'\beta$ is called a "best linear predictor" or "linear projection".

Moreover, if the conditional expectation of y given x is linear it turns out that it coincides with the linear predictor. If on the other hand $E(y \mid x)$ is nonlinear, the linear projection is an optimal approximation to it in the sense that

$$\beta = \arg \min_b E\left\{ [E(y \mid x) - x'b]^2 \right\}. \tag{A.5}$$

This is why sometimes the notation $E^*(y \mid x) = x'\beta$ is used, which emphasizes the proximity of the linear projection and conditional expectation concepts (e.g. Goldberger, 1991).[1]

Therefore, β is a useful quantity if we are interested in a linear prediction of y given x, or if we are interested in studying how the mean of y changes for different values of x, and we think that $E(y \mid x)$ is linear or approximately linear.

Linear regression may also be of interest as a structural or causal relationship between y and x if we have a priori reasons to believe that the unobservable determinants of y are uncorrelated with x.

Instrumental Variables   If we are interested in a structural relationship between y, x, and an unobservable variable u

$$y = x'\delta + u, \tag{A.6}$$

such that u is correlated with at least some of the components of x, clearly $\delta \neq \beta$ in general.

In many situations of interest in econometrics, δ can be regarded as the solution to moment equations of the form

$$E\left[z(y - x'\delta) \right] = 0 \tag{A.7}$$

where z is a vector of instrumental variables that a priori can be assumed to be uncorrelated with u.[2]

If $E(zx')$ has full rank, the system of equations (A.7) has a unique solution. Moreover, if z and x are of the same dimension

$$\delta = \left[E(zx') \right]^{-1} E(zy). \tag{A.8}$$

Examples of (A.7) include an equation from the classical supply and demand simultaneous system, and a regression model with measurement errors in the regressors.

Equations (A.2) and (A.7) can be described as "moment problems" because the parameters of interest solve moment equations.

---

[1]Nevertheless, whereas $E(y \mid x)$ is a characteristic of the conditional distribution of y given x, $E^*(y \mid x)$ is a characteristic of the joint distribution. That is, if we keep constant the distribution of $y \mid x$ but change the marginal distribution of x, $E(y \mid x)$ remains constant while $E^*(y \mid x)$ changes unless $E^*(y \mid x) = E(y \mid x)$.

[2]The vectors x and z may have elements in common. For example, a constant term.

The Analogy Principle According to the analogy principle, given a representative sample $\{y_i, x_i, z_i\}_{i=1}^{N}$, we choose as a candidate estimator for a population characteristic, the same characteristic defined in the sample (Manski, 1988). In this way, the sample linear regression coefficients solve

$$\frac{1}{N} \sum_{i=1}^{N} x_i \left(y_i - x_i' \widehat{\beta} \right) = 0 \tag{A.9}$$

giving rise to the standard OLS formula:

$$\widehat{\beta} = \left(\sum_{i=1}^{N} x_i x_i' \right)^{-1} \sum_{i=1}^{N} x_i y_i. \tag{A.10}$$

Similarly, the simple instrumental variable estimator, with as many instruments as explanatory variables, solves

$$\frac{1}{N} \sum_{i=1}^{N} z_i \left(y_i - x_i' \widehat{\delta} \right) = 0, \tag{A.11}$$

yielding

$$\widehat{\delta} = \left(\sum_{i=1}^{N} z_i x_i' \right)^{-1} \sum_{i=1}^{N} z_i y_i. \tag{A.12}$$

Generalized Moment Problems Suppose now that the number of instruments in z exceeds the number of explanatory variables in x. Let z and x be of orders r and k, respectively, and let $d = (y, x')'$. If we assume that $r > k$, the truth of (A.7) requires that the $r \times (k+1)$ matrix $E(zd')$ has reduced rank k. Otherwise it could not be the case that

$$E(zu) = E(zd') \begin{pmatrix} 1 \\ \delta \end{pmatrix} = 0, \tag{A.13}$$

and at least some of the moment conditions would not hold.

However, even if $E(zd')$ has reduced rank in the population, its sample counterpart

$$\frac{1}{N} \sum_{i=1}^{N} z_i d_i'$$

will not have reduced rank in general because of sample error. Therefore, there will be no single value $\widehat{\delta}$ that satisfies the r equations (A.11), and different estimates of δ will be obtained from the solution to different subsets of k equations.

This situation modifies the nature of the estimation problem and makes assertion (A.7) empirically refutable. Following Sargan (1958), we consider estimators that solve k linear combinations of the r sample moment equations (A.11):

$$\frac{1}{N}\Gamma_N \sum_{i=1}^{N} z_i \left(y_i - x_i'\widehat{\delta} \right) = 0 \tag{A.14}$$

for an optimal choice of the $k \times r$ matrix of coefficients Γ_N. Moreover, we can test the overidentifying restrictions by testing whether the rank of the matrix $N^{-1} \sum_{i=1}^{N} z_i d_i'$ is significantly greater than k.

These issues are addressed in the following section in the context of a more general class of moment problems.

A.2   General Formulation

We consider parameters that are defined by a set of moment equations (or orthogonality conditions) of the form

$$E\psi(w,\theta) = 0 \tag{A.15}$$

where:

w is a $p \times 1$ random vector,

ψ is a $r \times 1$ vector of functions,

θ is a $k \times 1$ vector of parameters such that $k \leq r$,

Θ is the parameter space (set of admissible values of θ).

We have a sample of N observations $(w_1, ..., w_N)$ and estimation of θ is based on the sample counterpart of (A.15) given by

$$b_N(c) = \frac{1}{N} \sum_{i=1}^{N} \psi(w_i, c). \tag{A.16}$$

We choose as an estimator of θ the value of c that minimizes the quadratic distance of $b_N(c)$ from zero:

$$\begin{aligned} \widehat{\theta} &= \arg\min_{c \in \Theta} \left(\frac{1}{N} \sum_{i=1}^{N} \psi(w_i, c) \right)' A_N \left(\frac{1}{N} \sum_{i=1}^{N} \psi(w_i, c) \right) \tag{A.17} \\ &= \arg\min_{c \in \Theta} s(c) \end{aligned}$$

where A_N is an $r \times r$, possibly random, non-negative definite weight matrix, whose rank is greater than or equal to k. The statistic $\widehat{\theta}$ is a GMM estimator of θ.

If the problem is just identified we have that $r = k$, the weight matrix is irrelevant, and $\widehat{\theta}$ solves

$$b_N\left(\widehat{\theta}\right) = 0. \tag{A.18}$$

A.3   Examples: 2SLS and 3SLS

Two Stage Least-Squares (2SLS)   Let us consider the single equation model

$$y_i = x_i'\theta + u_i \tag{A.19}$$

together with the assumption

$$E(z_i u_i) = 0 \tag{A.20}$$

where z_i is an $r \times 1$ vector of instruments and $r > k$. Thus, in this example $w_i = (y_i, x_i', z_i')'$, $\psi(w_i, \theta) = z_i(y_i - x_i'\theta)$, and the sample moment conditions are

$$b_N(c) = \frac{1}{N}\sum_{i=1}^{N} z_i(y_i - x_i'c) = \frac{1}{N}Z'(y - Xc) \tag{A.21}$$

where we are using the notation $y = (y_1, ..., y_N)'$, $X = (x_1, ..., x_N)'$, and $Z = (z_1, ..., z_N)'$. This is the example that was used in the introductory section. Since $r > k$ there is no solution to the system $b_N(c) = 0$.

The 2SLS estimator of θ minimizes the GMM objective function

$$b_N(c)' A_N b_N(c) = N^{-2}(y - Xc)' Z A_N Z'(y - Xc) \tag{A.22}$$

for $A_N = (Z'Z/N)^{-1}$. This choice of weight matrix will be motivated later in the GMM context. Let us note now that since the first-order conditions from (A.22) are

$$X'Z A_N Z'(y - Xc) = 0, \tag{A.23}$$

the form of the 2SLS estimator is

$$\widehat{\theta}_{2SLS} = \left[X'Z(Z'Z)^{-1}Z'X\right]^{-1}X'Z(Z'Z)^{-1}Z'y. \tag{A.24}$$

Moreover, this equals

$$\widehat{\theta}_{2SLS} = \left(\widehat{X}'\widehat{X}\right)^{-1}\widehat{X}'y \tag{A.25}$$

where $\widehat{X}$ is the matrix of fitted values in a multivariate regression of X on Z:

$$\widehat{X} = Z\widehat{\Pi}' \tag{A.26}$$

with $\widehat{\Pi} = X'Z(Z'Z)^{-1}$.

Thus, following the classic interpretation of 2SLS that justifies its name, in the first stage X is regressed on Z to obtain $\widehat{X}$, whereas in the second stage we obtain $\widehat{\theta}_{2SLS}$ as a regression of y on $\widehat{X}$.

Note also that we have

$$\widehat{\theta}_{2SLS} = \left(\widehat{X}'X\right)^{-1} \widehat{X}'y. \tag{A.27}$$

That is, the 2SLS estimator can also be interpreted as the simple IV estimator that uses $\widehat{X}$ as instrument. Specifically, it solves the k moment equations:

$$\sum_{i=1}^{N} \widehat{x}_i \left(y_i - x_i'\widehat{\theta}_{2SLS}\right) = 0 \tag{A.28}$$

where $\widehat{x}_i = \widehat{\Pi}z_i$. So, 2SLS uses as instruments the linear combinations of the z_i that best predict x_i.

Three Stage Least-Squares (3SLS)   We turn to consider a system of g equations

$$y_{1i} \;\;=\;\; x_{1i}'\theta_1 + u_{1i} \tag{A.29}$$

$$\vdots$$

$$y_{gi} \;\;=\;\; x_{gi}'\theta_g + u_{gi}$$

whose errors are orthogonal to a common $r_0 \times 1$ vector of instruments z_i. Thus, in this example there are $r = gr_0$ moment conditions given by

$$E\left(z_i u_{1i}\right) \;\;=\;\; 0 \tag{A.30}$$

$$\vdots$$

$$E\left(z_i u_{gi}\right) \;\;=\;\; 0.$$

Convenient compact notations for these moments are:

$$E\left(u_i \otimes z_i\right) \equiv E\left(Z_i' u_i\right) \equiv E\left[Z_i'\left(y_i - X_i\theta\right)\right] = 0 \tag{A.31}$$

where $u_i = (u_{1i}, ..., u_{gi})'$, $Z_i = I_g \otimes z_i'$, $y_i = (y_{1i}, ..., y_{gi})'$, $\theta = \left(\theta_1', ..., \theta_g'\right)'$, and

$$X_i = \begin{pmatrix} x_{1i}' & & 0 \\ & \ddots & \\ 0 & & x_{gi}' \end{pmatrix}.$$

Accordingly, the sample orthogonality conditions are

$$b_N\left(c\right) \;\;=\;\; \frac{1}{N}\sum_{i=1}^{N} Z_i'\left(y_i - X_i c\right) = \frac{1}{N}\sum_{i=1}^{N} \begin{pmatrix} z_i\left(y_{1i} - x_{1i}'c_1\right) \\ \vdots \\ z_i\left(y_{gi} - x_{gi}'c_g\right) \end{pmatrix}$$

$$= \frac{1}{N} \begin{pmatrix} Z'(y_1 - X_1 c_1) \\ \vdots \\ Z'(y_g - X_g c_g) \end{pmatrix} = \frac{1}{N} (I_g \otimes Z')(y - Xc) \quad \text{(A.32)}$$

where $Z = (z_1, ..., z_N)'$ is an $N \times r_0$ matrix similar to that used in the 2SLS example, and we analogously define $y_1, ..., y_g$ and $X_1, ..., X_g$. Moreover, $y = (y_1', ..., y_g')'$ and X is a block diagonal matrix with blocks $X_1, ..., X_g$.

The 3SLS estimator of θ minimizes the GMM criterion

$$b_N(c)' A_N b_N(c)$$

with weight matrix given by

$$A_N = \left(\frac{1}{N} \sum_{i=1}^{N} Z_i' \widehat{\Omega} Z_i \right)^{-1} = \left(\frac{1}{N} \sum_{i=1}^{N} \widehat{\Omega} \otimes z_i z_i' \right)^{-1} = N \left(\widehat{\Omega} \otimes Z'Z \right)^{-1} \quad \text{(A.33)}$$

where $\widehat{\Omega}$ is the 2SLS residual covariance matrix:

$$\widehat{\Omega} = \frac{1}{N} \sum_{i=1}^{N} \widehat{u}_i \widehat{u}_i' \quad \text{(A.34)}$$

and $\widehat{u}_i = y_i - X_i \widehat{\theta}_{2SLS}$.

Therefore:

$$\widehat{\theta}_{3SLS} = \left[\left(\sum_i X_i' Z_i \right) A_N \left(\sum_i Z_i' X_i \right) \right]^{-1} \left(\sum_i X_i' Z_i \right) A_N \left(\sum_i Z_i' y_i \right) \quad \text{(A.35)}$$

or

$$\widehat{\theta}_{3SLS} = \left[X' \left(\widehat{\Omega}^{-1} \otimes Z (Z'Z)^{-1} Z' \right) X \right]^{-1} X' \left(\widehat{\Omega}^{-1} \otimes Z (Z'Z)^{-1} Z' \right) y. \quad \text{(A.36)}$$

Moreover, in parallel with the earlier development for 2SLS, the 3SLS formula can be written as

$$\widehat{\theta}_{3SLS} = \left(\sum_i \widehat{X}_i' \widehat{\Omega}^{-1} \widehat{X}_i \right)^{-1} \sum_i \widehat{X}_i' \widehat{\Omega}^{-1} y_i \quad \text{(A.37)}$$

where $\widehat{X}_i$ is a block diagonal matrix with blocks $\widehat{x}_{1i}', ..., \widehat{x}_{gi}'$ and

$$\widehat{x}_{ji} = \widehat{\Pi}_j z_i \quad (j = 1, ..., g) \quad \text{(A.38)}$$

with $\widehat{\Pi}_j = \sum_i x_{ji} z_i' \left(\sum_i z_i z_i' \right)^{-1}$.

Expression (A.37) corresponds to the interpretation of 3SLS on which its name is based. Namely, the first two stages coincide with those of 2SLS for each of the g equations, whereas in the third stage we obtain $\widehat{\theta}_{3SLS}$ as GLS of y_i on $\widehat{X}_i$ weighted by the inverse of $\widehat{\Omega}$. Note that replacing $\widehat{\Omega}$ by an identity matrix in (A.37) we obtain a compact expression for the 2SLS estimators of all the θ.

Finally, we also have

$$\widehat{\theta}_{3SLS} = \left(\sum_i \widehat{X}_i' \widehat{\Omega}^{-1} X_i \right)^{-1} \sum_i \widehat{X}_i' \widehat{\Omega}^{-1} y_i, \qquad (A.39)$$

so that $\widehat{\theta}_{3SLS}$ can also be interpreted as a simple IV estimator of the full system that uses $\widehat{\Omega}^{-1} \widehat{X}_i$ as instrument and solves the moment conditions

$$\sum_{i=1}^{N} \widehat{X}_i' \widehat{\Omega}^{-1} \left(y_i - X_i \widehat{\theta}_{3SLS} \right) = 0. \qquad (A.40)$$

A.4   Consistency of GMM Estimators

A general method for establishing consistency in the case of estimators that minimize a continuous function is provided by the following theorem of Amemiya (1985). Precursors of this type of theorem were employed by Sargan (1959) in his analysis of the asymptotic properties of nonlinear in parameters IV estimators, and by Jennrich (1969) and Malinvaud (1970) in their proofs of the consistency of nonlinear least-squares. A comprehensive discussion can be found in Newey and McFadden (1994).

Consistency Theorem   Let us assume the following:

(a) The parameter space Θ is a compact subset of R^k such that $\theta \in \Theta$.

(b) The estimation criterion $s_N(w_1, ..., w_N, c) = s_N(c)$ is a continuous function in $c \in \Theta$ for all $(w_1, ..., w_N)$.

(c) $s_N(c)$ converges uniformly in probability to a nonstochastic function $s_\infty(c)$, which has a unique minimum at $c = \theta$, i.e.:

$$\sup_{\Theta} |s_N(c) - s_\infty(c)| \xrightarrow{p} 0 \text{ as } N \to \infty. \qquad (A.41)$$

Let us define an estimator $\widehat{\theta}_N$ as the value that minimizes $s_N(c)$:

$$\widehat{\theta}_N = \arg \min_{\Theta} s_N(c). \qquad (A.42)$$

Then $\text{plim}_{N \to \infty} \widehat{\theta}_N = \theta$. (Proof: See Amemiya, 1985, p. 107.)

Application to GMM Estimators In this case we have

$$s_N(c) = b_N(c)' A_N b_N(c) \tag{A.43}$$

with $b_N(c) = N^{-1} \sum_{i=1}^{N} \psi(w_i, c)$.

The previous theorem can be applied under the following assumptions:

1. Θ is compact, and $\psi(w, c)$ is continuous in $c \in \Theta$ for each w.

2. $A_N \xrightarrow{p} A_0$ and A_0 is positive semi-definite.

3. $E[\psi(w, c)]$ exists for all $c \in \Theta$ and $A_0 E[\psi(w, c)] = 0$ only if $c = \theta$ (identification condition).

4. $b_N(c)$ converges in probability uniformly in c to $E[\psi(w, c)]$.

Note that with these assumptions

$$s_\infty(c) = E[\psi(w, c)]' A_0 E[\psi(w, c)] \geq 0, \tag{A.44}$$

which has a unique minimum of zero at $c = \theta$.

Condition 4 states that $b_N(c)$ satisfies a uniform law of large numbers, and it ensures that the uniform convergence assumption of the theorem is satisfied. More primitive conditions for stationary or *iid* data are discussed by Hansen (1982), and Newey and McFadden (1994).

A.5 Asymptotic Normality

One way to establish the asymptotic normality of GMM estimators is to proceed as in the analysis of consistency. That is, to treat GMM as a special case within the class of estimators that minimize some objective function (*extremum* estimators). A general theorem for extremum estimators adapted from Amemiya (1985) is as follows.

Asymptotic Normality Theorem for Extremum Estimators Let us make the assumptions:

(a) We have $\widehat{\theta}_N = \arg\min_\Theta s_N(c)$ such that $\operatorname{plim}_{N\to\infty} \widehat{\theta}_N = \theta$, where $s_N(c)$ has first and second derivatives in a neighbourhood of θ, and θ is an interior point of Θ.

(b) Asymptotic normality of the gradient:[3]

$$\sqrt{N} \frac{\partial s_N(\theta)}{\partial c} \xrightarrow{d} \mathcal{N}(0, \mathcal{W}) \tag{A.45}$$

---

[3]We use the notation $\partial s_N(\theta)/\partial c$ as an abbreviation of

$$\frac{\partial s_N(c)}{\partial c}\bigg|_{c=\theta}.$$

(c) Convergence of the Hessian: for any $\widetilde{\theta}_N$ such that $\widetilde{\theta}_N \xrightarrow{p} \theta$

$$\frac{\partial^2 s_N\left(\widetilde{\theta}_N\right)}{\partial c \partial c'} \xrightarrow{p} H \qquad (A.46)$$

where H is a non-singular non-stochastic matrix.

Then

$$\sqrt{N}\left(\widehat{\theta}_N - \theta\right) \xrightarrow{d} \mathcal{N}\left(0, H^{-1}WH^{-1}\right). \qquad (A.47)$$

Proof. We can proceed as if $\widehat{\theta}_N$ were an interior point of Θ since consistency of $\widehat{\theta}_N$ for θ and the assumption that θ is interior to Θ implies that the probability that $\widehat{\theta}_N$ is not interior goes to zero as $N \to \infty$.

Using the mean value theorem (and writing $\widehat{\theta}$ for shortness):

$$0 = \frac{\partial s_N\left(\widehat{\theta}\right)}{\partial c_j} = \frac{\partial s_N\left(\theta\right)}{\partial c_j} + \sum_{\ell=1}^{k} \frac{\partial^2 s_N\left(\widetilde{\theta}_{[j]}\right)}{\partial c_j \partial c_\ell}\left(\widehat{\theta}_\ell - \theta_\ell\right) \quad (j = 1, ..., k) \quad (A.48)$$

where $\widehat{\theta}_\ell$ is the ℓ-th element of $\widehat{\theta}$, and $\widetilde{\theta}_{[j]}$ denotes a $k \times 1$ random vector such that $\left\|\widetilde{\theta}_{[j]} - \theta\right\| \leq \left\|\widehat{\theta} - \theta\right\|$. The expansion has to be made element by element since $\widetilde{\theta}_{[j]}$ may be different for each j.

Note that $\widehat{\theta} \xrightarrow{p} \theta$ implies $\widetilde{\theta}_{[j]} \xrightarrow{p} \theta$. In view of assumption (c) this implies

$$\frac{\partial^2 s_N\left(\widetilde{\theta}_N\right)}{\partial c_j \partial c'_\ell} \xrightarrow{p} (j, \ell) \text{ element of } H. \qquad (A.49)$$

Hence,

$$0 = \sqrt{N}\frac{\partial s_N\left(\theta\right)}{\partial c} + \left[H + o_p\left(1\right)\right]\sqrt{N}\left(\widehat{\theta} - \theta\right) \qquad (A.50)$$

and

$$-H^{-1}\left[H + o_p\left(1\right)\right]\sqrt{N}\left(\widehat{\theta} - \theta\right) = H^{-1}\sqrt{N}\frac{\partial s_N\left(\theta\right)}{\partial c}. \qquad (A.51)$$

Finally, using assumption (b) and Cramer's theorem the result follows. ∎

Note that this theorem requires twice differentiability of the objective function. However, asymptotic normality for GMM can be easily proved when $b_N\left(c\right)$ only has first derivatives if we directly use the first-order conditions. An alternative specific result for GMM along these lines is as follows.

Asymptotic Normality Theorem for GMM   We make the following assumptions in addition to those used for consistency:

5. θ is in the interior of Θ, and $\psi(w, c)$ is (once) continuously differentiable in Θ.

6. The quantity $D_N(c) = \partial b_N(c)/\partial c'$ converges in probability uniformly in c to a non-stochastic matrix $D(c)$, and $D(c)$ is continuous at $c = \theta$.

7. $\sqrt{N} b_N(\theta)$ satisfies a central limit theorem:

$$\sqrt{N} b_N(\theta) = \frac{1}{\sqrt{N}} \sum_{i=1}^{N} \psi(w_i, \theta) \xrightarrow{d} \mathcal{N}(0, V_0). \qquad (A.52)$$

8. For $D_0 = D(\theta)$, $D_0' A_0 D_0$ is non-singular.

Then

$$\sqrt{N}\left(\widehat{\theta} - \theta\right) \xrightarrow{d} \mathcal{N}(0, W_0) \qquad (A.53)$$

where W_0 is given by the sandwich formula

$$W_0 = (D_0' A_0 D_0)^{-1} D_0' A_0 V_0 A_0 D_0 (D_0' A_0 D_0)^{-1}. \qquad (A.54)$$

Proof. The GMM estimator satisfies the first-order conditions

$$D_N'\left(\widehat{\theta}\right) A_N b_N\left(\widehat{\theta}\right) = 0. \qquad (A.55)$$

Moreover, in view of condition 6 and the consistency of $\widehat{\theta}$:

$$D_0' A_0 \sqrt{N} b_N\left(\widehat{\theta}\right) = o_p(1). \qquad (A.56)$$

Next, using a first-order expansion, we have

$$D_0' A_0 \left[\sqrt{N} b_N(\theta) + D_N(\theta) \sqrt{N}\left(\widehat{\theta} - \theta\right)\right] = o_p(1). \qquad (A.57)$$

Hence

$$(D_0' A_0 D_0) \sqrt{N}\left(\widehat{\theta} - \theta\right) = -D_0' A_0 \sqrt{N} b_N(\theta) + o_p(1) \qquad (A.58)$$

and

$$\sqrt{N}\left(\widehat{\theta} - \theta\right) = -(D_0' A_0 D_0)^{-1} D_0' A_0 \sqrt{N} b_N(\theta) + o_p(1). \qquad (A.59)$$

Finally, from the central limit theorem for $\sqrt{N} b_N(\theta)$ the result follows. ∎

Note that the conditions of this result imply the first two conditions of the asymptotic normality theorem for extremum estimators but not the third one, which requires twice differentiability of $b_N(c)$. From a different angle, the theorem for extremum estimators can be regarded as a special case of a result based on GMM-like first-order conditions with estimating equation given by $\partial s_N\left(\widehat{\theta}\right)/\partial c = 0$ (cf. Hansen, 1982; Newey and McFadden, 1994).

As long as the relevant moments exist, V_0 is given by

$$
\begin{aligned}
V_0 &= \lim_{N\to\infty} Var\left(\frac{1}{\sqrt{N}}\sum_{i=1}^{N}\psi\left(w_i,\theta\right)\right) \\
&= \lim_{N\to\infty}\frac{1}{N}\sum_{i=1}^{N}\sum_{j=1}^{N}E\left[\psi\left(w_i,\theta\right)\psi\left(w_j,\theta\right)'\right].
\end{aligned}
\tag{A.60}
$$

With independent observations, V_0 reduces to

$$
V_0 = \lim_{N\to\infty}\frac{1}{N}\sum_{i=1}^{N}E\left[\psi\left(w_i,\theta\right)\psi\left(w_i,\theta\right)'\right],
\tag{A.61}
$$

and with *iid* observations

$$
V_0 = E\left[\psi\left(w_i,\theta\right)\psi\left(w_i,\theta\right)'\right].
\tag{A.62}
$$

Given our focus on *iid* observations, in the sequel we assume that V_0 is given by (A.62).[4] Similarly, we take the $r \times k$ matrix D_0 to be given by

$$
D_0 = E\left(\frac{\partial\psi\left(w_i,\theta\right)}{\partial c'}\right).
\tag{A.63}
$$

A.6   Estimating the Asymptotic Variance

To obtain a consistent estimate of W_0 we just replace A_0, D_0, and V_0 in (A.54) by their sample counterparts A_N, $\widehat{D}$, and $\widehat{V}$, where the last two are given by

$$
\widehat{D} = \frac{1}{N}\sum_{i=1}^{N}\frac{\partial\psi\left(w_i,\widehat{\theta}\right)}{\partial c'}
\tag{A.64}
$$

$$
\widehat{V} = \frac{1}{N}\sum_{i=1}^{N}\psi\left(w_i,\widehat{\theta}\right)\psi\left(w_i,\widehat{\theta}\right)'.
\tag{A.65}
$$

In this way we obtain

$$
\widehat{W}_N = \left(\widehat{D}'A_N\widehat{D}\right)^{-1}\widehat{D}'A_N\widehat{V}A_N\widehat{D}\left(\widehat{D}'A_N\widehat{D}\right)^{-1}.
\tag{A.66}
$$

---

[4]Depending on the context we may suppress the i subscript for convenience and simply write $E\left[\psi\left(w,\theta\right)\psi\left(w,\theta\right)'\right]$.

Thus, the concluding result from the discussion so far is

$$\left(\widehat{W}_N/N\right)^{-1/2}\left(\widehat{\theta}_N - \theta\right) \xrightarrow{d} \mathcal{N}\left(0, I\right),\tag{A.67}$$

which justifies the approximation of the joint distribution of the random vector $\left(\widehat{W}_N/N\right)^{-1/2}\left(\widehat{\theta}_N - \theta\right)$ by a $\mathcal{N}\left(0, I\right)$ when N is large.

The squared root of the diagonal elements of $\widehat{W}_N/N$ are the asymptotic standard errors of the components of $\widehat{\theta}_N$, and $\widehat{W}_N/N$ itself is sometimes referred to as the *estimated asymptotic variance matrix* of $\widehat{\theta}_N$.

Example: 2SLS with *iid* observations   In this case we have

$$\psi\left(w_i, \theta\right) = z_i\left(y_i - x_i'\theta\right) = z_i u_i.\tag{A.68}$$

The expressions for A_0, D_0, and V_0 are given by

$$\begin{align}
A_0 &= \left[E\left(z_i z_i'\right)\right]^{-1} \tag{A.69}\\
D_0 &= E\left(z_i x_i'\right) \tag{A.70}\\
V_0 &= E\left(u_i^2 z_i z_i'\right), \tag{A.71}
\end{align}$$

and their sample counterparts are

$$A_N = \left(\frac{1}{N}\sum_{i=1}^{N} z_i z_i'\right)^{-1} = N\left(Z'Z\right)^{-1}\tag{A.72}$$

$$\widehat{D} = \frac{1}{N}\sum_{i=1}^{N} z_i x_i' = \frac{1}{N}Z'X\tag{A.73}$$

$$\widehat{V} = \frac{1}{N}\sum_{i=1}^{N}\widehat{u}_i^2 z_i z_i' = \frac{1}{N}\sum_{i=1}^{N}\left(y_i - x_i'\widehat{\theta}_{2SLS}\right)^2 z_i z_i'.\tag{A.74}$$

Hence, the estimated asymptotic variance matrix of 2SLS is

$$\begin{align}
\widehat{W}_N/N &= \left(\widehat{X}'\widehat{X}\right)^{-1}\left(X'Z\right)\left(Z'Z\right)^{-1}\left(\sum_{i=1}^{N}\widehat{u}_i^2 z_i z_i'\right)\left(Z'Z\right)^{-1}\left(Z'X\right)\left(\widehat{X}'\widehat{X}\right)^{-1}\\
&= \left(\widehat{X}'\widehat{X}\right)^{-1}\left(\sum_{i=1}^{N}\widehat{u}_i^2 \widehat{x}_i \widehat{x}_i'\right)\left(\widehat{X}'\widehat{X}\right)^{-1}\tag{A.75}
\end{align}$$

where as before $\widehat{X} = Z\left(Z'Z\right)^{-1}\left(Z'X\right) = Z\widehat{\Pi}'$ with rows $\widehat{x}_i = \widehat{\Pi}z_i$.

Homoskedastic Case Under conditional homoskedasticity u_i^2 is mean independent of z_i:

$$E\left(u_i^2 \mid z_i\right) = \sigma^2, \tag{A.76}$$

in which case the variance matrix of the 2SLS moment conditions particularizes to:

$$V_0 \equiv E\left[E\left(u_i^2 \mid z_i\right) z_i z_i'\right] = \sigma^2 E\left(z_i z_i'\right). \tag{A.77}$$

Hence, in this case

$$W_0 = \sigma^2 \left\{E\left(x_i z_i'\right)\left[E\left(z_i z_i'\right)\right]^{-1} E\left(z_i x_i'\right)\right\}^{-1} = \sigma^2 \left[E\left(\Pi z_i z_i' \Pi'\right)\right]^{-1} \tag{A.78}$$

where $\Pi = E\left(x_i z_i'\right)\left[E\left(z_i z_i'\right)\right]^{-1}$.

Therefore, letting the 2SLS residual variance be

$$\widehat{\sigma}^2 = \frac{1}{N} \sum_{i=1}^{N} \widehat{u}_i^2, \tag{A.79}$$

an alternative consistent estimate of W_0 under homoskedasticity is

$$\widetilde{W}_N/N = \widehat{\sigma}^2 \left[X'Z\left(Z'Z\right)^{-1} Z'X\right]^{-1} = \widehat{\sigma}^2 \left(\widehat{X}'\widehat{X}\right)^{-1}, \tag{A.80}$$

which is the standard formula for the 2SLS estimated asymptotic variance matrix.

Standard errors and tests of hypothesis calculated from (A.75) are robust to heteroskedasticity, whereas those calculated from (A.80) are not. However, $\widehat{W}_N$ depends on fourth-order moments of the data whereas $\widetilde{W}_N$ only depends on second-order moments. This fact may imply that under homoskedasticity, for given N, the quality of the asymptotic approximation is poorer for the robust statistics. So in practice there may be a finite-sample trade-off in the choice between (A.75) and (A.80).

A.7 Optimal Weight Matrix

So far we have not considered the problem of choosing the matrix A_N, but clearly given the form of the asymptotic variance of $\widehat{\theta}$, different choices of A_0 will give rise to GMM estimators with different precision (at least in large samples).

It is a matter of deciding which linear combinations of a given set of orthogonality conditions are optimal for the estimation of θ. This is a different question from the problem of constructing optimal orthogonality conditions from conditional moments, which will be considered in Appendix B. The following optimality result takes the specification of orthogonality conditions as given.

The result is that an optimal choice of A_N is such that A_0 is equal to V_0^{-1} up to an arbitrary positive multiplicative constant k:

$$A_0 = kV_0^{-1}. \tag{A.81}$$

For a GMM estimator with such A_0, the asymptotic covariance matrix is given by

$$\left(D_0'V_0^{-1}D_0\right)^{-1}. \tag{A.82}$$

We can prove that this is an optimal choice showing that for any other A_0:[5]

$$\left(D_0'A_0D_0\right)^{-1}D_0'A_0V_0A_0D_0\left(D_0'A_0D_0\right)^{-1} - \left(D_0'V_0^{-1}D_0\right)^{-1} \geq 0. \tag{A.83}$$

To see this, note that this difference is equivalent to

$$\overline{D}\left[I - H\left(H'H\right)^{-1}H'\right]\overline{D}' \tag{A.84}$$

where

$$\overline{D} = \left(D_0'A_0D_0\right)^{-1}D_0'A_0V_0^{1/2} \tag{A.85}$$
$$H = V_0^{-1/2}D_0. \tag{A.86}$$

Moreover, (A.84) is a positive semi-definite matrix since $\left[I - H\left(H'H\right)^{-1}H'\right]$ is idempotent.

Therefore, in order to obtain an optimal estimator we need a consistent estimate of V_0 up to scale. In general, this will require us to obtain a preliminary suboptimal GMM estimator, which is then used in the calculation of an estimate like (A.65).

Example: 2SLS Under conditional homoskedasticity, $V_0 = \sigma^2 E\left(z_i z_i'\right)$, in which case the 2SLS limiting weight matrix (A.69) is a multiple of V_0^{-1}, and therefore 2SLS is optimal. Moreover, a consistent estimate of the 2SLS asymptotic variance is given by (A.80).

However, if the conditional variance of u_i given z_i depends on z_i, then 2SLS is suboptimal in the GMM class, and $\widetilde{W}_N$ is not a consistent estimate of the asymptotic variance of 2SLS.

Under heteroskedasticity, we can still do valid asymptotic inference with 2SLS since $\widehat{W}_N$ in (A.75) remains a consistent estimate of W_0.

---

[5]The weak inequality notation $B \geq 0$ applied to a matrix here denotes that B is positive semi-definite.

A two-step optimal GMM estimator is given by

$$\widetilde{\theta} = \left[X'Z \left(\sum_{i=1}^{N} \widehat{u}_i^2 z_i z_i' \right)^{-1} Z'X \right]^{-1} X'Z \left(\sum_{i=1}^{N} \widehat{u}_i^2 z_i z_i' \right)^{-1} Z'y. \qquad (A.87)$$

This estimator is of the same form as 2SLS but it replaces the 2SLS weight matrix $(Z'Z)^{-1}$ by the robust choice $\left(\sum_{i=1}^{N} \widehat{u}_i^2 z_i z_i' \right)^{-1}$ based on 2SLS residuals (cf. White, 1982).

Semi-parametric Asymptotic Efficiency   We obtained (A.82) as the best asymptotic variance that can be achieved by an estimator within the GMM class. An interesting theoretical question is whether a different type of estimator based on the same information could be more efficient asymptotically than optimal GMM. The answer is that no additional efficiency gains are possible since, as shown by Chamberlain (1987), (A.82) is a semi-parametric information bound. That is, (A.82) is the best one can do if all that is known about the distribution of w is that it satisfies the moment restrictions in (A.15).

Chamberlain's argument proceeds as follows. Suppose that the w_i are *iid* observations with a multinomial distribution with known finite support given by $\{\xi_1, ..., \xi_q\}$ and corresponding probabilities $\pi_1, ..., \pi_q$. Suppose all that is known about these probabilities is that they add up to one

$$\sum_{j=1}^{q} \pi_j = 1 \qquad (A.88)$$

and that they satisfy the moment restrictions (A.15):

$$\sum_{j=1}^{q} \psi\left(\xi_j, \theta\right) \pi_j = 0. \qquad (A.89)$$

Since this is a parametric likelihood problem, we can obtain the asymptotic Cramer-Rao information bound for θ. Chamberlain (1987) showed that this bound corresponds to (A.82). Thus the optimal GMM variance is the lower bound on asymptotic variance that can be achieved in the multinomial case, regardless of knowledge of the support of the distribution of w.

Next, Chamberlain argued that any distribution can be approximated arbitrarily well by a multinomial. He used a formal approximation argument to show that the restriction to finite support is not essential, thus characterizing (A.82) as a semi-parametric information bound.

A.8   Testing the Overidentifying Restrictions

When $r > k$ there are testable restrictions implied by the econometric model. Estimation of θ sets to zero k linear combinations of the r sample orthogonality conditions $b_N(c)$. So, when the model is right, there are $r - k$ linearly independent combinations of $b_N\left(\widehat{\theta}\right)$ that should be close to zero but are not exactly equal to zero.

The main result here is that a minimized optimal GMM criterion scaled by N has an asymptotic chi-square distribution with $r - k$ degrees of freedom:

$$Ns\left(\widehat{\theta}\right) = Nb_N\left(\widehat{\theta}\right)' \widehat{V}^{-1} b_N\left(\widehat{\theta}\right) \xrightarrow{d} \chi^2_{r-k} \qquad (A.90)$$

where $\widehat{\theta}$ is an optimal estimator and $\widehat{V}$ is a consistent estimate of V_0.

A statistic of this form is called a Sargan test statistic in the instrumental-variable context, and more generally a J or a Hansen test statistic (cf. Sargan, 1958, 1959; and Hansen, 1982).

As a sketch of the argument, note that factoring $\widehat{V}^{-1} = \widehat{C}\widehat{C}'$, in view of (A.52)

$$\sqrt{N}\widehat{C}'b_N(\theta) \xrightarrow{d} N(0, I_r). \qquad (A.91)$$

Moreover, letting $\widehat{G} = \widehat{C}'\widehat{D}$ we have

$$\begin{aligned}
\sqrt{N}\left(\widehat{\theta} - \theta\right) &= -\left(\widehat{D}'\widehat{V}^{-1}\widehat{D}\right)^{-1} \widehat{D}'\widehat{V}^{-1}\sqrt{N}b_N(\theta) + o_p(1) \\
&= -\left(\widehat{G}'\widehat{G}\right)^{-1} \widehat{G}'\sqrt{N}\widehat{C}'b_N(\theta) + o_p(1). \qquad (A.92)
\end{aligned}$$

Now, using a first-order expansion for $b_N\left(\widehat{\theta}\right)$ and combining the result with (A.92):

$$\begin{aligned}
h &\equiv \sqrt{N}\widehat{C}'b_N\left(\widehat{\theta}\right) = \sqrt{N}\widehat{C}'b_N(\theta) + \widehat{C}'\widehat{D}\sqrt{N}\left(\widehat{\theta} - \theta\right) + o_p(1) \\
&= \left[I_r - \widehat{G}\left(\widehat{G}'\widehat{G}\right)^{-1} \widehat{G}'\right] \sqrt{N}\widehat{C}'b_N(\theta) + o_p(1). \qquad (A.93)
\end{aligned}$$

Since the limit of $\left[I_r - \widehat{G}\left(\widehat{G}'\widehat{G}\right)^{-1} \widehat{G}'\right]$ is idempotent and has rank $r - k$, $h'h \xrightarrow{d} \chi^2_{r-k}$, from which (A.90) follows.

Incremental Sargan Tests Let us consider a partition

$$\psi(w, \theta) = \begin{pmatrix} \psi_1(w, \theta) \\ \psi_2(w, \theta) \end{pmatrix} \qquad (A.94)$$

where $\psi_1(w, \theta)$ and $\psi_2(w, \theta)$ are of orders r_1 and r_2, respectively. Suppose that $r_1 > k$ and that we wish to test the restrictions

$$E\psi_2(w, \theta) = 0 \qquad (A.95)$$

taking $E\psi_1(w, \theta) = 0$ as a maintained hypothesis.

From the earlier result we know that

$$N s_1 \left(\widehat{\theta}_{[1]} \right) = N b_{1N} \left(\widehat{\theta}_{[1]} \right)' \widehat{V}_1^{-1} b_{1N} \left(\widehat{\theta}_{[1]} \right) \xrightarrow{d} \chi^2_{r_1 - k} \qquad (A.96)$$

where $b_{1N}(c) = N^{-1} \sum_{i=1}^{N} \psi_1(w_i, c)$, $\widehat{V}_1$ is a consistent estimate of the covariance matrix $E \left[\psi_1(w, \theta) \psi_1(w, \theta)' \right]$, and $\widehat{\theta}_{[1]}$ is the minimizer of $s_1(c)$.

Then it can be shown that

$$S_d = N s \left(\widehat{\theta} \right) - N s_1 \left(\widehat{\theta}_{[1]} \right) \xrightarrow{d} \chi^2_{r_2} \qquad (A.97)$$

and that S_d is asymptotically independent of $N s_1 \left(\widehat{\theta}_{[1]} \right)$.

Therefore, the incremental statistic S_d can be used to test (A.95), having previously tested the validity of $E \psi_1(w, \theta) = 0$ or maintaining their validity a priori.

To prove (A.97), note that in view of (A.93) we have:

$$h \equiv \sqrt{N} \widehat{C}' b_N \left(\widehat{\theta} \right) = \left[I_r - G \left(G'G \right)^{-1} G' \right] \sqrt{N} C' b_N (\theta) + o_p(1) \qquad (A.98)$$

$$h_1 \equiv \sqrt{N} \widehat{C}_1' b_{1N} \left(\widehat{\theta}_{[1]} \right) = \left[I_{r_1} - G_1 \left(G_1' G_1 \right)^{-1} G_1' \right] \sqrt{N} C_1' b_{1N} (\theta) + o_p(1)$$

where G and C denote the probability limits of $\widehat{G}$ and $\widehat{C}$, respectively, and we are using similar definitions of G_1, C_1, $\widehat{G}_1$, and $\widehat{C}_1$ applied to the first r_1 moments. Thus, we have $G = C'D_0$ and $G_1 = C_1' D_{10}$, with $D_0 = (D_{10}', D_{20}')'$.

Next, consider an orthogonal transformation of the two blocks of moments:

$$\psi_i^* = \begin{pmatrix} \psi_{1i} \\ \psi_{2i}^* \end{pmatrix} = \begin{pmatrix} I & 0 \\ -H_{21} & I \end{pmatrix} \begin{pmatrix} \psi_{1i} \\ \psi_{2i} \end{pmatrix} = H \psi_i \qquad (A.99)$$

where for shortness we are writing $\psi_i = \psi(w_i, \theta)$, etc., and

$$H_{21} = E \left(\psi_{2i} \psi_{1i}' \right) \left[E \left(\psi_{1i} \psi_{1i}' \right) \right]^{-1}. \qquad (A.100)$$

Also, let us denote $b_N^*(\theta) = H b_N(\theta)$, $D_0^* = H D_0$, and $C^{*\prime} = C' H^{-1}$. With these notations, we can rewrite (A.98) as:

$$h = \left[I_r - G \left(G'G \right)^{-1} G' \right] \sqrt{N} C^{*\prime} b_N^* (\theta) + o_p(1). \qquad (A.101)$$

Clearly, G is unaffected by the transformation since $G = C'D_0 = C^{*\prime} D_0^*$. Moreover, because of block-orthogonality, $C^{*\prime}$ is block diagonal with elements C_1' and $C_2^{*\prime}$, say. Hence, G_1 contains the top r_1 rows of G:

$$G = C^{*\prime} D_0^* = \begin{pmatrix} C_1' & 0 \\ 0 & C_2^{*\prime} \end{pmatrix} \begin{pmatrix} D_{10} \\ D_{20}^* \end{pmatrix} = \begin{pmatrix} G_1 \\ G_2^* \end{pmatrix}. \qquad (A.102)$$

Therefore, letting $M = I_r - G \left(G'G \right)^{-1} G'$ and

$$M_1 = \left(\begin{array}{cc} \left[I_{r_1} - G_1 \left(G_1' G_1 \right)^{-1} G_1' \right] & 0 \\ 0 & 0 \end{array} \right),$$

we can write

$$\left(\begin{array}{c} h_1 \\ 0 \end{array} \right) = M_1 \sqrt{N} C^{*\prime} b_N^* \left(\theta \right) + o_p \left(1 \right) \tag{A.103}$$

and

$$h'h - h_1' h_1 = N b_N^* \left(\theta \right)' C^* \left(M - M_1 \right) C^{*\prime} b_N^* \left(\theta \right) + o_p \left(1 \right). \tag{A.104}$$

Finally, notice that $(M - M_1)$ is symmetric and idempotent with rank $r - r_1$, and also

$$(M - M_1) M_1 = 0, \tag{A.105}$$

from which (A.97) and the asymptotic independence between S_d and $N s_1 \left(\widehat{\theta}_{[1]} \right)$ follow.

Example: 2SLS We may consider a test of the validity of a subset of instruments for the model

$$y = X\theta + u, \tag{A.106}$$

where the $N \times r$ data matrix of instruments is partitioned as $Z = \left(Z_1 \vdots Z_2 \right)$, Z_1 is $N \times r_1$ and Z_2 is $N \times r_2$.

Thus,

$$\sum_{i=1}^{N} \psi \left(w_i, \theta \right) = \left(\begin{array}{c} Z_1' u \\ Z_2' u \end{array} \right). \tag{A.107}$$

In this example S_d performs a test of the validity of the additional instruments Z_2 given the validity of Z_1.

If $k = 1$ and $r = 2$, x_i, z_{1i}, and z_{2i} are scalar variables, and the single parameter θ satisfies the two moment conditions

$$\begin{aligned} E\left[z_{1i} \left(y_i - \theta x_i \right) \right] &= 0 \\ E\left[z_{2i} \left(y_i - \theta x_i \right) \right] &= 0. \end{aligned} \tag{A.108}$$

So the Sargan test is testing just one overidentifying restriction, which can be written as the equality of two simple IV estimating coefficients:

$$\frac{E\left(z_{1i} y_i \right)}{E\left(z_{1i} x_i \right)} = \frac{E\left(z_{2i} y_i \right)}{E\left(z_{2i} x_i \right)}. \tag{A.109}$$

Irrelevance of Unrestricted Moments Let us suppose that the sample moment vector consists of two components

$$b_N\left(\theta\right) = \begin{pmatrix} b_{1N}\left(\theta_1\right) \\ b_{2N}\left(\theta\right) \end{pmatrix} \begin{array}{c} r_1 \times 1 \\ r_2 \times 1 \end{array} \tag{A.110}$$

corresponding to a partition $\theta = \left(\theta_1', \theta_2'\right)' \in \Theta_1 \times \Theta_2$ of dimensions k_1 and k_2, respectively. The first component of $b_N\left(\theta\right)$ depends only on θ_1 whereas the second depends on both θ_1 and θ_2. We assume that $r_1 \geq k_1$, but $r_2 = k_2$. Moreover, $\partial b_{2N}\left(c\right)/\partial c_2'$ is non-singular for all c, so that $b_{2N}\left(\theta\right)$ are effectively unrestricted moments.

Suppose that we are primarily interested in the estimation of θ_1. We wish to compare two different GMM estimators of θ_1. The first one is a joint estimator of θ_1 and θ_2 using all the moments:

$$\widehat{\theta} = \begin{pmatrix} \widehat{\theta}_1 \\ \widehat{\theta}_2 \end{pmatrix} = \arg\min_c b_N\left(c\right)' V^{-1} b_N\left(c\right) = \arg\min_c s_N\left(c\right). \tag{A.111}$$

The other is a separate estimator of θ_1 based on the first r_1 moments:

$$\widetilde{\theta}_1 = \arg\min_{c_1} b_{1N}\left(c_1\right)' V_{11}^{-1} b_{1N}\left(c_1\right) = \arg\min_c s_N^*\left(c_1\right) \tag{A.112}$$

where V_{11} consists of the first r_1 rows and columns of V.

The result is that as long as $b_{2N}\left(\theta\right)$ are unrestricted moments:[6]

$$\widehat{\theta}_1 = \widetilde{\theta}_1. \tag{A.113}$$

Moreover, since $s_N\left(\widehat{\theta}\right) = s_N^*\left(\widetilde{\theta}_1\right)$, provided V is an optimal weight matrix, the Sargan test statistics of $b_N\left(\theta\right)$ and $b_{1N}\left(\theta_1\right)$ coincide.

To see this, we need to show that $s_N^*\left(c_1\right)$ coincides with $s_N\left(c\right)$ concentrated with respect to c_2. Let us write

$$s_N\left(c\right) = b_{1N}\left(c_1\right)' V^{11} b_{1N}\left(c_1\right) + 2 b_{1N}\left(c_1\right)' V^{12} b_{2N}\left(c\right) + b_{2N}\left(c\right)' V^{22} b_{2N}\left(c\right) \tag{A.114}$$

where

$$V^{-1} = \begin{pmatrix} V^{11} & V^{12} \\ V^{21} & V^{22} \end{pmatrix},$$

and let $\widehat{\theta}_2\left(c_1\right)$ be the minimizer of $s_N\left(c\right)$ with respect to c_2 for given c_1.

---

[6] A similar result for minimum distance is in Chamberlain (1982, Proposition 9b).

In general, $\widehat{\theta}_2(c_1)$ satisfies the first-order conditions

$$\frac{\partial s_N(c)}{\partial c_2} = 2\left(\frac{\partial b_{2N}(c)}{\partial c_2'}\right)'\left[V^{22}b_{2N}(c) + V^{21}b_{1N}(c_1)\right] = 0, \qquad (A.115)$$

but if $b_{2N}(c)$ are unrestricted, $\widehat{\theta}_2(c_1)$ satisfies

$$b_{2N}\left(c_1, \widehat{\theta}_2(c_1)\right) = -\left(V^{22}\right)^{-1}V^{21}b_{1N}(c_1). \qquad (A.116)$$

Therefore, the concentrated criterion is given by

$$\begin{aligned}
s_N\left(c_1, \widehat{\theta}_2(c_1)\right) &= b_{1N}(c_1)'\left[V^{11} - V^{12}\left(V^{22}\right)^{-1}V^{21}\right]b_{1N}(c_1) \qquad (A.117) \\
&= b_{1N}(c_1)'V_{11}^{-1}b_{1N}(c_1),
\end{aligned}$$

which coincides with $s_N^*(c_1)$ in view of the formulae for partitioned inverses.

B

Optimal Instruments in Conditional Models

B.1 Introduction

So far the starting point of our discussion has been an $r \times 1$ vector of orthogonality conditions of the form

$$E\psi(w, \theta) = 0. \tag{B.1}$$

Given these moment restrictions we obtained asymptotically efficient GMM estimators of θ.

However, we are often interested in models that imply an infinite number of orthogonality conditions. In particular, this is the case with models defined by conditional moment restrictions. For example, the linear regression model

$$E(y \mid x) = x'\theta \tag{B.2}$$

implies that

$$E[h(x)(y - x'\theta)] = 0 \tag{B.3}$$

for any function h such that the expectation exists, and therefore in general an infinite set of unconditional moment restrictions.

Note, however, that the number of restrictions is finite if x is discrete and only takes a finite number of different values. For example, suppose that x is a single $0 - 1$ binary variable. Let $h_0(x)$ and $h_1(x)$ be the indicator functions of the events $x = 0$ and $x = 1$, respectively, so that $h_0(x) = 1 - x$ and $h_1(x) = x$. Clearly, any other function of x will be a linear combination of these two. Therefore, in this case (B.2) only implies two moment restrictions:

$$E[h_0(x)(y - x\theta)] \quad = \quad 0$$

$$E\left[h_1\left(x\right)\left(y-x\theta\right)\right] \quad = \quad 0. \tag{B.4}$$

Similarly, if x is discrete with q points of support $\left(\xi_1, ..., \xi_q\right)$, the conditional moment restriction (B.2) implies q unconditional moments:

$$E\left[h_j\left(x\right)\left(y-x\theta\right)\right] = 0\left(j = 1, ..., q\right) \tag{B.5}$$

where $h_j\left(x\right) = 1\left(x = \xi_j\right)$ (cf. Chamberlain, 1987).[1]

The question that we address here is whether it is possible to find a finite set of optimal orthogonality conditions that give rise to asymptotically efficient estimators, in the sense that their asymptotic variance cannot be reduced by using additional orthogonality conditions.

We begin by solving the problem for the linear regression model which is the most familiar context, and next we use the same procedure for increasingly more complex models. The most general case that we consider, a set of nonlinear simultaneous implicit equations, nests all the others as special cases.

In all cases we assume the identification of the parameters that we wish to estimate. Moreover, except in a cursory way, we do not consider explicitly specific feasible estimators. Instead, the focus of our discussion is in finding the optimal instruments for each type of model.

We only consider optimal instruments for *iid* observations. The analysis of optimal instruments for dependent observations is more complicated. Moreover, the *iid* assumption is sufficiently general to cover panel data models in a fixed T, large N setting.

Amemiya (1977) obtained the optimal instruments for a nonlinear simultaneous equation model with homoskedastic and serially uncorrelated errors. The form of the optimal instruments for a conditional mean model with dependent observations was derived by Hansen (1985). Chamberlain (1987) found that the optimal IV estimator attains the semi-parametric efficiency bound for conditional moment restrictions. Newey (1993) provides a survey of the literature and discussion of nonparametric estimation of the optimal instruments in the *iid* case.

B.2   Linear Regression

The model is

$$y = x'\theta + u \tag{B.6}$$

$$E\left(u \mid x\right) = 0, \tag{B.7}$$

where y is a scalar variable, and x and θ are $k \times 1$.

---

[1]We use $1\left(A\right)$ to denote the indicator function of event A, such that $1\left(A\right) = 1$ if A is true and $1\left(A\right) = 0$ otherwise.

Let $z = z(x)$ denote a $p \times 1$ vector of functions of x such that $p \geq k$. Then z is a vector of valid instruments since

$$E\left[z\left(y - x'\theta\right)\right] = 0. \tag{B.8}$$

The optimal GMM estimator based on a given set of orthogonality conditions $E\psi(w, \theta) = 0$ and *iid* observations has asymptotic variance

$$\left(D_0' V_0^{-1} D_0\right)^{-1} \tag{B.9}$$

where $D_0 = E\left[\partial\psi(w, \theta)/\partial c'\right]$ and $V_0 = E\left[\psi(w, \theta)\,\psi(w, \theta)'\right]$ (see Section A.7). In our case $\psi(w, \theta) = z(y - x'\theta)$, and therefore

$$
\begin{aligned}
D_0 &= -E\left(zx'\right) & \text{(B.10)}\\
V_0 &= E\left(u^2 zz'\right) = E\left[\sigma^2(x)\,zz'\right] & \text{(B.11)}
\end{aligned}
$$

where

$$E\left(u^2 \mid x\right) = \sigma^2(x). \tag{B.12}$$

Hence, the expression for (B.9) is

$$\left\{E\left(xz'\right) E\left[\sigma^2(x)\,zz'\right]^{-1} E\left(zx'\right)\right\}^{-1} \tag{B.13}$$

The optimal instruments in this case are

$$z^*(x) = \frac{x}{\sigma^2(x)}. \tag{B.14}$$

Setting $z = z^*(x)$ the asymptotic variance (B.13) for the optimal instruments takes the form[2]

$$\left[E\left(\frac{xx'}{\sigma^2(x)}\right)\right]^{-1}. \tag{B.15}$$

To show that $z^*(x)$ are the optimal instruments we prove that for any other z:

$$E\left(\frac{xx'}{\sigma^2(x)}\right) - E\left(xz'\right) E\left[\sigma^2(x)\,zz'\right]^{-1} E\left(zx'\right) \geq 0. \tag{B.16}$$

Letting $x^\dagger = x/\sigma(x)$, $z^\dagger = \sigma(x) z$, and $w = \left(x^{\dagger\prime}, z^{\dagger\prime}\right)'$, the *lhs* of (B.16) can be rewritten as

$$E\left(x^\dagger x^{\dagger\prime}\right) - E\left(x^\dagger z^{\dagger\prime}\right)\left[E\left(z^\dagger z^{\dagger\prime}\right)\right]^{-1} E\left(z^\dagger x^{\dagger\prime}\right) = H'E\left(ww'\right) H \tag{B.17}$$

where

$$H' = \left(I\colon - E\left(x^\dagger z^{\dagger\prime}\right)\left[E\left(z^\dagger z^{\dagger\prime}\right)\right]^{-1}\right). \tag{B.18}$$

Clearly, $E\left(ww'\right) \geq 0$ since for any a of the same dimension as w, we have $a'E\left(ww'\right) a = E\left(\zeta^2\right) \geq 0$ with $\zeta = a'w$. Therefore, $H'E\left(ww'\right) H \geq 0$ also, which shows that (B.15) is a lower bound for variances of the form (B.13).

---

[2]The optimal choice of instruments is up to a multiplicative constant, since any $b(x) c$ for constant $c \neq 0$ does not change the asymptotic variance.

Thus, for example, if we consider an optimal GMM estimator that uses an augmented instrument set

$$z = \begin{pmatrix} z^* (x) \\ h (x) \end{pmatrix}$$

for some $h(x)$, there is no improvement in the asymptotic variance which remains equal to (B.15).

The direct implication of this result is that the estimator $\tilde{\theta}$ that solves

$$\sum_{i=1}^{N} z^* (x_i) \left(y_i - x_i' \tilde{\theta} \right) = 0 \qquad (B.19)$$

is optimal. Note that the optimal instrument has the same dimension as θ, so that no further weighting of the moments is required.

Of course, we have just reviewed the Gauss–Markov result and $\tilde{\theta}$ is nothing more than the unfeasible GLS estimator of θ:

$$\tilde{\theta} = \left(\sum_{i=1}^{N} \frac{x_i x_i'}{\sigma^2 (x_i)} \right)^{-1} \sum_{i=1}^{N} \frac{x_i y_i}{\sigma^2 (x_i)}. \qquad (B.20)$$

This estimator is unfeasible because the form of $\sigma^2 (.)$ is unknown.

Homoskedasticity   Under homoskedasticity $\sigma^2 (x) = \sigma^2$ for all x and the optimal variance (B.15) becomes

$$\sigma^2 \left[E (xx') \right]^{-1}. \qquad (B.21)$$

The optimal instruments are the x themselves since σ becomes an irrelevant constant, so that OLS is optimal.

Note that all we are saying is that OLS attains the asymptotic variance bound when $\sigma^2 (x)$ happens to be constant, but this constancy is not taken into account in the calculation of the bound. If we incorporate the homoskedasticity assumption in estimation the bound for θ may be lowered as we show later in Section B.6.

Feasible GLS   The efficiency result suggests to consider feasible GLS estimators that use estimated optimal instruments $\widehat{z}^* (x_i) = x_i / \widehat{\sigma}^2 (x_i)$ where $\widehat{\sigma}^2 (x_i)$ is an estimate of $\sigma^2 (x_i)$. If there is a known (or presumed) functional form of the heteroskedasticity $\sigma^2 (x_i, \gamma)$, we can set $\widehat{\sigma}^2 (x_i) = \sigma^2 (x_i, \widehat{\gamma})$ using a consistent estimator $\widehat{\gamma}$ of γ. For example, we can use squared OLS residuals $\widehat{u}_i$ to obtain a regression estimate of γ of the form

$$\widehat{\gamma} = \arg \min_{b} \sum_{i=1}^{N} \left[\widehat{u}_i^2 - \sigma^2 (x_i, b) \right]^2. \qquad (B.22)$$

Under correct specification and appropriate regularity conditions, it is well known that feasible and unfeasible GLS have the same asymptotic distribution.

Alternatively, $\hat{\sigma}^2(x_i)$ could be a nonparametric estimator of the conditional variance. A nearest neighbour estimate that lead to an asymptotically efficient feasible GLS was discussed by Robinson (1987).

B.3   Nonlinear Regression

The model is

$$y = f(x, \theta) + u \tag{B.23}$$

$$E(u \mid x) = 0 \tag{B.24}$$

where y is a scalar variable, θ is $k \times 1$, and $f(x, \theta)$ is some differentiable nonlinear function of x and θ.

As before, we consider an arbitrary vector of instruments $z = z(x)$ and the moments

$$E[z(y - f(x, \theta))] = 0. \tag{B.25}$$

The only difference with the linear case is that now

$$D_0 = -E(zf_1') \tag{B.26}$$

where

$$f_1 \equiv f_1(x, \theta) = \frac{\partial f(x, \theta)}{\partial c}. \tag{B.27}$$

Therefore, the expression for the asymptotic variance (B.9) is

$$\left\{ E(f_1 z') E\left[\sigma^2(x) zz'\right]^{-1} E(zf_1') \right\}^{-1}. \tag{B.28}$$

Following the steps of the linear case, the optimal instruments are

$$z^*(x) = \frac{f_1(x, \theta)}{\sigma^2(x)} \tag{B.29}$$

and the corresponding variance

$$\left[E\left(\frac{f_1(x, \theta) f_1(x, \theta)'}{\sigma^2(x)} \right) \right]^{-1} \tag{B.30}$$

This variance is achieved by the unfeasible IV estimator $\tilde{\theta}$ that solves the nonlinear sample moment equations:

$$q_N(c) = \sum_{i=1}^{N} \frac{f_1(x_i, \theta)}{\sigma^2(x_i)} [y_i - f(x_i, c)] = 0. \tag{B.31}$$

This estimator is unfeasible on two accounts. In common with the linear case, $\tilde{\theta}$ depends on the conditional variance $\sigma^2(x_i)$, which is an unknown function of x_i.

But it also depends on the vector of partial derivatives $f_1(x_i, \theta)$ evaluated at θ, which are known functions of x_i and the unknown true values of the parameters. It can be shown that substituting θ in (B.31) by a consistent estimator we still get an asymptotically efficient estimator. Alternatively, instead of keeping the optimal instrument fixed we can update it in the estimation. This is precisely what nonlinear least-squares does, which we discuss next.

Nonlinear Least-Squares   The generalized nonlinear least-squares estimator minimizes

$$\min_c \sum \frac{[y_i - f(x_i, c)]^2}{\sigma^2(x_i)} \tag{B.32}$$

and its first-order conditions are

$$\sum_{i=1}^{N} \frac{f_1(x_i, c)}{\sigma^2(x_i)} [y_i - f(x_i, c)] = 0, \tag{B.33}$$

which are similar to (B.31) except for the replacement of θ by c in the optimal instruments. It can be easily shown that the estimator that solves (B.33) is asymptotically equivalent to $\tilde{\theta}$. Of course, to obtain a feasible estimator one still has to replace $\sigma^2(x_i)$ by an estimate as in the linear case.

Finally, note that in the homoskedastic case, the variance term becomes irrelevant and we obtain the ordinary nonlinear least-squares formulae.

B.4   Nonlinear Structural Equation

The model is

$$\rho(y, x, \theta) = u \tag{B.34}$$

$$E(u \mid x) = 0 \tag{B.35}$$

where now y is a vector of endogenous variables and $\rho(.,.,.)$ is a scalar function that usually will only depend on a subset of the conditioning variables x.

Again, considering an arbitrary instrument vector $z = z(x)$ with moments $E[z\rho(y, x, \theta)] = 0$ we obtain an expression for V_0 equal to (B.11) and

$$D_0 = E[z\rho_1(y, x, \theta)'] \tag{B.36}$$

where

$$\rho_1(y, x, \theta) = \frac{\partial \rho(y, x, \theta)}{\partial c}. \tag{B.37}$$

Note that $\rho_1(y, x, \theta)$ may depend on y and hence it is not a valid instrument in general. So we consider instead its conditional expectation given x

$$b(x) = E[\rho_1(y, x, \theta) \mid x]. \tag{B.38}$$

Moreover, by the law of iterated expectations

$$D_0 = E\left[zb\left(x\right)'\right]. \tag{B.39}$$

Now we can argue as in the case of the regression models, so that the optimal instruments are

$$z^*\left(x\right) = \frac{b\left(x\right)}{\sigma^2\left(x\right)} = E\left(\frac{\partial\rho\left(y,x,\theta\right)}{\partial c}\mid x\right)\sigma^{-2}\left(x\right), \tag{B.40}$$

and the optimal variance

$$\left[E\left(\frac{b\left(x\right)b\left(x\right)'}{\sigma^2\left(x\right)}\right)\right]^{-1}. \tag{B.41}$$

This variance is achieved by the unfeasible IV estimator $\widetilde{\theta}$ that satisfies the sample moment equations:

$$\sum_{i=1}^{N}\frac{b\left(x_i\right)}{\sigma^2\left(x_i\right)}\rho\left(y_i,x_i,\widetilde{\theta}\right) = 0. \tag{B.42}$$

The difference with nonlinear regression is that now both $b\left(x_i\right)$ and $\sigma^2\left(x_i\right)$ are unknown functions of x_i. A parametric approach to feasible estimation is to specify functional forms for $b\left(x_i\right)$ and $\sigma^2\left(x_i\right)$, and substitute suitable estimates in (B.42). 2SLS can be regarded as an example of this approach and this is discussed below. On the other hand, there are two nonparametric approaches to feasible estimation. One is the "plug-in" method that replaces $b\left(x_i\right)$ and $\sigma^2\left(x_i\right)$ in (B.42) by nonparametric regression estimates. Another is to consider a GMM estimator based on an expanding set of instruments as N tends to infinity for a pre-specified class of functions (cf. Newey, 1990, 1993, for discussion and references).

Linear Structural Equation   Letting $y = \left(y_1, y_2'\right)'$, $x = \left(x_1', x_2'\right)'$, and $w = \left(y_2', x_1'\right)'$, we have

$$\rho\left(y,x,\theta\right) = y_1 - w'\theta \tag{B.43}$$

where y_1 is the (first) element of y, and w contains the remaining components of y and the conditioning variables that are included in the equation.

In this case

$$b\left(x\right) = -E\left(w\mid x\right) = -\left(\begin{array}{c} E\left(y_2\mid x\right) \\ x_1 \end{array}\right), \tag{B.44}$$

so that the unfeasible optimal IV estimator is

$$\widetilde{\theta} = \left(\sum_{i=1}^{N}\frac{b\left(x_i\right)}{\sigma^2\left(x_i\right)}w_i'\right)^{-1}\sum_{i=1}^{N}\frac{b\left(x_i\right)}{\sigma^2\left(x_i\right)}y_{1i}. \tag{B.45}$$

If $E\left(w\mid x\right)$ is linear and $\sigma^2\left(x\right)$ is constant:

$$E\left(w\mid x\right) \quad = \quad \Pi x$$

$$\sigma^2(x) \;\; = \;\; \sigma^2$$

where $\Pi = E(wx')[E(xx')]^{-1}$, the asymptotic variance (B.41) becomes

$$\sigma^2\left[\Pi E(xx')\Pi'\right]^{-1} = \sigma^2\left\{E(wx')[E(xx')]^{-1}E(xw')\right\}^{-1}, \qquad (\text{B.46})$$

which is the 2SLS asymptotic variance under homoskedasticity.[3]

In effect, 2SLS is the IV estimator that uses the sample linear projection $\widehat{\Pi}x$ as an estimate of the optimal instrument. It achieves the variance bound when $E(w\mid x)$ is linear and $\sigma^2(x)$ is constant, but this information is not used in the specification of the estimation problem.

We saw in Section A.7 that if there is heteroskedasticity the two-step GMM estimator (A.87) is asymptotically more efficient than 2SLS. In the current notation two-step GMM solves

$$\sum_{i=1}^{N}\widehat{\Gamma}x_i\left(y_{1i} - w_i'\widehat{\theta}_{GMM2}\right) = 0 \qquad (\text{B.47})$$

where

$$\widehat{\Gamma} = \sum_{i=1}^{N} w_i x_i'\left(\sum_{i=1}^{N}\widehat{u}_i^2 x_i x_i'\right)^{-1} \qquad (\text{B.48})$$

Thus, both GMM2 and 2SLS are using linear combinations of x as instruments.[4] Under heteroskedasticity, GMM2 is combining optimally a non-optimal set of orthogonality conditions. So, it is more efficient than 2SLS but inefficient relative to the IV estimator that uses $E(w\mid x)/\sigma^2(x)$ as instruments.

B.5   Multivariate Nonlinear Regression

We now consider a multivariate nonlinear regression

$$y_1 \;\; = \;\; f_{[1]}(x,\theta) + u_1$$

$$\vdots$$

$$y_g \;\; = \;\; f_{[g]}(x,\theta) + u_g \qquad (\text{B.49})$$

with $E(u_j\mid x) = 0$ $(j = 1, ..., g)$, or in compact notation

$$y = f(x,\theta) + u \qquad (\text{B.50})$$

$$E(u\mid x) = 0 \qquad (\text{B.51})$$

where θ is $k \times 1$, and y, $f(x,\theta)$, and u are $g \times 1$ vectors.

---

[3]Note that replacing Π by $\widehat{\Pi}$ has no effect on the asymptotic distribution.

[4]$\widehat{\Gamma}$ is a consistent estimate of the coefficients of a linear projection of $E(w\mid x)/\sigma(x)$ on $\sigma(x)x$:

$$\Gamma = E\left[E(w\mid x)x'\right]\left\{E\left[\sigma^2(x)xx'\right]\right\}^{-1} = E(wx')\left[E(u^2xx')\right]^{-1}.$$

This is a nonlinear system of "seemingly unrelated regression equations" (SURE) that places no restrictions on the second moments of the errors. There may be correlation among the errors of different equations, and their conditional variances and covariances may be heteroskedastic. Let the conditional variance matrix of u given x be

$$E\left(uu' \mid x\right) = \Omega\left(x\right), \tag{B.52}$$

which we assume to be nonsingular with probability one.

Let $Z = Z\left(x\right)$ denote a $g \times p$ matrix of functions of x such that $p \geq k$. Then we can form the moment conditions

$$E\left\{Z'\left[y - f\left(x, \theta\right)\right]\right\} = 0. \tag{B.53}$$

Proceeding as in the previous cases we have

$$D_0 = -E\left(Z'F_1\right) \tag{B.54}$$

where F_1 is the $g \times k$ matrix of partial derivatives

$$F_1 \equiv F_1\left(x, \theta\right) = \frac{\partial f\left(x, \theta\right)}{\partial c'}. \tag{B.55}$$

Moreover,

$$V_0 = E\left(Z'uu'Z\right) = E\left(Z'\Omega\left(x\right)Z\right). \tag{B.56}$$

Therefore, the optimal GMM variance based on (B.53) is

$$\left\{E\left(F_1'Z\right)\left[E\left(Z'\Omega\left(x\right)Z\right)\right]^{-1}E\left(Z'F_1\right)\right\}^{-1}. \tag{B.57}$$

The optimal instruments are

$$Z^*\left(x\right) = \Omega^{-1}\left(x\right)F_1 \tag{B.58}$$

in which case the asymptotic variance is

$$\left[E\left(F_1'\Omega^{-1}\left(x\right)F_1\right)\right]^{-1}. \tag{B.59}$$

To show that $Z^*\left(x\right)$ are the optimal instruments we just use a multivariate version of the argument employed in Section B.2. We need to prove that for any other Z:

$$E\left(F_1'\Omega^{-1}\left(x\right)F_1\right) - E\left(F_1'Z\right)\left[E\left(Z'\Omega\left(x\right)Z\right)\right]^{-1}E\left(Z'F_1\right) \geq 0. \tag{B.60}$$

Letting $F_1^\dagger = \Omega^{-1/2}\left(x\right)F_1$, $Z^\dagger = \Omega^{1/2}\left(x\right)Z$, and $W = \left(F_1^\dagger \vdots Z^\dagger\right)$, the *lhs* of (B.60) can be rewritten as

$$E\left(F_1^{\dagger'}F_1^\dagger\right) - E\left(F_1^{\dagger'}Z^\dagger\right)\left[E\left(Z^{\dagger'}Z^\dagger\right)\right]^{-1}E\left(Z^{\dagger'}F_1^\dagger\right) = H'E\left(W'W\right)H \tag{B.61}$$

where

$$H' = \left(I \vdots - E\left(F_1^{\dagger\prime} Z^\dagger \right) \left[E\left(Z^{\dagger\prime} Z^\dagger \right) \right]^{-1} \right). \tag{B.62}$$

Since $H' E \left(W'W \right) H \geq 0$, (B.59) is a variance bound.[5]

The unfeasible optimal IV estimator solves

$$\sum_{i=1}^{N} F_1' \left(x_i, \theta \right) \Omega^{-1} \left(x_i \right) \left[y_i - f\left(x_i, c \right) \right] = 0. \tag{B.63}$$

Under homoskedasticity $\Omega \left(x \right) = \Omega$, but in the multivariate case the error variance still plays a role in the construction of the optimal instruments.

Multivariate Nonlinear Least-Squares   This estimator minimizes

$$\sum_{i=1}^{N} \left[y_i - f\left(x_i, c \right) \right]' \Omega^{-1} \left(x_i \right) \left[y_i - f\left(x_i, c \right) \right] \tag{B.64}$$

with first-order conditions given by

$$\sum_{i=1}^{N} F_1' \left(x_i, c \right) \Omega^{-1} \left(x_i \right) \left[y_i - f\left(x_i, c \right) \right] = 0. \tag{B.65}$$

The same remarks we made for the single-equation case apply here. The estimators that solve (B.63) and (B.65) can be shown to be asymptotically equivalent. Moreover, a feasible estimator replaces $\Omega \left(x_i \right)$ by an estimated variance matrix. Under homoskedasticity this is simply given by

$$\widehat{\Omega} = \frac{1}{N} \sum_{i=1}^{N} \widehat{u}_i \widehat{u}_i'$$

where the $\widehat{u}_i$ are preliminary consistent residuals.

B.6   Nonlinear Simultaneous Equation System

Finally, we consider a system of implicit nonlinear simultaneous equations

$$\rho_{[1]} \left(y, x, \theta \right) = u_1$$
$$\vdots$$
$$\rho_{[g]} \left(y, x, \theta \right) = u_g \tag{B.66}$$

with $E\left(u_j \mid x \right) = 0$ $(j = 1, ..., g)$. The structural model (B.34) can be regarded as a single equation from this system, so that the notation in both cases is

---

[5]Note that $\Omega^{-1} \left(x \right) F_1 \left(x, \theta \right) C$, where C is any $k \times k$ non-singular matrix of constants, are also optimal instruments, and that the variance bound does not depend on C.

similar, i.e. y and x are vectors of endogenous and conditioning variables, respectively. In a compact notation we have

$$\rho(y, x, \theta) = u \qquad \text{(B.67)}$$

$$E(u \mid x) = 0 \qquad \text{(B.68)}$$

where $\rho(y, x, \theta)$ and u are $g \times 1$ vectors.

As in the multivariate regression case, we take an arbitrary $g \times p$ instrument matrix $Z = Z(x)$ and form the moments

$$E[Z'\rho(y, x, \theta)] = 0. \qquad \text{(B.69)}$$

In this case the expression for V_0 is the same as (B.56) and D_0 is given by

$$D_0 = E[Z'P_1(y, x, \theta)] = E\{Z'E[P_1(y, x, \theta) \mid x]\} = E[Z'B(x)] \qquad \text{(B.70)}$$

where $P_1(y, x, \theta)$ is the $g \times k$ matrix of partial derivatives

$$P_1(y, x, \theta) = \frac{\partial \rho(y, x, \theta)}{\partial c'}, \qquad \text{(B.71)}$$

and $B(x)$ denotes their conditional expectations given x:

$$B(x) = E[P_1(y, x, \theta) \mid x]. \qquad \text{(B.72)}$$

The components of $P_1(y, x, \theta)$ are not valid instruments in general because of their dependence on y. So we consider instead $B(x)$, which are optimal predictors of $P_1(y, x, \theta)$ given x.

The optimal instruments are

$$Z^*(x) = \Omega^{-1}(x) B(x) \qquad \text{(B.73)}$$

and the corresponding variance bound is

$$\{E[B(x)'\Omega^{-1}(x) B(x)]\}^{-1}. \qquad \text{(B.74)}$$

This variance is achieved by the unfeasible IV estimator $\tilde{\theta}$ that satisfies the sample moment equations:

$$\sum_{i=1}^{N} B(x_i)' \Omega^{-1}(x_i) \rho\left(y_i, x_i, \tilde{\theta}\right) = 0. \qquad \text{(B.75)}$$

The optimal IV estimator can also be expressed as the minimizer of a quadratic objective function. Since the number of moments equals the number of parameters, the choice of weight matrix is statistically irrelevant, but a computationally useful objective function is

$$\left(\sum_{i=1}^{N} \rho(y_i, x_i, c)' Z_i^*\right) \left(\sum_{i=1}^{N} Z_i^{*'} Z_i^*\right)^{-1} \left(\sum_{i=1}^{N} Z_i^{*'} \rho(y_i, x_i, c)\right) \qquad \text{(B.76)}$$

where $Z_i^* = \Omega^{-1}(x_i) B(x_i)$.

The same comments we made for the single structural equation case regarding strategies to feasible estimation apply also here, so we shall not elaborate further.

Linear Simultaneous Equation System The 3SLS estimator considered in Section A.3 is an example of a feasible IV estimator that adopts a parametric specification of the optimal instruments. In the 3SLS context, $\rho(y_i, x_i, c)$ is a linear system, $B(x_i)$ contains sample linear projections, and $\Omega(x_i)$ is replaced by the unconditional covariance matrix of 2SLS residuals.

Specifically, we have

$$\rho(y, x, \theta) = y_1 - W\theta \qquad (\text{B.77})$$

where y_1 is a $g \times 1$ (sub) vector of the endogenous variables y whose coefficients are normalized to one, $\theta = \left(\theta'_1 ... \theta'_g\right)'$ and W is a $g \times k$ block diagonal matrix containing both endogenous and exogenous explanatory variables:[6]

$$W = \begin{pmatrix} w'_1 & & 0 \\ & \ddots & \\ 0 & & w'_g \end{pmatrix} \qquad (\text{B.78})$$

In this case

$$B(x) = -E(W \mid x) = -\begin{pmatrix} E(w'_1 \mid x) & & 0 \\ & \ddots & \\ 0 & & E(w'_g \mid x) \end{pmatrix} \qquad (\text{B.79})$$

so that the unfeasible optimal IV estimator solves

$$\theta = \left(\sum_{i=1}^{N} B(x_i)' \Omega^{-1}(x_i) W_i\right)^{-1} \sum_{i=1}^{N} B(x_i)' \Omega^{-1}(x_i) y_{1i}. \qquad (\text{B.80})$$

If $E(W \mid x)$ is linear and $\Omega(x)$ is constant:

$$E(W \mid x) = X\Pi^{\dagger}$$
$$\Omega(x) = \Omega$$

where $X = (I_g \otimes x')$ and $\Pi^{\dagger} = [E(X'X)]^{-1} E(X'W)$, the variance bound (B.74) coincides with the asymptotic variance of 3SLS:

$$\left[\Pi^{\dagger\prime} E\left(X'\Omega^{-1}X\right)\Pi^{\dagger}\right]^{-1}. \qquad (\text{B.81})$$

Indeed, the 3SLS estimator solves

---

[6]If $y_1 - W\theta$ represents the errors of a complete system then $y_1 = y$, but distinguishing between y and y_1 our notation also accommodates incomplete linear systems.

$$\sum_{i=1}^{N} \widehat{\Pi}^{\dagger\prime} X_i' \widehat{\Omega}^{-1} \left(y_{1i} - W_i \widehat{\theta}_{3SLS} \right) = 0 \tag{B.82}$$

where $\widehat{\Pi}^{\dagger} = \left(\sum_i X_i' X_i \right)^{-1} \sum_i X_i' W_i$ and $\widehat{\Omega}$ is the sample covariance matrix of 2SLS residuals.

Homoskedastic Linear Regression Nonlinear simultaneous equations are a useful motivation for (B.66), hence the title of this section. However, the conditional moment restrictions framework has broader applicability. Here we consider a linear regression model subject to homoskedasticity as an example of (B.66).

The model is

$$y = x'\beta + u \tag{B.83}$$

$$\begin{aligned} E\left(u \mid x\right) &= 0 & \text{(B.84)} \\ E\left(u^2 \mid x\right) &= \sigma^2. & \text{(B.85)} \end{aligned}$$

Thus, we have $\theta = \left(\beta', \sigma^2\right)'$ and

$$\rho(y, x, \theta) = \begin{pmatrix} y - x'\beta \\ (y - x'\beta)^2 - \sigma^2 \end{pmatrix}. \tag{B.86}$$

Moreover,

$$P_1(y, x, \theta) = \frac{\partial \rho(y, x, \theta)}{\partial c'} = -\begin{pmatrix} x' & 0 \\ 2ux' & 1 \end{pmatrix} \tag{B.87}$$

$$B(x) = E\left(\frac{\partial \rho(y, x, \theta)}{\partial c'} \mid x \right) = -\begin{pmatrix} x' & 0 \\ 0 & 1 \end{pmatrix}. \tag{B.88}$$

Also,

$$\Omega(x) = \begin{pmatrix} \sigma^2 & E\left(u^3 \mid x\right) \\ E\left(u^3 \mid x\right) & E\left(u^4 \mid x\right) - \sigma^4 \end{pmatrix}. \tag{B.89}$$

If $E\left(u^3 \mid x\right) = 0$, the variance bound becomes

$$\left\{ E\left[B(x)' \Omega^{-1}(x) B(x) \right] \right\}^{-1} = \begin{pmatrix} \sigma^{-2} E\left(xx'\right) & 0 \\ 0 & E\left[1/Var\left(u^2 \mid x\right) \right] \end{pmatrix}^{-1} \tag{B.90}$$

Thus, there is no efficiency gain from incorporating the homoskedasticity assumption in estimation since we obtain the same bound that we got using (B.84) only. However, if $E\left(u^3 \mid x\right) \neq 0$ there is a lower variance bound for β than the one given in (B.21) (cf. MaCurdy, 1982a).

Simultaneous System with Heteroskedasticity of Known Form   Extending the argument in the previous example, let us consider now a nonlinear simultaneous system with a heteroskedastic conditional covariance matrix of known parametric form.[7] The model is

$$\rho^{\dagger}\left(y, x, \beta\right) = u \tag{B.91}$$

$$E\left(u \mid x\right) = 0 \tag{B.92}$$

$$E\left(uu' \mid x\right) = \Omega^{\dagger}\left(x, \gamma\right). \tag{B.93}$$

Thus, we have $\theta = \left(\beta', \gamma'\right)'$, $c = \left(b', g'\right)'$, and[8]

$$\rho\left(y, x, \beta\right) = \left(\begin{array}{c} \rho^{\dagger}\left(y, x, \beta\right) \\ vech\left[\rho^{\dagger}\left(y, x, \beta\right) \rho^{\dagger}\left(y, x, \beta\right)' - \Omega^{\dagger}\left(x, \gamma\right)\right] \end{array} \right). \tag{B.94}$$

In this case we have[9]

$$P_{1}\left(y, x, \theta\right) = \left(\begin{array}{cc} P_{1}^{\dagger}\left(y, x, \theta\right) & 0 \\ LK\left[u \otimes P_{1}^{\dagger}\left(y, x, \theta\right)\right] & -G_{1}\left(x, \gamma\right) \end{array} \right), \tag{B.95}$$

where

$$P_{1}^{\dagger}\left(y, x, \theta\right) = \frac{\partial \rho^{\dagger}\left(y, x, \beta\right)}{\partial b'}$$

$$G_{1}\left(x, \gamma\right) = \frac{\partial vech\Omega^{\dagger}\left(x, \gamma\right)}{\partial g'},$$

and L and K are matrices of constants such that $vech\left(uu'\right) = Lvec\left(uu'\right)$, and $\left(u \otimes P_{1}^{\dagger}\right) + \left(P_{1}^{\dagger} \otimes u\right) = K\left(u \otimes P_{1}^{\dagger}\right)$, respectively. Also,

$$B\left(x\right) = E\left[P_{1}\left(y, x, \theta\right) \mid x\right] = \left(\begin{array}{cc} E\left[P_{1}^{\dagger}\left(y, x, \theta\right) \mid x\right] & 0 \\ LKE\left[u \otimes P_{1}^{\dagger}\left(y, x, \theta\right) \mid x\right] & -G_{1}\left(x, \gamma\right) \end{array} \right). \tag{B.96}$$

Note that now in general $E\left[u \otimes P_{1}^{\dagger}\left(y, x, \theta\right) \mid x\right] \neq 0$, since $P_{1}^{\dagger}\left(y, x, \theta\right)$ depends on y, and therefore its elements may be correlated with those of u. This

---

[7]Note that in our context, homoskedasticity (with or without covariance restrictions) is just a special case of heteroskedasticity of known parametric form.

[8]The *vech* operator stacks by rows the lower triangle of a square matrix. It is used to avoid redundant elements, given the symmetry of the covariance matrix.

[9]We are using

$$\frac{\partial vec\left(uu'\right)}{\partial b'} = \left(\frac{\partial u}{\partial b'} \otimes u\right) + \left(u \otimes \frac{\partial u}{\partial b'}\right).$$

is in contrast with the regression case, where $\rho^\dagger\left(y, x, \beta\right) = y - f\left(x, \beta\right)$, so that $P_1^\dagger$ does not depend on y.

Moreover, using the fact that $vech\left(uu'\right) = L\left(u \otimes u\right)$,

$$\Omega\left(x\right) = \begin{pmatrix} \Omega^\dagger\left(x, \gamma\right) & E\left(uu' \otimes u' \mid x\right) L' \\ LE\left(uu' \otimes u \mid x\right) & LE\left(uu' \otimes uu' \mid x\right) L' \end{pmatrix}. \tag{B.97}$$

This matrix is block diagonal if the conditional third-order moments of the us are zero. However, even if $E\left(uu' \otimes u \mid x\right) = 0$, the variance bound is not block diagonal between β and γ because $B\left(x\right)$ is not block diagonal. Therefore, there is an efficiency gain from incorporating the conditional covariance restrictions in the estimation of β. There is, of course, a trade-off between robustness and efficiency, since estimates of β that exploit the covariance restrictions may be inconsistent if these restrictions turn out to be false.

Finally, note that if the covariance matrix depends on both β and γ, so that

$$E\left(uu' \mid x\right) = \Omega^\dagger\left(x, \beta, \gamma\right), \tag{B.98}$$

the off-diagonal term of $B\left(x\right)$ has an additional non-zero term which is given by $-\partial vech\Omega^\dagger\left(x, \beta, \gamma\right)/\partial b'$. In such case there is an obvious efficiency gain from incorporating the covariance structure in the estimation of β, even if $P_1^\dagger$ does not depend on endogenous variables.

References

Abowd, J. M. and D. Card (1989): "On the Covariance Structure of Earnings and Hours Changes", *Econometrica*, 57, 411–445.

Ahn, S. and P. Schmidt (1995): "Efficient Estimation of Models for Dynamic Panel Data", *Journal of Econometrics*, 68, 5–27.

Aigner, D. J., C. Hsiao, A. Kapteyn, and T. Wansbeek (1984): "Latent Variable Models in Econometrics", in Griliches, Z. and M. D. Intriligator (eds.), *Handbook of Econometrics*, vol. 2, Elsevier Science, Amsterdam.

Alonso-Borrego, C. and M. Arellano (1999): "Symmetrically Normalized Instrumental-Variable Estimation Using Panel Data", *Journal of Business & Economic Statistics*, 17, 36–49.

Altonji, J. G. and A. Siow (1987): "Testing the Response of Consumption to Income Changes with (Noisy) Panel Data", *Quarterly Journal of Economics*, 102, 293–328.

Alvarez, J. (1999): "Dynamics and Seasonality in Quarterly Panel Data: An Analysis of Earnings Mobility in Spain", Working Paper 9914, CEMFI, Madrid.

Alvarez, J. and M. Arellano (1998): "The Time Series and Cross-Section Asymptotics of Dynamic Panel Data Estimators", Working Paper 9808, CEMFI, Madrid (forthcoming in *Econometrica*, 2003).

Amemiya, T. (1971): "The Estimation of the Variances in a Variance-Components Model", *International Economic Review*, 12, 1–3.

Amemiya, T. (1977): "The Maximum Likelihood and the Nonlinear Three-Stage Least Squares Estimator in the General Nonlinear Simultaneous Equation Model", *Econometrica*, 45, 955–968.

Amemiya, T. (1985): *Advanced Econometrics*, Blackwell, Oxford.

Amemiya, T. and T. E. MaCurdy (1986): "Instrumental-variable Estimation of an Error-components Model", *Econometrica*, 54, 869–881.

Andersen, E. B. (1970): "Asymptotic Properties of Conditional Maximum Likelihood Estimators", *Journal of the Royal Statistical Society*, Series B, 32, 283–301.

Anderson, T. W. and C. Hsiao (1981): "Estimation of Dynamic Models with Error Components", *Journal of the American Statistical Association*, 76, 598–606.

Anderson, T. W. and C. Hsiao (1982): "Formulation and Estimation of Dynamic Models Using Panel Data", *Journal of Econometrics*, 18, 47–82.

Angrist, J. D. and W. N. Evans (1998): "Children and Their Parents Labor Supply: Evidence from Exogenous Variation in Family Size", *American Economic Review*, 88, 450–477.

Arellano, M. (1985): "Estimation and Testing of Dynamic Econometric Models from Panel Data", Ph.D. Thesis, London School of Economics.

Arellano, M. (1987): "Computing Robust Standard Errors for Within-Group Estimators", *Oxford Bulletin of Economics and Statistics*, 49, 431–434.

Arellano, M. (1989a): "On the Efficient Estimation of Simultaneous Equations with Covariance Restrictions", *Journal of Econometrics*, 42, 247–265.

Arellano, M. (1989b): "An Efficient GLS Estimator of Triangular Models with Covariance Restrictions", *Journal of Econometrics*, 42, 267–273.

Arellano, M. (1990): "Testing for Autocorrelation in Dynamic Random Effects Models", *Review of Economic Studies*, 57, 127–134.

Arellano, M. (1993): "On the Testing of Correlated Effects with Panel Data", *Journal of Econometrics*, 59, 87–97.

Arellano, M. (2000): "Modelling Optimal Instrumental Variables for Panel Data Models", Working Paper, CEMFI, Madrid.

Arellano, M. (2002): "Sargan's Instrumental Variables Estimation and the Generalized Method of Moments", *Journal of Business & Economic Statistics*, 20, 450–459.

Arellano, M. and S. R. Bond (1988): "Dynamic Panel Data Estimation Using DPD—A Guide for Users", Institute for Fiscal Studies, Working Paper 88/15, London.

Arellano, M. and S. R. Bond (1991): "Some Tests of Specification for Panel Data: Monte Carlo Evidence and an Application to Employment Equations", *Review of Economic Studies*, 58, 277–297.

Arellano, M. and O. Bover (1995): "Another Look at the Instrumental-Variable Estimation of Error-Components Models", *Journal of Econometrics*, 68, 29–51.

Arellano, M. and B. Honoré (2001): "Panel Data Models: Some Recent Developments", in Heckman, J. J. and E. Leamer (eds.), *Handbook of Econometrics*, vol. 5, chapter 53, North-Holland.

Arellano, M., L. P. Hansen, and E. Sentana (1999): "Underidentification?", unpublished manuscript, CEMFI, Madrid.

Ashenfelter, O. and D. Card (1985): "Using the Longitudinal Structure of Earnings to Estimate the Effect of Training Programs", *Review of Economics and Statistics*, 67, 648–660.

Ashenfelter, O. and A. Krueger (1994): "Estimates of the Economic Return to Schooling from a New Sample of Twins", *American Economic Review*, 84, 1157–1173.

Balestra, P. and M. Nerlove (1966): "Pooling Cross Section and Time Series Data in the Estimation of a Dynamic Model: The Demand for Natural Gas", *Econometrica*, 34, 585–612.

Baltagi, B. H. (1995): *Econometric Analysis of Panel Data*, John Wiley, Chichester.

Barro, R. J. and X. Sala-i-Martin (1995): *Economic Growth*, McGraw-Hill, New York.

Becker, G., M. Grossman, and K. Murphy (1994): "An Empirical Analysis of Cigarette Addiction", *American Economic Review*, 84, 396–418.

Bekker, P.A. (1994): "Alternative Approximations to the Distributions of Instrumental Variable Estimators", *Econometrica*, 62, 657–681.

Benhabib, J. and M. M. Spiegel (2000): "The Role of Financial Development in Growth and Investment", *Journal of Economic Growth*, 5, 341–360.

Bhargava, A. and J. D. Sargan (1983): "Estimating Dynamic Random Effects Models from Panel Data Covering Short Time Periods", *Econometrica*, 51, 1635–1659.

Blundell, R. and R. Smith (1991): "Initial Conditions and Efficient Estimation in Dynamic Panel Data Models", *Annales d'Economie et de Statistique*, 20/21, 109–123.

Blundell, R. and S. Bond (1998): "Initial Conditions and Moment Restrictions in Dynamic Panel Data Models", *Journal of Econometrics*, 87, 115–143.

Blundell, R. and S. Bond (2000): "GMM Estimation with Persistent Panel Data: An Application to Production Functions", *Econometric Reviews*, 19, 321–340.

Blundell, R., S. Bond, M.P. Devereux, and F. Schiantarelli (1992): "Investment and Tobin's Q: Evidence from Company Panel Data", *Journal of Econometrics*, 51, 233–257.

Bond, S. and C. Meghir (1994): "Dynamic Investment Models and the Firm's Financial Policy", *Review of Economic Studies*, 61, 197–222.

Bond, S. R., A. Hoeffler, and J. Temple (2001): "GMM Estimation of Empirical Growth Models", CEPR Discussion Paper 3048, London.

Bover, O. (1991): "Relaxing Intertemporal Separability: A Rational Habits Model of Labor Supply Estimated from Panel Data", *Journal of Labor Economics*, 9, 85–100.

Bover, O. and N. Watson (2000): "Are There Economies of Scale in the Demand for Money by Firms? Some Panel Data Estimates", Working Paper 0008, Research Department, Bank of Spain.

Breusch, T. S., G. E. Mizon, and P. Schmidt (1989): "Efficient Estimation Using Panel Data", *Econometrica*, 57, 695–700.

Browning, M., A. Deaton, and M. Irish (1985): "A Profitable Approach to Labor Supply and Commodity Demand over the Life-Cycle", *Econometrica*, 53, 503–543.

Carrasco, R. (2001): "Binary Choice with Binary Endogenous Regressors in Panel Data: Estimating the Effect of Fertility on Female Labor Participation", *Journal of Business & Economic Statistics*, 19, 385–394.

Caselli, F., G. Esquivel, and F. Lefort (1996): "Reopening the Convergence Debate: A New Look at Cross-Country Growth Empirics", *Journal of Economic Growth*, 1, 363–389.

Chamberlain, G. (1982): "Multivariate Regression Models for Panel Data", *Journal of Econometrics*, 18, 5–46.

Chamberlain, G. (1984): "Panel Data", in Griliches, Z. and M. D. Intriligator (eds.), *Handbook of Econometrics*, vol. 2, Elsevier Science, Amsterdam.

Chamberlain, G. (1985): "Heterogeneity, Omitted Variable Bias, and Duration Dependence", in Heckman, J. J. and B. Singer (eds.), *Longitudinal Analysis of Labor Market Data*, Cambridge University Press, Cambridge.

Chamberlain, G. (1987): "Asymptotic Efficiency in Estimation with Conditional Moment Restrictions", *Journal of Econometrics*, 34, 305–334.

Chamberlain, G. (1992a): "Efficiency Bounds for Semiparametric Regression", *Econometrica*, 60, 567–596.

Chamberlain (1992b): Comment: Sequential Moment Restrictions in Panel Data", *Journal of Business & Economic Statistics*, 10, 20–26.

Chamberlain, G. (1993): "Feedback in Panel Data Models", unpublished manuscript, Department of Economics, Harvard University.

Chamberlain, G. (2000): "Econometrics and Decision Theory", *Journal of Econometrics*, 95, 255–283.

Chamberlain, G. and K. Hirano (1999): "Predictive Distributions Based on Longitudinal Earnings Data", *Annales d'Économie et de Statistique*, 55–56, 211–242.

Chowdhury, G. and S. Nickell (1985): "Hourly Earnings in the United States: Another Look at Unionization, Schooling, Sickness, and Unemployment Using PSID Data", *Journal of Labor Economics*, 3, 38–69.

Cox, D. R. and N. Reid (1987): "Parameter Orthogonality and Approximate Conditional Inference" (with discussion), *Journal of the Royal Statistical Society*, Series B, 49, 1–39.

Crepon, B., F. Kramarz, and A. Trognon (1997): "Parameters of Interest, Nuisance Parameters and Orthogonality Conditions. An Application to Autoregressive Error Component Models", *Journal of Econometrics*, 82, 135–156.

Deaton, A. (1991): "Saving and Liquidity Constraints", *Econometrica*, 59, 1221–1248.

Forbes, K. J. (2000): "A Reassessment of the Relationship Between Inequality and Growth", *American Economic Review*, 90, 869–887.

Forni, M. and L. Reichlin (1998): "Let's Get Real: A Factor Analytical Approach to Disaggregated Business Cycle Dynamics", *Review of Economic Studies*, 65, 453–473.

Geweke, J. and M. Keane (2000): "An Empirical Analysis of Earnings Dynamics Among Men in the PSID: 1968–1989", *Journal of Econometrics*, 96, 293–356.

Goldberger, A. S. (1978): "The Genetic Determination of Income: Comment", *American Economic Review*, 68, 960–969.

Goldberger, A. S. (1991): *A Course in Econometrics*, Harvard University Press.

Granger, C. W. J. (1969): "Investigating Causal Relations by Econometric Models and Cross-Spectral Methods", *Econometrica*, 37, 424–438.

Griliches, Z. (1977): "Estimating the Returns to Schooling: Some Econometric Problems", *Econometrica*, 45, 1–22.

Griliches, Z. (1979): "Sibling Models and Data in Economics: Beginnings of a Survey", *Journal of Political Economy*, 87, S37-S64.

Griliches, Z. and J. A. Hausman (1986): "Errors in Variables in Panel Data", *Journal of Econometrics*, 31, 93–118.

Griliches, Z. and J. Mairesse (1998): "Production Functions: The Search for Identification", in Strom, S. (ed.), *Econometrics and Economic Theory in the 20th Century*, The Ragnar Frisch Centennial Symposium, Cambridge University Press, Cambridge.

Hahn, J. (1997): "Efficient Estimation of Panel Data Models with Sequential Moment Restrictions", *Journal of Econometrics*, 79, 1–21.

Hahn, J. (1999): "How Informative Is the Initial Condition in the Dynamic Panel Model with Fixed Effects?", *Journal of Econometrics*, 93, 309–326.

Hahn, J. and G. Kuersteiner (2002): "Asymptotically Unbiased Inference for a Dynamic Panel Model with Fixed Effects When Both n and T are Large", *Econometrica*, 70, 1639–1657.

Hall, R. and F. Mishkin (1982): "The Sensitivity of Consumption to Transitory Income: Estimates from Panel Data on Households", *Econometrica*, 50, 461–481.

Hansen, L. P. (1982): "Large Sample Properties of Generalized Method of Moments Estimators", *Econometrica*, 50, 1029–1054.

Hansen, L. P. (1985): "A Method of Calculating Bounds on the Asymptotic Covariance Matrices of Generalized Method of Moments Estimators", *Journal of Econometrics*, 30, 203–238.

Hansen, L. P., J. Heaton, and A. Yaron (1996): "Finite Sample Properties of Some Alternative GMM Estimators", *Journal of Business & Economic Statistics*, 14, 262–280.

Harris, R. D. F. and E. Tzavalis (1999): "Inference for Unit Roots in Dynamic Panels where the Time Dimension is Fixed", *Journal of Econometrics*, 91, 201–226.

Hause, J. C. (1980): ""The Fine Structure of Earnings and the On-the-Job Training Hypothesis", *Econometrica*, 48, 1013–1029.

Hausman, J. A. (1978): "Specification Tests in Econometrics", *Econometrica*, 46, 1251–1272.

Hausman, J. A. and W. E. Taylor (1981): "Panel Data and Unobservable Individual Effects", *Econometrica*, 49, 1377–1398.

Hausman, J. A., W. K. Newey, and J. L. Powell (1995): "Nonlinear Errors in Variables Estimation of Some Engel Curves", *Journal of Econometrics*, 65, 205–233.

Hayashi, F. and C. Sims (1983): "Nearly Efficient Estimation of Time Series Models with Predetermined, But Not Exogenous, Instruments", *Econometrica*, 51, 783–798.

Hayashi, F. and T. Inoue (1991): "The Relation Between Firm Growth and Q with Multiple Capital Goods: Theory and Evidence from Panel Data on Japanese Firms", *Econometrica*, 59, 731–753.

Heckman, J. J. and T. E. MaCurdy (1980): "A Life Cycle Model of Female Labour Supply." *Review of Economic Studies*, 47, 47–74.

Hildreth, C. (1949): "Preliminary Considerations Regarding Time Series and/ or Cross Section Studies", Cowles Commission Discussion Paper, Statistics No. 333.

Hildreth, C. (1950): "Combining Cross Section Data and Time Series Data", Cowles Commission Discussion Paper, No. 347.

Hirano, K. (2002): "Semiparametric Bayesian Inference in Autoregressive Panel Data Models", *Econometrica*, 70, 781–799.

Hoch, I. (1962): "Estimation of Production Function Parameters Combining Time-Series and Cross-Section Data", *Econometrica*, 30, 34–53.

Holtz-Eakin, D. (1988): "Testing for Individual Effects in Autoregressive Models", *Journal of Econometrics*, 39, 297–307.

Holtz-Eakin, D., W. Newey, and H. Rosen (1988): "Estimating Vector Autoregressions with Panel Data", *Econometrica*, 56, 1371–1395.

Horowitz, J. L. (1998): *Semiparametric Methods in Econometrics*, Springer-Verlag, New York.

Horowitz, J. L. and M. Markatou (1996): "Semiparametric Estimation of Regression Models for Panel Data", *Review of Economic Studies*, 63, 145–168.

Hsiao, C. (1986): *Analysis of Panel Data*, Cambridge University Press, Cambridge.

Hsiao, C., M. H. Pesaran, and A. K. Tahmiscioglu (2002): "Maximum Likelihood Estimation of Fixed Effects Dynamic Panel Data Models Covering Short Time Periods", *Journal of Econometrics*, 109, 107–150.

Hurwicz, L. (1950): "Least Squares Bias in Time Series", in Koopmans, T. C. (ed.), *Statistical Inference in Dynamic Economic Models*, Cowles Commission Monograph No. 10, John Wiley, New York.

Imbens, G. (1997): "One-step Estimators for Over-identified Generalized Method of Moments Models", *Review of Economic Studies*, 64, 359–383.

Imbens, G., R. Spady, and P. Johnson (1998): "Information Theoretic Approaches to Inference in Moment Condition Models", *Econometrica*, 66, 333–357.

Islam, N. (1995): "Growth Empirics: A Panel Data Approach", *Quarterly Journal of Economics*, 110, 1127–1170.

Jennrich, R. I. (1969): "Asymptotic Properties of Non-Linear Least Squares Estimators", *Annals of Mathematical Statistics*, 40, 633–643.

Jöreskog, K. G. and D. Sörbom (1977): "Statistical Models and Methods for Analysis of Longitudinal Data", in Aigner, D. J. and A. S. Goldberger (eds.), *Latent Variables in Socio-Economic Models*, North-Holland, Amsterdam.

Keane, M. and D. Runkle (1992): "On the Estimation of Panel-Data Models with Serial Correlation When Instruments Are Not Strictly Exogenous", *Journal of Business & Economic Statistics*, 10, 1–9.

Kiefer, N. M. (1980): "Estimation of Fixed Effect Models for Time Series of Cross-Sections with Arbitrary Intertemporal Covariance", *Journal of Econometrics*, 14, 195–202.

King, M., E. Sentana, and S. Wadhwani (1994): "Volatility and Links Between National Stock Markets", *Econometrica*, 62, 901–933.

Kiviet, J. F. (1995): "On Bias, Inconsistency, and Efficiency of Various Estimators in Dynamic Panel Data Models", *Journal of Econometrics*, 68, 53–78.

Kruiniger, H. (1998): "Conditional Maximum Likelihood Estimation of Dynamic Panel Data Models", University College London Economics Paper 98-04.

Lahiri, K. and P. Schmidt (1978): "On the Estimation of Triangular Structural Systems", *Econometrica*, 46, 1217–1221.

Lancaster, T. (2000): "The Incidental Parameter Problem Since 1948", *Journal of Econometrics*, 95, 391–413.

Lancaster, T. (2002): "Orthogonal Parameters and Panel Data", *Review of Economic Studies*, 69, 647–666.

Levine, R., N. Loayza, and T. Beck (2000): "Financial Intermediation and Growth: Causality and Causes", *Journal of Monetary Economics*, 46, 31–77.

Lillard, L. and R. J. Willis (1978): "Dynamic Aspects of Earnings Mobility", *Econometrica*, 46, 985–1012.

Lillard, L. and Y. Weiss (1979): "Components of Variation in Panel Earnings Data: American Scientists 1960–1970", *Econometrica*, 47, 437–454.

MaCurdy, T. E. (1981): "An Empirical Model of Labor Supply in a Life-Cycle Setting", *Journal of Political Economy*, 89, 1059–1085.

MaCurdy, T. E. (1982a): "Using Information on the Moments of Disturbances to Increase the Efficiency of Estimation", NBER Technical Paper 22, Cambridge, MA.

MaCurdy, T. E. (1982b): "The Use of Time Series Processes to Model the Error Structure of Earnings in a Longitudinal Data Analysis", *Journal of Econometrics*, 18, 83–114.

MaCurdy, T. E. (1985): "Interpreting Empirical Models of Labor Supply in an Intertemporal Framework with Uncertainty", in Heckman, J. J. and B. Singer (eds.), *Longitudinal Analysis of Labor Market Data*, Cambridge University Press, Cambridge.

Maddala, G. S. (1971): "The Use of Variance Components Models in Pooling Cross Section and Time Series Data", *Econometrica*, 39, 351–358.

Magnus, J. R. and H. Neudecker (1988): *Matrix Differential Calculus with Applications in Statistics and Econometrics*, John Wiley, Chichester.

Malinvaud, E. (1970): "The Consistency of Nonlinear Regressions", *Annals of Mathematical Statistics*, 41, 956–969.

Mankiw, N. G., D. Romer, and D. N. Weil (1992): "A Contribution to the Empirics of Economic Growth", *Quarterly Journal of Economics*, 107, 407–437.

Manski, C. (1988): *Analog Estimation Methods in Econometrics*, Chapman and Hall, London.

Mariger, R.-P. and K. Shaw (1993): "Unanticipated Aggregate Disturbances and Tests of the Life-Cycle Consumption Model Using Panel Data", *Review of Economics and Statistics*, 75, 48–56.

Mulligan, C. B. (1997): "Scale Economies, the Value of Time, and the Demand for Money: Longitudinal Evidence from Firms", *Journal of Political Economy*, 105, 1061–1079.

Mundlak, Y. (1961): "Empirical Production Function Free of Management Bias", *Journal of Farm Economics*, 43, 44–56.

Mundlak, Y. (1978): "On the Pooling of Time Series and Cross Section Data", *Econometrica*, 46, 69–85.

Nerlove, M. (1967), "Experimental Evidence on the Estimation of Dynamic Economic Relations from a Time Series of Cross-Sections", *Economic Studies Quarterly*, 18, 42–74.

Nerlove, M. (1971), "Further Evidence on the Estimation of Dynamic Economic Relations from a Time Series of Cross Sections", *Econometrica*, 39, 359–387.

Newey, W. K. (1990): "Efficient Instrumental Variables Estimation of Nonlinear Models", *Econometrica*, 58, 809–837.

Newey, W. K. (1993): "Efficient Estimation of Models with Conditional Moment Restrictions", in Maddala, G. S., C. R. Rao, and H. D. Vinod (eds.), *Handbook of Statistics*, Vol. 11, Elsevier Science.

Newey, W. K. and K. D. West (1987): "A Simple, Positive Semi-Definite, Heteroskedasticity and Autocorrelation Consistent Covariance Matrix", *Econometrica*, 55, 703–708.

Newey, W. and D. McFadden (1994): "Large Sample Estimation and Hypothesis Testing", in Engle, R. F. and D. L. McFadden (eds.) *Handbook of Econometrics*, IV, Ch. 36, North-Holland.

Newey, W. K. and R. J. Smith (2002): "Asymptotic Bias and Equivalence of GMM and GEL Estimators", unpublished manuscript, University of Bristol.

Neyman, J. and E. L. Scott (1948): "Consistent Estimation from Partialy Consistent Observations", *Econometrica*, 16, 1–32.

Nickell, S. (1981): "Biases in Dynamic Models with Fixed Effects", *Econometrica*, 49, 1417–1426.

Pakes, A. and Z. Griliches (1984): "Estimating Distributed Lags in Short Panels with an Application to the Specification of Depreciation Patterns and Capital Stock Constructs", *Review of Economic Studies*, 51, 243–262.

Pesaran, M. H. and R. Smith (1995): "Estimating Long-Run Relationships from Dynamic Heterogeneous Panels", *Journal of Econometrics*, 68, 79–113.

Phillips, P. C. B. (1983): "Exact Small Sample Theory in the Simultaneous Equations Model", in Griliches, Z. and M. D. Intriligator (eds.), *Handbook of Econometrics*, vol. 1, North-Holland, Amsterdam, Ch. 8.

Phillips, P. C. B. and H. R. Moon (2000): "Nonstationary Panel Data Analysis: An Overview of Some Recent Developments", *Econometric Reviews*, 19(3).

Qin, J. and J. Lawless (1994): "Empirical Likelihood and General Estimating Equations", *Annals of Statistics*, 22, 300–325.

Richard, J.-F. (1975): "A Note on the Information Matrix of the Multivariate Normal Distribution", *Journal of Econometrics*, 3, 57–60.

Robinson, P. (1987): "Asymptotically Efficient Estimation in the Presence of Heteroskedasticity of Unknown Form", *Econometrica*, 55, 875–891.

Rothenberg, T. J. (1973): *Efficient Estimation with A Priori Information*, Cowles Foundation Monograph no. 23, Yale University Press, New Haven, CT.

Runkle, D. E. (1991): "Liquidity Constraints and the Permanent Income Hypothesis: Evidence from Panel Data", *Journal of Monetary Economics*, 97, 73–98.

Sargan, J. D. (1958): "The Estimation of Economic Relationships Using Instrumental Variables", *Econometrica*, 26, 393–415.

Sargan, J. D. (1959): "The Estimation of Relationships with Autocorrelated Residuals by the Use of Instrumental Variables", *Journal of the Royal Statistical Society. Series B*, 21, 91–105.

Sargan, J. D. (1964): "Three-Stage Least-Squares and Full Maximum Likelihood Estimates", *Econometrica*, 32, 77–81.

Sargent, T. J. (1978): "Estimation of Dynamic Labor Demand Schedules Under Rational Expectations", *Journal of Political Economy*, 86, 1009–1044.

Schiantarelli, F. and A. Sembenelli (1993): "Asymmetric Adjustment Costs and the Estimation of Euler Equations for Employment: An Application to U.K. Panel Data", in van-Ours, J., G. Pfann, and G. Ridder (eds.), *Labor Demand and Equilibrium Wage Formation*, Contributions to Economic Analysis, vol. 213, North-Holland.

Sims, C. A. (1972): "Money, Income, and Causality", *American Economic Review*, 62, 540–552.

Taubman, P. (1976a): "The Determinants of Earnings: Genetics, Family, and Other Environments: A Study of White Male Twins", *American Economic Review*, 66, 858–870.

Taubman, P. (1976b): "Earnings, Education, Genetics, and Environment", *Journal of Human Resources*, 11, 447–461.

Tiao, G. C. and M. M. Ali (1971): "Analysis of Correlated Random Effects: Linear Model with Two Random Components", *Biometrika*, 58, 37–51.

Vuong, Q. H. (1989): "Likelihood Ratio Tests for Model Selection and Non-Nested Hypotheses", *Econometrica*, 57, 307–333.

Wallace, T. D. and A. Hussain (1969): "The Use of Error Components Models in Combining Cross-Section and Time-Series Data", *Econometrica*, 37, 55–72.

Wansbeek, T. (2001): "GMM Estimation in Panel Data Models with Measurement Error", *Journal of Econometrics*, 104, 259–268.

Wansbeek, T. and E. Meijer (2000): *Measurement Error and Latent Variables in Econometrics*, North-Holland, Amsterdam.

White, H. (1982): "Instrumental Variables Regression with Independent Observations", *Econometrica*, 50, 483–499.

White, H. (1984): *Asymptotic Theory for Econometricians*, Academic Press, New York.

Zeldes, S. P. (1989): "Consumption and Liquidity Constraints: An Empirical Investigation", *Journal of Political Economy*, 97, 305–346.

Ziliak, J. P. (1997): "Efficient Estimation with Panel Data when Instruments Are Predetermined: An Empirical Comparison of Moment-Condition Estimators", *Journal of Business & Economic Statistics*, 15, 419–431.

Index

Abowd and Card model, *see* labour supply
analogy principle, 179
Anderson–Hsiao IV estimator, 88, 170
Arellano–Bond serial correlation test, 121–123, 168
Arellano–Bover estimator, *see* GMM, system estimators
asymptotics in T and N
    of GMM, 90–91
    of LIML, 172
    of stacked IV, 169–170
    of within-groups, 87–88

Balestra–Nerlove GLS estimator, 35
Becker, Grossman, and Murphy model, 130–132
best linear predictor, *see* linear projection
between-group estimator, 35, 37, 39, 41
Bhargava–Sargan estimator, *see* MLE

Caselli, Esquivel, and Lefort model, *see* growth and convergence
Chamberlain's minimum distance estimator, 22–23
Chamberlain's optimal forward filter, 155, 159
characteristic function, empirical, 45
conditional MLE, *see* MLE, conditional likelihood
conditional moment restrictions, 199

constant term, estimation of, 35, 39, 112, 136, 164
consumption models, *see also* Hall and Mishkin
    cigarette addiction, 130–132
    Zeldes Euler equation, 145–147
continuously updated GMM, 73, 118, 172
correlated effects, tests of
    generalized Wald test, 41
    Hausman test, 39
    incremental overidentifying restrictions, 42
    likelihood ratio test, 36
country and state panel data, 1, 130–132, 148–149
covariance restrictions, tests of
    in dynamic models, 141
    incremental Sargan, 73
    LR tests and non-normality, 74
crude GMM in first-differences, 90–91

DPD program (Dynamic Panel Data), 117, 166
dummy-variable least-squares, 16, *see* within-group estimators
dynamic factor models, 61

empirical likelihood estimation, 172–174
error components
    graphical diagnostic of normality, 46

227

Printed and bound by CPI Group (UK) Ltd, Croydon, CR0 4YY